IT
SECURITY +
EXAM
ULTIMATE GUIDE

Ultimate Guide to the It Security+ Exam: Your complete path to exam success with real-world insights, interactive tools, and exclusive flashcards

This resource aims to help individuals prepare for the CompTIA Security+ Exam. Despite this, neither the authors nor the publisher offer any assurances regarding the accuracy or completeness of the content herein. All warranties, explicit or implicit, particularly those of suitability for a given purpose, are disclaimed.

Legal Note:

This material is intended to offer reliable information related to its focus area. It's provided under the presumption that the publisher is not offering legal, accounting, or any other form of professional advice. If you require specialized counsel, consult a qualified professional for assistance.

Disclaimer:

The content in this resource is solely for educational and informational purposes. It is not an officially recognized exam guide by CompTIA. The publisher and the author make no guarantees regarding the reliability or completeness of this material and explicitly renounce all warranties, including but not limited to those concerning its suitability for specific objectives. No promises are made or implied by any sales or promotional activities.

The recommendations and approaches included in this material may not be universally applicable. Neither the author nor the publisher are responsible for any damages or losses resulting from the usage of this material, including but not limited to, loss of profits or any other form of financial loss, incidental or consequential damages.

SUMMARY

Introduction:

Introduction: Mastering the CompTIA Security+ Exam

Welcome to the comprehensive guide that aims to give you with all the necessary things that permit you to master the CompTIA Security+ exam. This exam serves as a critical benchmark for best practices in IT security, establishing the main knowledge required of any cybersecurity role. Not only does it open the door to an illustrious career in cybersecurity, but it also proves to employers that you possess the hands-on skills and technical acumen needed to safeguard critical assets.

Why CompTIA Security+?

In this new era, cybersecurity is no longer a luxury or an afterthought; it's a necessity. With constant news of data breaches, cyber threats, and online scams, organizations are on high alert. This translates to an ever-increasing demand for certified and competent cybersecurity professionals who can protect an organization's infrastructure, data, and personnel. Holding a CompTIA Security+ certification not only elevates your career prospects but also adds value to your skillset, arming you with the knowledge to navigate an ever-changing cyber world.

What Will You Learn?

In this guide, we take a real-world, practical approach to the material, catering to both newcomers and experienced professionals. You'll dive into various topics such as:

- Introduction to Cyber Security: Understand the landscape of cybersecurity, including the types, nature, and mechanisms of cyber threats.
- Networks and Infrastructure: Unpack the core components of networking and how to secure them.
- Cryptography: Decrypt the world of ciphers, keys, and cryptographic protocols.
- Identity and Access Management: Learn how authenticize and authorize work hand-in-hand to secure an enterprise.
- Risk Management: Understand how to assess, mitigate, and manage risks effectively.
- Security Technologies and Tools: Get familiar with the tools that safeguard an organization from threats.
- Threats, Attacks, and Vulnerabilities: Recognize the arsenal of cyber threats and how to mitigate them.
- Security Operations and Incident Responses: Understand the immediate steps to take when a security incident occurs.

Practical Tone and Exam-Centric Content

The narrative of this guide revolves around a practical, real-world approach enriched by interactive learning, self-assessment, and real-world scenarios. We provide diagrams, charts, quizzes, and practice questions that align with key exam topics, pitfalls, and tips. Each chapter builds logically from basic to advanced topics, structuring your learning path towards exam success. This ensures a conducive learning atmosphere, making your CompTIA Security+ exam preparation as streamlined and effective as possible.

So, are you ready to embark on this exciting journey to becoming a CompTIA Security+ certified professional? Let's dive in.

Preface: Your Journey to CompTIA Security+ Certification Starts Here

Dear Aspiring Cybersecurity Professional,

As you hold this guide in your hands, or view it on your screen, you're taking a critical step toward bolstering your career in cybersecurity. The CompTIA Security+ exam is more than just a test; it's a doorway into a world of opportunities in the cybersecurity field—a world that needs trained and certified professionals more than ever.

Why This Guide?

You may wonder why another guide on the CompTIA Security+ exam? The answer is simple: This isn't just another study guide. It's a comprehensive, interactive toolkit that fuses theory with practice, providing you with the real-world skills you need to excel not just in the exam but also in the field of cybersecurity.

Our Approach

Our approach aligns perfectly with the requirements and the narrative tone set by the CompTIA Security+ exam. We emphasize real-world applicability, practical exercises, and an exam-centric focus. You'll find visual aids, interactive quizzes, and a wealth of supplementary resources to enrich your learning journey.

What's Ahead?

In the chapters that follow, we cover the entire spectrum of topics that you'll face in the exam. From the foundations of cybersecurity to the intricacies of network protocols, from identity management to threat mitigation—we have it all. The guide is structured in a logical sequence, ensuring that you build your knowledge base from the ground up.

Features to Look Forward To

- Real-World Scenarios: Practical exercises based on real-world situations to prepare you for the types of challenges you will face.
- Exam-Centric Content: Key focus on topics that are critical to the exam, peppered with tips and pitfalls to watch out for.
- Interactive Learning: Practice questions and quizzes interspersed throughout the guide to provide a hands-on learning experience.
- Structured Learning: We start with the basics and then take you through advanced topics, making it easier for you to digest the material.
- Accessible Language: Complex jargon and concepts are broken down into straightforward language to ensure easy comprehension.
- Self-Assessment: Checklists and reflection questions to gauge your readiness for the exam.

Your Companion in Success

Consider this guide your mentor, your companion in success. We are thrilled to be part of your journey toward cybersecurity excellence. We know that the road ahead is challenging, but with commitment, focused preparation, and the right resources—success is not just a possibility; it's a guarantee.

Welcome aboard, and let's embark on this exciting journey together.

Best wishes for a successful and enriching experience,

The Team Behind "Mastering the CompTIA Security+ Exam"

Understanding the CompTIA Security+ Exam

The CompTIA Security+ exam serves as a critical benchmark for IT professionals seeking to establish themselves in the field of cybersecurity. Often viewed as a foundational certification, Security+ is designed to validate the skills and knowledge you need to perform core security functions, making it an ideal stepping-stone for a career in information security.

What It Covers

The exam spans a wide range of topics, from network security, cryptography, and risk management, to identity and access management, cloud security, and more. While the exam is comprehensive, it's not overwhelmingly specialized, making it attainable for those who have a broad understanding of cybersecurity principles.

Why It's Important

Cybersecurity threats continue to evolve, becoming increasingly sophisticated and pervasive. The Security+ exam is designed to equip you with the most current, real-world skills needed to tackle these threats. By validating these skills, you become a more competitive candidate in the job market, and you can prove to employers that you possess the practical knowledge needed to secure their networks and data.

Exam Format

The Security+ exam typically consists of a mix of multiple-choice questions, performance-based questions, and possibly some drag-and-drop type questions. This diversified format tests not just rote memorization but also practical skills and scenario-based problem-solving. It's a timed exam, adding a level of time-management pressure to the already rigorous content.

Exam-Taking Skills

One of the unique features of Security+ is its emphasis on applying knowledge in real-world settings. As such, simply memorizing terms and concepts won't be enough. Understanding how to implement security measures in various scenarios is key to both passing the exam and succeeding in real-world roles.

Practical Applications

Beyond the exam, Security+ serves as a foundational layer for any aspiring or current IT professional who will deal with network security issues. Many organizations even require Security+ certification as a baseline qualification for their IT staff, which speaks volumes about its industry relevance.

Continued Learning

Although passing the Security+ exam is an accomplishment, it's also just a starting point. The world of cybersecurity is vast and continuously evolving. Successful professionals frequently update their skills and knowledge, often pursuing more specialized certifications and training programs after attaining the Security+ certification.

In summary, the CompTIA Security+ exam is much more than just a test; it's a career-enabler. Whether you're just starting your career or looking to elevate your existing role in the IT sector, the Security+ certification offers a path to gain the skills, validation, and credibility needed to succeed in the ever-changing world of cybersecurity.

1) Cybersecurity

The Importance of Cyber Security

In a world fervently driven by digital transformation, the essence of cybersecurity has never been more pivotal. Every facet of society, be it business, government, or personal interactions, is interwoven with digital threads. The conveniences and advancements brought about by the digital era are numerous; however, they come with a complex array of security concerns. Cybersecurity, the way to protect systems, networks, and programs from digital attacks, has thus become a crucial pillar in maintaining the integrity, confidentiality, and availability of information.

As we delve deeper into the digital abyss, the potential threats and malicious activities also evolve, rendering the stakes higher than ever. Cyber threats no longer merely target large corporations or governments; they have trickled down to impact individuals and small businesses alike. The repercussions of a cyber-attack can be profound, often resulting in financial loss, identity theft, loss of critical data, and damage to reputation.

The importance of cybersecurity extends beyond just monetary implications. It's about safeguarding the fundamental rights of individuals and organizations. It's about ensuring a safe digital environment where innovation and ideas flourish without the looming shadow of malicious intent. Moreover, in a regulatory landscape that's becoming increasingly stringent, adhering to cybersecurity norms is not just about best practices but about legal compliance and maintaining trust.

A robust cybersecurity posture is not a luxury but a necessity in today's scenario. It's the unsung hero that works tirelessly behind the scenes to ensure the digital frontier remains secure. Different elements of cybersecurity like network security, information security, and incident management form the bulwark against the nefarious designs of cyber criminals.

Preparing for a career in cybersecurity, particularly through a rigorous examination like CompTIA Security+, equips individuals with the requisite knowledge and skills to combat the ever-evolving threat landscape. It provides a solid foundation to understand the various components of cybersecurity and how they interlink to create a resilient security posture.

The journey through this guide is not just about preparing for an examination; it's about embarking on a meaningful and impactful career that plays a critical role in shaping a safe digital future. As you traverse through the chapters, you'll not only learn the technicalities but grasp the essence of why cybersecurity is the linchpin in the digital era.

Understanding the importance of cybersecurity is the first step in a rewarding journey towards becoming a proficient and certified cybersecurity professional. Through this guide, you're not just studying for an exam; you're preparing to become a sentinel in the digital realm, ever vigilant and ready to thwart the malicious intents that lurk in the digital shadows.

This introduction creates the premise for the following chapters, each of which will dive deeper into the critical aspects of cybersecurity, preparing you thoroughly for the CompTIA Security+ examination and a fulfilling career in safeguarding the digital frontier.

Cybersecurity is not merely a technical requirement but a crucial societal need. The digital age, while brimming with potential, is also fraught with peril. Cyber threats, once a concern relegated to the realm of tech-savvy individuals and enterprises, now touch every facet of society. The importance for a robust cybersecurity measures transcends industries and borders. Today, the protection of digital assets and data is a concern shared by individuals, small businesses, corporations, and nation-states alike.

Let's delve into some key aspects that underscore the indispensable role of cybersecurity in today's global digital landscape:

Economic Implications:

Cyber-attacks can wreak havoc on the economy of a nation. From disrupting the operations of businesses, both large and small, to instigating financial fraud, the economic repercussions are vast and varied. A single breach can cost an organization millions, if not billions, impacting not just its bottom line but also its market reputation and customer trust.

National Security Concerns:

The realm of cybersecurity extends into national security. Sophisticated cyber-attacks on critical infrastructure, like energy grids or financial systems, can have far-reaching consequences, affecting the lives of millions. The defense against such high-stakes threats is an integral aspect of a nation's security apparatus.

Privacy and Identity Protection:

In a world where personal data is a valuable commodity, the importance of cybersecurity in safeguarding individual privacy cannot be overstated. Protecting sensitive information from unauthorized access and identity theft is a fundamental aspect of digital safety.

Compliance and Legal Obligations:

With an increase in data breaches, there's a growing emphasis on legal frameworks and compliance mandates surrounding data protection. Adhering to these regulatory requirements is crucial for avoiding legal repercussions and maintaining a reputable business standing.

Technological Advancements:

As technology evolves at a rapid pace, so does the sophistication of cyber threats. The advent of technologies like IoT, AI, and blockchain presents new challenges and attack vectors. A robust cybersecurity framework is essential for harnessing the benefits of these technologies securely.

Public Awareness and Education:

Cybersecurity isn't solely the domain of IT professionals; it's a societal concern. Public awareness and education on cyber hygiene practices are crucial for fostering a culture of cybersecurity, making individuals and organizations more resilient against cyber threats.

Innovation and Competitive Edge:

In a competitive market, having robust cybersecurity measures can provide a significant edge. It fosters a culture of innovation by providing a safe environment for companies and individuals to develop and invest in new technologies and solutions.

Talent Development and Employment Opportunities:

The growing demand for cybersecurity professionals underscores the sector's significance. Pursuing a career in cybersecurity, validated by certifications like CompTIA Security+, is not only a prudent professional choice but also a contribution to addressing the global cybersecurity skills gap.

Global Cooperation:

Cybersecurity is a global concern that necessitates international cooperation. Collaborative efforts across nations are crucial for developing and enforcing cybersecurity standards, sharing threat intelligence, and promoting a secure global digital environment

Future-Proofing:

Preparing for emerging threats and future challenges is a quintessential aspect of cybersecurity. It's about staying ahead of the curve, anticipating potential risks, and building resilient systems capable of withstanding the evolving threat landscape.

As you embark on the journey through this guide, each page turned is a step towards not merely understanding but mastering the cybersecurity realm. The knowledge and skills you acquire will not only prepare you for the CompTIA Security+ examination but also equip you to be a vanguard in the ongoing battle against cyber threats. The importance of cybersecurity is a multifaceted topic, with each facet having real-world implications that resonate across personal, organizational, and global domains.

The subsequent chapters will dive into the technical and practical aspects of cybersecurity, aligned with the CompTIA Security+ exam objectives. The foundational understanding established in this chapter will provide a solid base as you delve deeper into the intricate and fascinating world of cybersecurity, gearing you towards acing the examination and making a meaningful impact in the cybersecurity domain.

Key Concepts and Terminologies

As we delve deeper into the field of cybersecurity, it's crucial to have a strong understanding of its fundamental principles and terms. This not only enhances your comprehension of the content in this guide but also serves as a stepping stone for your development into a skilled cybersecurity expert. Let's demystify key cybersecurity concepts and terms that you'll encounter frequently in this guide and on the CompTIA Security+ exam.

1. Information Assurance (IA):

This term denotes the managerial practices employed to safeguard the confidentiality, availability, authenticity, integrity, and protection of information and data.

2. Elements of Security Concern: Threat, Vulnerability, and Risk:

Threat: A possible hazard capable of exploiting system vulnerabilities.

Vulnerability: A system flaw that is susceptible to being exploited by threats.

Risk: The potential negative impact that could arise if a vulnerability is exploited by a threat.

3. Malware:

Short for "malicious software," malware includes a range of damaging software types, such as viruses, worms, ransomware, trojans, and spyware.

4. Phishing:

A form of cyber-attack where the attacker poses as a credible source to collect personal and financial information from the target.

5. Firewall:

A device designed to oversee and regulate network traffic based on predefined security parameters.

6. Encryption:

The technique of transforming data into a coded format to block unauthorized access.

7. Identity Verification and Access Control:

Authentication: The process of confirming the identity of an individual or system.

Authorization: The act of deciding whether an authenticated party has permission to access specific resources.

8. Intrusion Detection and Prevention Systems (IDS/IPS):

IDS: Scans network traffic for unusual activity and sends out warnings when such activity is identified.

IPS: Takes action based on IDS alerts to neutralize potential threats.

9. Virtual Private Network (VPN):

A technology that establishes a secure communication channel over an insecure network, maintaining data confidentiality.

10. Incident Management:

The strategy for dealing with the consequences of a security violation or cyber-attack.

11. Update Management:

The method for keeping software programs current with the most recent security enhancements.

12. Zero-Day Weakness:

An unknown software flaw that poses a significant risk until it is rectified.

13. Manipulative Tactics (Social Engineering):

The act of convincing individuals to disclose sensitive information or undertake actions that jeopardize security.

14. Data Preservation (DLP):

Techniques and utilities deployed to prevent the unauthorized loss, misuse, or access of confidential data.

15. Information Security Governance:

Documentation that provides a framework of rules, procedures, and guidelines to assure an organization's information security.

16. Regulatory Adherence in Cybersecurity:

Compliance with pertinent legal standards, rules, guidelines, and cybersecurity regulations.

17. Digital Investigations (Forensics):

The scientific approach to examining and interpreting data to provide evidence in cybercrime or security incidents.

    18. Cloud Safeguards:

Measures, technologies, and rules applied to secure data, apps, and infrastructure within cloud settings.

    19. Endpoint Protection:

Security measures implemented when the organizational network is accessed via remote hardware like phones and laptops.

    20. Safety-First Programming (Secure Coding):

Methodologies and procedures aimed at creating software resilient to security threats. These key concepts and terminologies form the lexicon of cybersecurity. Having a firm understanding of these terms will enrich your comprehension as you navigate through the diverse topics covered in the subsequent chapters. Each term and concept here is a glimpse into the vast and intricate world of cybersecurity you are about to explore. As you prepare for the CompTIA Security+ examination, familiarizing yourself with these terms is a step towards mastering the language of cybersecurity, enabling you to engage with the material in a meaningful and insightful manner.

This section serves as a glossary, a reference you can turn to as you encounter these terms throughout your study. The essence of cybersecurity lies in the nuanced understanding of these concepts, and as you delve deeper, you will find these terms intertwining, forming the complex yet fascinating fabric of cybersecurity.

21. Access Control:

  - A cornerstone of cybersecurity, access control determines the authorization levels individuals or systems have within a digital environment. Its models like Mandatory Access Control (MAC), Discretionary Access Control (DAC), and Role-Based Access Control (RBAC) define these authorization levels differently.

22. Biometrics:

  - This authentication method hinges on unique physical or behavioral traits that machines can measure and verify, such as fingerprint or eye retina scans.

23. Botnets:

  - These are clusters of computers compromised by malicious software, orchestrated as a collective without the owners' awareness, typically for nefarious activities like spam distribution or initiating Distributed Denial of Service (DDoS) attacks.

24. DDoS Attacks:

  - Aimed at derailing the standard operations of specific servers, services, or networks, these attacks inundate the targets with an overwhelming volume of online traffic.

25. Multi-Factor Authentication (MFA):

  - MFA bolsters security by necessitating multiple authentication steps from distinct credential categories before permitting user login or transactions.

26. Honeypots:

  - Serving as bait, honeypots are fabricated systems or networks designed to lure and capture cyber intruders attempting unauthorized system access.

27. SIEM (Security Information and Event Management):

  - By aggregating and analyzing logs and other security-centric documents, SIEM solutions furnish a comprehensive insight into an enterprise's information security landscape.

28. VPN (Virtual Private Network):

  - VPNs bridge private networks over public ones, facilitating data transmission across shared or public networks as though the computing devices were directly tethered to the private network.

29. Wireless Security:

  - This involves the strategies employed to safeguard wireless networks from unauthorized intrusion and threats.

30. Penetration Testing:

  - This is a sanctioned cyber assault simulation on a computer system, conducted to appraise the system's security robustness.

31. Cryptography:

- Entails the exploration and application of methods for ensuring secure data communication and storage.

32. Application Security:
   - This domain is dedicated to shielding software and devices from threats and vulnerabilities.

33. Endpoint Detection and Response (EDR):
   - EDR frameworks facilitate real-time endpoint system event monitoring and detection, enabling swift threat mitigation actions.

34. Mobile Security:
   - This covers the defenses against threats and vulnerabilities targeting mobile apps and devices.

35. Identity and Access Management (IAM):
   - These frameworks are devised to ascertain that individuals access the appropriate resources, at the apt times, for justified reasons.

Each of these terms and concepts further contributes to building a robust understanding of the cybersecurity domain. As we explore these terms, we delve into the various mechanisms, strategies, and tools employed by cybersecurity professionals to safeguard information and ensure a secure digital environment.

Moreover, understanding the interrelationships between these terms is crucial. For instance, how IAM strategies intertwine with concepts like MFA and Biometrics to ensure robust authentication and authorization mechanisms, or how technologies like SIEM and EDR are employed in tandem to enhance incident detection and response capabilities. Cybersecurity is a multi-dimensional domain with each concept and term opening up avenues for deeper exploration and understanding. As you navigate through this guide, you will find these terms becoming more familiar, their implications more apparent, and their significance more profound.

The objective is not just to acquaint you with these terms, but to instill a holistic understanding that will be necessary as a solid foundation as you prepare for the CompTIA Security+ examination and beyond. Each chapter ahead will delve into these concepts in detail, illustrating their practical applications, and preparing you for the scenarios you might encounter in the examination and your subsequent professional endeavors.

Historical Evolution of Cyber Threats

The landscape of cyber threats has witnessed a dramatic evolution over the years. From rudimentary viruses to sophisticated state-sponsored cyber-attacks, the spectrum of cyber threats has expanded significantly, mirroring the rapid advancements in technology. Understanding the historical trajectory of cyber threats provides invaluable insights into the current cybersecurity landscape and prepares us for the challenges ahead.

1. The Dawn of Cyber Threats (1970s - 1980s):
   - The inception of cyber threats can be traced back to the 1970s and 1980s, with the emergence of the first computer viruses and worms. The notable ones included the Creeper virus and the Morris Worm. These early forms of malware were primarily experimental or prank-driven rather than malicious in intent.

2. The Emergence of Malware and Internet-born Threats (1990s):
   - With the popularization of the internet in the 1990s, the nature of cyber threats evolved. The decade saw the rise of malware, with infamous examples like the Melissa virus and the ILOVEYOU worm causing widespread disruption. These incidents underscored the potential damage cyber threats could inflict on a global scale.

3. The Advent of Modern Cyber Threats (2000s):
   - The new millennium witnessed a surge in cyber threats with a more malicious intent. The landscape saw the proliferation of spyware, adware, and phishing scams. Cyber threats like the Mydoom and Slammer worms caused substantial financial and data losses, signaling the urgency for enhanced cybersecurity measures.

4. State-Sponsored Attacks and Advanced Persistent Threats (2010s):
   - The 2010s marked the era of state-sponsored cyber-attacks and Advanced Persistent Threats (APTs). Notable incidents like Stuxnet and the Sony Pictures hack showcased the geopolitical implications of cyber threats. APTs, often backed by nation-states, demonstrated a high degree of sophistication and persistence.

5. The Rise of Ransomware and Cryptojacking (2010s - 2020s):

- Ransomware attacks like WannaCry and NotPetya highlighted the lucrative nature of cyber-attacks. Simultaneously, the rise of cryptocurrencies led to the emergence of cryptojacking, where attackers illicitly mine cryptocurrencies using victims' computing resources.

6. Emerging Threats in the Age of IoT and AI (2020s):

- The proliferation of Internet of Things (IoT) devices and Artificial Intelligence (AI) has ushered in a new era of cyber threats. The expanding attack surface now includes smart devices, industrial control systems, and even autonomous vehicles. Furthermore, attackers are leveraging AI to enhance the sophistication of their attacks.

7. The Pandemic Era (2020 - Present):

- The COVID-19 pandemic exacerbated cybersecurity challenges. The shift to remote work and the accelerated digital transformation led to a spike in cyber-attacks, including phishing, ransomware, and attacks on healthcare facilities.

8. The Future of Cyber Threats:

- Looking ahead, we anticipate an increasingly complex threat landscape. The evolution of quantum computing, 5G technology, and the continuous integration of AI and IoT will invariably introduce novel threat vectors. The cybersecurity community must remain vigilant and innovative to stay ahead of malicious actors.

The history of cyber threats paints a narrative of an escalating arms race between cyber adversaries and defenders. Each advancement in technology brings forth new opportunities for innovation and, concurrently, new avenues for exploitation. As you prepare for the CompTIA Security+ examination, understanding this historical evolution enriches your perspective on the current cybersecurity challenges and prepares you for the multifaceted nature of cyber threats you might encounter in your cybersecurity career.

The subsequent chapters will delve deeper into the mechanics of these threats, the defenses crafted to thwart them, and the best practices that have emerged from these historical experiences, all aimed at equipping you with the knowledge and skills necessary to navigate the ever-evolving cyber threat landscape.

9. Cyber Espionage and Data Breaches (Late 2000s - 2010s):

- This era saw a substantial rise in cyber espionage activities and data breaches. Intrusions into corporate and governmental networks to steal sensitive data became a common tactic among nation-state actors and cybercriminals. Prominent incidents such as the Target breach in 2013 and the OPM breach in 2015 highlighted the severe implications of data exfiltration and exposed the vulnerabilities inherent in complex network systems.

10. The Emergence of DarkWeb and Cyber Criminal Markets (2010s):

- The rise of dark web platforms and cyber criminal markets facilitated the buying, selling, and trading of malware, exploit kits, and stolen data. This underground economy fueled the rapid evolution and dissemination of cyber threats, making cybersecurity a continually escalating challenge.

11. The Elevation of Cybersecurity Legislation and International Norms (2010s - 2020s):

- The growing recognition of cyber threats led to a global push for more robust cybersecurity legislation and international norms. Countries started developing national cybersecurity strategies, and international bodies like the United Nations began addressing cybersecurity on the global stage.

12. The Expanding Landscape of Mobile and Cloud-Based Threats (2010s - 2020s):

- The widespread adoption of mobile devices and cloud services altered the cyber threat landscape. Threat actors developed new methods to exploit these technologies, leading to the emergence of mobile malware and cloud misconfiguration issues.

13. Supply Chain Attacks (2010s - 2020s):

- Supply chain attacks, like the SolarWinds incident in 2020, showcased a sophisticated attack vector where threat actors infiltrate the supply chain to compromise a broader network of targets. This incident underscored the interconnectedness of the digital ecosystem and the amplified risks associated with supply chain vulnerabilities.

14. The Intersection of Physical and Cyber Threats (2010s - 2020s):

- The convergence of physical and cyber threats, epitomized by incidents like the Ukrainian power grid attack in 2015, demonstrated the real-world implications of cyber-attacks. Such incidents blurred the lines between the digital and physical realms, emphasizing the holistic nature of modern security challenges.

15. The Growing Concern Over Privacy and Surveillance (2010s - 2020s):
- Amid the escalating cyber threat landscape, concerns over privacy and surveillance became paramount. Revelations about mass surveillance programs and debates on encryption backdoors brought attention to the delicate balance between security and privacy in the digital age.

16. Cybersecurity Awareness and Education (2010s - 2020s):
- The escalating frequency and impact of cyber threats led to a surge in cybersecurity awareness and education. Organizations began investing in cybersecurity training, and academic institutions started offering specialized cybersecurity programs to address the growing skills gap in the field.

17. The Development of Cyber Insurance Markets (2010s - 2020s):
- The recognition of cyber threats as a significant risk factor led to the development of cyber insurance markets. Organizations started considering cyber insurance as a part of their risk management strategies to mitigate the financial impact of cyber incidents.

Real-world Scenario: Impact of a Cyber Breach

The chilling morning of November 30, 2013, marked a black day in the annals of cybersecurity history. Retail giant Target Corporation became the prey of a nefarious cyber-attack, the ripples of which reverberated across the global retail industry, jolting organizations into recognizing the dire necessity of robust cybersecurity measures.

The attack was meticulously crafted. The adversaries first infiltrated a small HVAC contractor that had a business relationship with Target. Utilizing a spear-phishing email, they implanted malware on the contractor's network, which eventually facilitated unauthorized access to Target's network. The attackers were relentless and sophisticated, maneuvering their way through the network until they reached the point-of-sale (POS) systems across various Target stores.

The malware, now residing on the POS systems, was engineered to scrape memory for unencrypted payment card data right at the moment when the cards were swiped for transactions. This ingenuous yet malicious strategy allowed the attackers to harvest massive amounts of payment card data, which were then exfiltrated to a remote server controlled by the attackers. Over a span of three weeks, the attackers looted data of at least 40 million payment cards and personal information of 70 million customers.

The aftermath was catastrophic. The breach cost Target over $290 million in legal fees and other expenses, not to mention a 46% drop in profits during the fourth quarter of 2013. The incident tarnished Target's brand reputation, and the company had to invest an additional $100 million to upgrade its cybersecurity infrastructure. The ripple effect transcended Target, sending shockwaves through the retail industry and prompting organizations worldwide to ramp up their cybersecurity measures.

The Target breach is a harrowing testament to the potential devastation a cyber-attack can inflict on an organization. It showcased the importance of not only having robust cybersecurity measures in place but also ensuring that the cybersecurity posture extends across the supply chain, enveloping all third-party vendors and business partners.

The lessons about Target breach are profound:

1. Third-Party Risk Management: The importance of vetting and managing security of third-party vendors and partners cannot be overstated. A weak link in the supply chain can serve as a conduit for attackers to infiltrate the network.

2. Proactive Cybersecurity Measures: Employing proactive measures such as regular security audits, penetration testing, and employee training can significantly bolster an organization's cybersecurity posture.

3. Incident Response Preparedness: Having a well-orchestrated incident response plan is crucial for timely detection and mitigation of a cyber-attack, minimizing potential damage.

4. Investment in Advanced Security Technologies: Employing advanced security technologies like endpoint detection and response (EDR), network segmentation, and encryption can provide robust defense mechanisms against sophisticated cyber threats.

5. Regulatory Compliance and Customer Trust: Ensuring compliance with industry regulations and building trust with customers by being transparent about cybersecurity practices is essential for brand reputation and customer loyalty.

The narrative of the Target breach is a stark reminder of the turbulent waters organizations navigate in the digital realm. As you prepare for the CompTIA Security+ examination, real-world incidents like the Target breach provide invaluable insights into the practical application of cybersecurity principles and the tangible impact cybersecurity has on organizations and individuals alike.

This real-world scenario lays the groundwork for the concepts and practices elucidated in the subsequent chapters of this guide, accentuating the importance of cybersecurity in a palpable and impactful manner.

6. Cybersecurity Awareness and Continuous Learning:

   - The Target breach underscored the importance of fostering a culture of cybersecurity awareness and continue to learn within an organization. Employees at every level should have an education about the common cyber threats and the best practices for mitigating these threats. Regular training programs, workshops, and awareness campaigns are crucial for building a resilient organization capable of defending against and responding to cyber threats.

7. Public-Private Partnerships and Information Sharing:

   - The incident highlighted the need for enhanced cooperation between the private sector and government agencies. Public-private partnerships can facilitate information sharing about emerging threats and best practices for preventing and responding to cyber attacks. Through collaborative efforts, the collective cybersecurity posture can be significantly bolstered, reducing the likelihood of successful attacks.

8. Consumer Protection and Data Privacy Laws:

   - In the wake of the breach, there was a renewed focus on consumer protection and data privacy laws. The incident spurred discussions among policymakers about the need for stronger regulations to protect consumer data and ensure that organizations are adhering to the highest standards of cybersecurity.

9. Cybersecurity Insurance:

   - The financial fallout from the breach also brought attention to the role of cybersecurity insurance in mitigating the financial risks associated with cyber incidents. Organizations began to recognize the value of having a cybersecurity insurance policy as part of their risk management strategy.

10. Reputation Management and Crisis Communication:

    - Effective communication with stakeholders, including customers, employees, and investors, is crucial during and after a cyber incident. The way an organization communicates about a breach can significantly impact its reputation and customer trust. A well-prepared crisis communication plan, which includes timely and transparent communication about the incident, is essential for managing the fallout and restoring trust.

11. Long-term Strategic Investments in Cybersecurity:

    - Post-incident, Target made substantial investments in enhancing its cybersecurity infrastructure, including the adoption of advanced security technologies and the establishment of a security operations center (SOC). This reflects a broader trend where organizations are making long-term strategic investments in cybersecurity to prevent future incidents and build resilience against evolving cyber threats.

12. Global Cybersecurity Standards and Best Practices:

    - The incident also underscored the importance of adhering to global cybersecurity standards and best practices. Implementing recognized frameworks and standards, such as the NIST Cybersecurity Framework or the ISO 27001 standard, can help organizations build a robust cybersecurity program that can withstand evolving threats.

13. Holistic Cybersecurity Approach:

    - The breach highlighted the necessity of a holistic approach to cybersecurity, encompassing not just technological solutions but also organizational processes, employee training, and a strong security culture. A multi-faceted approach to cybersecurity is essential for effectively managing the complex array of cyber threats faced by modern organizations. The detailed exploration of the Target breach illustrates the multifaceted impact a cyber-attack can have on an organization and its stakeholders. It provides a comprehensive perspective on the real-world implications of cyber threats, emphasizing the critical importance of robust cybersecurity measures. As you delve deeper into this guide and prepare for the CompTIA Security+ examination, keep in mind the tangible consequences of cyber threats and the essential role cybersecurity professionals play in safeguarding organizations against such adversities.

Interactive Quiz: Cyber Security Basics

1. What is a firewall designed to do?
   - a) Heat a building
   - b) Block unauthorized access
   - c) Provide a user interface
   - d) Cool down servers
2. What does HTTPS stand for?
   - a) HyperText Translation Protocol Secure
   - b) Hyper Transfer Text Protocol System
   - c) HyperText Transfer Protocol Secure
   - d) HyperText Transport Protocol System
3. What is malware short for?
   - a) Malfunctioning software
   - b) Malevolent software
   - c) Malicious software
   - d) Malware does not have a long form
4. What is the main purpose of data encryption?
   - a) To speed up data transfer
   - b) To make data unreadable without the key
   - c) To increase data size
   - d) To repair corrupted data
5. What is a VPN?
   - a) Variable Personal Network
   - b) Virtual Personal Network
   - c) Virtual Private Network
   - d) Variable Private Network
6. What is phishing?
   - a) A type of sport
   - b) A type of online scam
   - c) A method of file transfer
   - d) A programming language
7. Which one is an operating system?
   - a) Python
   - b) Windows
   - c) HTTP
   - d) CSS
8. What does IoT stand for?
   - a) Internet of Trials
   - b) Information of Technology
   - c) Internet of Things
   - d) Internal Optical Transfer
9. Which of these is an example of a strong password?
   - a) password123
   - b) 123456
   - c) Pa$$w0rD!
   - d) qwerty

10. What is a DDoS attack?
    - a) Direct Disk Operation Service
    - b) Double Data Operational Security
    - c) Distributed Denial of Service
    - d) Digital Data Operating System
11. What is the primary purpose of antivirus software?
    - a) To speed up computer performance
    - b) To detect and remove malware
    - c) To manage passwords
    - d) To provide a firewall
12. What does 2FA stand for?
    - a) Two-Factor Addition
    - b) Two-File Access
    - c) Two-Factor Authentication
    - d) Two-Firewall Addition
13. What is the common port number for HTTP?
    - a) 25
    - b) 80
    - c) 443
    - d) 22
14. What is ransomware?
    - a) A type of music genre
    - b) A software that locks files and demands payment for their release
    - c) A form of digital currency
    - d) A data storage solution
15. What is a cookie in the context of web browsing?
    - a) A snack
    - b) A device driver
    - c) A small file that stores user settings
    - d) A type of malware
16. What does CAPTCHA stand for?
    - a) Computerized Application Performance Tracking and Control Algorithm
    - b) Certified Advanced Programming Test for Computerized Hardware Analysis
    - c) Complete Analysis for Potential Threats and Cyber Activities
    - d) Completely Automated Public Turing test to tell Computers and Humans Apart
17. What does URL stand for?
    - a) Universal Relay Location
    - b) Unified Relay Language
    - c) Uniform Resource Locator
    - d) Universal Resource Locator

18. What is a brute-force attack?
- a) A logical error in a program
- b) An attempt to crack a password by trying all possible combinations
- c) A type of spam email
- d) An outdated encryption algorithm

19. What does CSRF stand for?
- a) Custom Security Response Format
- b) Cross-Site Request Forgery
- c) Cyber Security Response Framework
- d) Central Server Request Function

20. What does SSD stand for?
- a) Super Speed Disk
- b) Secure System Drive
- c) Solid State Drive
- d) Security Software Disk

21. What is a zero-day vulnerability?
- a) A fake vulnerability
- b) A vulnerability known for zero days
- c) A vulnerability that is unknown to the vendor
- d) A very low-risk vulnerability

22. What is BYOD?
- a) Buy Your Own Device
- b) Borrow Your Office Desk
- c) Bring Your Own Device
- d) Build Your Own Drive

23. What is a honeypot?
- a) A kitchen utensil
- b) A type of malware
- c) A trap set to detect or deflect unauthorized access
- d) A secure storage solution

24. What does PII stand for?
- a) Personal Identifiable Information
- b) Private Internet Index
- c) Personally Identifiable Information
- d) Public Information Interface

25. What does a digital signature provide?
- a) A handwritten signature
- b) Authentication and integrity
- c) Faster internet speeds
- d) Access to premium content

26. What is a botnet?
- a) A type of fish
- b) A group of computers controlled without their owners' knowledge
- c) A digital book network

- d) A type of strong, flexible net

27. What is the primary purpose of social engineering?
- a) Building social connections
- b) Manipulating people into revealing confidential information
- c) Engineering social media algorithms
- d) Designing social network systems

28. What is an intranet?
- a) A public network
- b) A private network within an organization
- c) A tool for creating websites
- d) A type of malware

29. What does UTM stand for?
- a) Universal Text Message
- b) Unified Threat Management
- c) Ultimate Technical Machine
- d) User

30. What does IDS stand for?
- a) Intrusion Detection System
- b) Internet Download Speed
- c) Information Data Service
- d) International Domain Server

31. What is hashing used for?
- a) Compressing files
- b) Encrypting data
- c) Verifying data integrity
- d) Increasing network speed

32. What does DMZ stand for?
- a) Digital Management Zone
- b) Demilitarized Zone
- c) Direct Memory Zone
- d) Dynamic Mail Zone

33. What does EDR stand for?
- a) Electronic Data Repository
- b) Endpoint Detection and Response
- c) Enterprise Data Routing
- d) Email Disaster Recovery

34. What is the most frequent type of cybersecurity attack?
- a) Social engineering
- b) Ransomware
- c) Phishing
- d) Man-in-the-middle

35. What is a keylogger?
- a) A device for keeping keys safe
- b) A tool for generating keys
- c) Software or hardware that records keystrokes
- d) A guide for keyboard shortcuts

36. What does MITM stand for?
  - a) Multiple Instance Transfer Mode
  - b) Media and Information Technology Management
  - c) Man-in-the-Middle
  - d) Mobile Internet and Telecommunication Model
37. What is steganography?
  - a) A study of asteroids
  - b) Hiding information within other information
  - c) A kind of encryption
  - d) A new branch of mathematics
38. What does SIEM stand for?
  - a) Security Information and Event Management
  - b) Simple Integrated Electronic Mail
  - c) Secure Internal Enterprise Model
  - d) Systemic Information Ecosystem Model
39. What is a cyber attack's primary aim?
  - a) To improve security
  - b) To steal, alter, or destroy data
  - c) To increase network speed
  - d) To provide updates for software
40. What does GDPR stand for?
  - a) Global Data Practice Regulation
  - b) General Digital Protection Rights
  - c) General Data Protection Regulation
  - d) Global Digital Policy Revie

ANSWERS

1. What is a firewall designed to do? Answer: b) Block unauthorized access Firewalls serve as barriers to keep out unapproved access to a network, not for temperature control or user interface functionalities.

2. What does HTTPS stand for? Answer: c) HyperText Transfer Protocol Secure HTTPS is an enhanced, secure version of HTTP, built to improve online safety.

3. What is malware short for? Answer: c) Malicious software Malware is essentially software engineered to damage, infiltrate, or compromise computers and networks.

4. What is the main purpose of data encryption? Answer: b) To make data unreadable without the key Encrypting data is meant to make it indecipherable to anyone lacking the appropriate decryption key.

5. What is a VPN? Answer: c) Virtual Private Network A VPN enables a secure online connection to another network over the internet.

6. What is phishing? Answer: b) A type of online scam Phishing attacks trick recipients via misleading emails to divulge personal information.

7. Which one is an operating system? Answer: b) Windows Windows is an operating system, unlike Python, HTTP, and CSS, which are not.

8. What does IoT stand for? Answer: c) Internet of Things IoT refers to the numerous physical devices that are connected to the internet nowadays.

9. Which of these is an example of a strong password? Answer: c) Pa$$w0rD! 'Pa$$w0rD!' is considered a strong password because it contains a mix of letters, numbers, and special characters.

10. What is a DDoS attack? Answer: c) Distributed Denial of Service DDoS aims to interfere with the normal traffic flow to a targeted server, network, or service.

11. What is the primary purpose of antivirus software? Answer: b) To detect and remove malware Antivirus software's main job is to identify and get rid of malware on your computer.

12. What does 2FA stand for? Answer: c) Two-Factor Authentication 2FA offers an additional security step during the login process.

13. What is the common port number for HTTP? Answer: b) 80 Port number 80 is the standard for HTTP communications.

14. What is ransomware? Answer: b) A software that locks files and demands payment for their release Ransomware encrypts your files and then asks for payment to unlock them.

15. What is a cookie in the context of web browsing? Answer: c) A small file that stores user settings Cookies store small bits of data to remember your website preferences.

16. What does CAPTCHA stand for? Answer: d) Completely Automated Public Turing test to tell Computers and Humans Apart CAPTCHAs are tests made to differentiate between human and automated inputs, often to prevent spam.

17. What does URL stand for? Answer: c) Uniform Resource Locator A URL specifies web addresses.

18. What is a brute-force attack? Answer: b) An attempt to crack a password by trying all possible combinations A brute-force attack entails trying all potential combinations to discover a password.

19. What does CSRF stand for? Answer: b) Cross-Site Request Forgery CSRF is an attack type that exploits vulnerabilities in a website.

20. What does SSD stand for? Answer: c) Solid State Drive SSD is a storage medium that utilizes integrated circuits to keep data.

21. What is a zero-day vulnerability? Answer: c) A vulnerability that is unknown to the vendor A zero-day vulnerability is a software flaw not yet known to those responsible for remedying it.

22. What is BYOD? Answer: c) Bring Your Own Device BYOD policies permit employees to bring their personal gadgets to work.

23. What is a honeypot? Answer: c) A trap set to detect or deflect unauthorized access A honeypot is designed to lure or catch unauthorized users.

24. What does PII stand for? Answer: c) Personally Identifiable Information PII is data that can be employed to identify an individual.

25. What does a digital signature provide? Answer: b) Authentication and integrity Digital signatures validate the sender's identity and ensure message integrity.

26. What is a botnet? Answer: b) A group of computers controlled without their owners' knowledge A botnet consists of multiple internet-connected devices operating one or more bots.

27. What is the primary purpose of social engineering? Answer: b) Manipulating people into revealing confidential information Social engineering manipulates people into giving away private information.

28. What is an intranet? Answer: b) A private network within an organization An intranet is restricted to users within the same organization.

29. What does UTM stand for? Answer: b) Unified Threat Management UTM is an all-in-one security solution that has revolutionized network security.

30. What does IDS stand for? Answer: a) Intrusion Detection System IDS monitors a network to spot malicious behavior or policy violations.

31. What is hashing used for? Answer: c) Verifying data integrity Hashing is mainly used to check the integrity of data as it is sent.

32. What does DMZ stand for? Answer: b) Demilitarized Zone DMZ is a subnetwork that exposes an organization's external services to a less secure network.

33. What does EDR stand for? Answer: b) Endpoint Detection and Response EDR is cybersecurity tech that continually monitors and responds to security threats.

34. What is the most frequent type of cybersecurity attack? Answer: c) Phishing Phishing commonly uses deceptive emails to execute cybersecurity attacks.

35. What is a keylogger? Answer: c) Software or hardware that records keystrokes A keylogger captures keyboard inputs on a computer.

36. What does MITM stand for? Answer: c) Man-in-the-Middle MITM attacks covertly alter or relay communications between two parties.

37. What is steganography? Answer: b) Hiding information within other information Steganography involves concealing one set of data within another.

38. What does SIEM stand for? Answer: a) Security Information and Event Management SIEM is an integrated solution for improving network security.

39. What is a cyber attack's primary aim? Answer: b) To steal, alter, or destroy data Typically, the goal of a cyber attack is to steal, modify, or erase data.

40. What does GDPR stand for? Answer: c) General Data Protection Regulation GDPR safeguards the personal data and privacy of individuals in the European Union.

2) Networks and Infrastructure

Understanding Networks

In the digital age, networks serve as the backbone of modern communication and business operations. They facilitate the seamless exchange of data between devices, individuals, and organizations, enabling a myriad of daily activities from emailing to online shopping. As we venture into this chapter, we'll unravel the fundamental concepts of networks, their significance, various types, and the basic components that constitute a network.

1. Importance of Networks:
   - Networks are pivotal for the functioning of contemporary societies and economies. They enable:
     - Communication: Allow instantaneous communication and collaboration between individuals and organizations globally.
     - Information Sharing: Facilitate the dissemination and access to information, enhancing knowledge and decision-making.
     - Resource Sharing: Enable sharing of resources like printers, files, and applications, optimizing operational efficiency.
     - Business Operations: Critical for carrying out business operations, customer interactions, and driving innovation.

2. Types of Network Configurations:
   - Networks differ based on dimensions, scope, and functionalities:
     - LAN (Localized Connection Networks): Links systems within a localized area like a residence, workspace, or campus.
     - WAN (Broad-Scope Networks): Covers extensive regions, typically beyond a city, connecting various localized networks.
     - MAN (Citywide Connection Networks): A halfway point between LAN and WAN, covering a large urban area.
     - PAN (Immediate Proximity Networks): Links gadgets within a confined space, often through technologies like Bluetooth or USB.

3. Core Network Elements:
   - The key components making up a network involve:
     - NICs (Network Connection Modules): The hardware that links computers to the network.
     - Data Traffic Managers (Switches): Specialized devices that send data solely to intended devices within the network.
     - Data Route Selectors (Routers): Gadgets that funnel data between a local network and external networks.
     - Wiring and Connective Hardware: The physical pathways linking all network devices.
     - Wireless Connection Points (Access Points): Hardware allowing wireless gadgets to join the network.
     - Security Barriers (Firewalls): Devices that scrutinize and manage incoming and outgoing data traffic based on pre-defined security guidelines.

4. Structure of Network Connections (Topologies):
   - The design of network elements significantly impacts network efficiency and operation:
     - Single-Path Topology: All devices share one communication line.
     - Centralized Star Topology: All gadgets are linked to a central data hub.
     - Closed-Circuit Topology: Each device links to two others, creating a loop.
     - Fully Interconnected Topology: Every device has a direct link to every other device.

5. Data Transmission Regulations (Protocols):
   - Regulations for seamless data transport include:
     - Basic Internet Protocols (TCP/IP): The backbone for most online interactions.
     - Web Page Protocols (HTTP/HTTPS): Protocols for web data exchange.
     - File Exchange Protocols (FTP): Rules for shifting files between networked computers.

6. Device Identifiers and Network Segmentation (IP and Subnetting):
   - Unique codes identify devices, and subnetting aids in logical division of networks.

7. Web-Based Naming System (DNS):
   - A structured naming method for online resources, both public and private.
8. The Imperatives of Secure Networking:
   - Network security measures are crucial for the safety and integrity of data:
     - Data Safeguards: Ensure confidential data remains secure.
     - Legal Compliance: Necessary for adhering to regulatory norms.
     - Data Integrity: Prevent unauthorized changes to data during transit.
     - Service Continuity: Ensures uninterrupted access to network services for authorized users.
9. Prevalent Security Risks:
   - Awareness of common network threats is essential:
     - Malicious Software: Includes various types of harmful software.
     - Service Denial Attacks: Targeted at disabling network resources.
     - Deceptive Data Collection (Phishing): Fraudulent acquisition of sensitive details.
     - Intercept Attacks (MitM): Unauthorized data interception.
     - Credential Cracking: Unauthorized access through password acquisition.
10. Enhancing Network Security:
   - Methods to strengthen network protection include:
     - Security Barriers (Firewalls): Separate trusted and risky networks.
     - Malware Detectors: Spot and neutralize harmful software.
     - Encrypted Network Extensions (VPNs): Secure data transmission over public networks.
     - Policy Violation Monitors (IDS): Spot and report unauthorized activities.
11. Network Oversight and Maintenance:
   - Vital for a secure and efficient network:
     - Traffic Pattern Studies: Helps spot anomalies or potential issues.
     - Operational Checks: Monitors network performance.
     - Activity Logs: Inspects for abnormal behavior or security threats.
     - Setup Control: Manages network configurations.
12. Upcoming Network Technologies:
   - Future trends in network technology include:
     - Controller-Based Networking (SDN): A new method for network management.
     - Faster Connectivity (5G and beyond): Poised to change network communications dramatically.
     - Device Networks (IoT): Links everyday gadgets, posing new networking challenges.
     - Near-Source Data Processing (Edge Computing): Handles data close to its point of generation.

Network Devices and Technologies

The robustness of a network largely depends on the devices and technologies that constitute it. In this section, we will dive deeper into the various network devices such as routers, switches, and firewalls, among others, and explore the technologies that enable networking. Understanding these components is pivotal for any IT professional, especially those looking to specialize in network security.

1. Routing Devices:
   - What They Do: Think of routing devices as traffic controllers, directing information flow between various networks, especially from local systems to the internet.
   - Essentials:
     - Path-Select Table: Pinpoints the most efficient routes for your data packets.
     - Public IP Sharing (NAT): Enables numerous local gadgets to utilize a single outward-facing IP address.
     - Dynamic IP Allocation (DHCP): Hands out IP addresses to devices within your network.
   - Security Highlights:

- Built-in Barriers: Many routing devices feature integrated firewalls for traffic scrutiny.
- Secured Remote Connections (VPN): VPN setups for secure off-site network access.

2. Data Switching Devices:
- What They Do: These are like switchboard operators, directing data solely to designated devices within a local network.
- Essentials:
  - Address Index: Uses MAC addresses to send packets to the right local destination.
  - Network Segmentation (VLANs): Permits creation of isolated data pathways in your network.
- Security Highlights:
  - Port Access Limits: Stops unauthorized gadgets from latching onto your network.
  - Traffic Rule Sets (ACLs): Enables traffic governance via set conditions.

3. Barrier Systems (Firewalls):
- What They Do: These are your network's bouncers, inspecting and managing data coming in or going out.
- Essentials:
  - Packet Rule: Examines data chunks and allows or blocks them based on preset criteria.
  - Context-Aware Checks (Stateful Inspection): Considers ongoing sessions for data management.
- Security Highlights:
  - Preemptive Safeguards (IPS): Detects and neutralizes potential security risks.
  - VPN Capabilities: Often comes with VPN features for encrypted off-site access.

4. Wire-Free Access Points (WAPs):
- What They Do: These are gateways for wireless gadgets to join the wired landscape.
- Essentials:
  - Network ID Broadcasting (SSID): Advertises the network for wireless connections.
  - Transmission Security (WPA2/WPA3): Provides secure wireless data transfer options.
- Security Highlights:
  - Device Whitelisting (MAC Filtering): Grants or denies network entry based on device identifiers.
  - Secure Entry Protocols: Ensures that only vetted users can connect.

5. Connective Materials:
- Discusses various cable types like Ethernet (Cat5, Cat6) and fiber optics, along with their connectors.

6. Protocol and Standard Guidelines:
- Covers essentials like Ethernet, TCP/IP, and the two Internet Protocol versions, IPv4 and IPv6.

7. High-Level Network Gear:
- Highlights the role of Load Balancers and Proxy Servers in advanced networking setups.

8. Next-Gen Network Tech:
- Discusses innovative trends like Software-Defined Networking (SDN) and 5G capabilities.

9. Diagnostic Utilities:
- Introduces tools like Wireshark for network traffic assessment and Network Management Systems for comprehensive network oversight.

10. Virtual Realms and NFV:
- Explains how virtualization and Network Function Virtualization are transforming network management, providing benefits like cost reduction and agile service deployment.

11. Service Quality Metrics (QoS):
- Discusses the concept of traffic prioritization for optimal network performance.

12. WAN Flexibility (SD-WAN):
- Explains how SD-WAN provides dynamic traffic management for wide-area networks.

13. Trouble-Shooting Arsenal:
- Includes tools like Ping, Traceroute, DNS Lookup, and network sniffers for diagnosing connectivity hitches.

14. Structural Blueprints:
   - Compares the physical layout and data flow schematics in network design.
15. Crisis Readiness and Continuity:
   - Explains the importance of disaster recovery and business continuity in network maintenance.
16. Cloud-Centric Networks:
   - Discusses the cloud as a tool for network management and analytics.
17. High-Availability Networks (CDNs):
   - Describes how CDNs optimize content delivery for better performance and lower latency.
18. Automated Workflows:
   - Introduces the concept of network automation and orchestration for streamlined network management.
19. Security Watchdogs (IDS & IPS):
   - Explains how Intrusion Detection and Prevention Systems monitor and take action against suspicious network activity.
20. On-The-Go Networking:
   - Discusses mobile network technologies, challenges, and security solutions.
21. Trust-Nothing Security (Zero Trust):
   - Explains the Zero Trust model of not assuming trustworthiness for any entity inside or outside the network perimeter, and the need for verification.

Network Design Principles

1. Redundancy:
   - What it Means: Redundancy in a network context is the act of duplicating key system components to enhance system reliability.
   - How it Works:
      - Double Routers: Deploying more than one router to make sure data flow is unaffected if one device stops working.
      - Replica Servers: Utilizing backup servers to maintain service availability even if the primary server goes offline.
      - Resource-Pooled Systems: Using clustered systems that pool resources to provide uninterrupted service during component failures.
   - Advantages:
      - Steady Uptime: Redundancy reduces the risk of service disruption.
      - Performance Boost: Load distribution across redundant components can improve performance.
   - Things to Consider:
      - Expense: Redundancy often involves additional expenditure for hardware or software.
      - Operational Complexity: A higher number of components can complicate management and diagnostics.
      - Ongoing Maintenance: Constant upkeep is required to ensure backup systems are operational.
   - Real-world Applications:
      - Traffic Distribution: Employing load balancing to prevent server overloads.
      - Auto-Switching: Using automatic failover for immediate system recovery during failures.
2. Scalability:
   - What it Means: Scalability refers to a network's ability to adapt and grow as workload increases.
   - How it Works:
      - Flexible Design: Using a modular approach that allows for easy upgrades or additions.
      - High-Capacity Devices: Employing routers and switches that can accommodate growing data flow.
      - Resource Maximization: Leveraging virtualization to optimize hardware resources.
   - Advantages:
      - Adaptability: Makes it easier to handle growth without a major redesign.
      - Budget-Friendly: Allows for piecemeal growth, lowering upfront costs.

- Things to Consider:
    - Stable Performance: Ensuring that performance isn't compromised as the network grows.
    - Ease of Management: Assessing management needs for a larger network.
    - Financial Implications: Budget considerations for scaling up.
  - Real-world Applications:
    - On-Demand Resources: Using cloud solutions that can scale as needed.
    - Growth-Friendly Infrastructure: Designing an architecture that minimizes the need for major changes when scaling.

3. Security:
   - What it Means: Network security encompasses the strategies and technologies for safeguarding network data from unauthorized access and threats.
    - How it Works:
      - Traffic Monitors: Using firewalls and intrusion detection and prevention systems to oversee network data flow.
      - Permission Barriers: Implementing strong access control methods to restrict unauthorized network access.
      - Data Safeguarding: Employing encryption protocols to protect data in transit.
      - Scheduled Security Checks: Running routine security reviews to find and rectify potential vulnerabilities.
    - Advantages:
      - Guarding Data: Provides a level of confidentiality, integrity, and data availability.
      - Regulatory Adherence: Facilitates compliance with legal and industry requirements.
    - Things to Consider:
      - Threat Monitoring: Ongoing vigilance for emerging threats.
      - Policy Governance: Crafting and enforcing comprehensive security rules.
      - User Education: Training users on how to maintain security.
    - Real-world Applications:
      - Multi-step Verification: Using multi-factor authentication for enhanced security when accessing network resources.
- Regular Patching and Updating: Ensuring that the network systems are updated with the latest security patches

4. Real-world Application:
     Incorporating these principles in real-world scenarios such as designing a network for a growing business, ensuring it has the redundancy to withstand hardware failures, the scalability to accommodate growth, and the security measures to protect sensitive data.
- Discussing real-world scenarios where these principles are applied, such as in a large organization where network redundancy, scalability, and security are critical for operations. Detailed analysis of a real-world scenario, explaining how the principles are implemented, challenges encountered, and solutions provided.

5. Best Practices:
   - Employing best practices in network design such as adhering to industry standards, continuous monitoring and maintenance, and staying updated on the latest in network technologies and security threats.
- Continuous Monitoring: Employing monitoring systems to track network performance, security, and the functioning of redundant systems.
- Disaster Recovery Planning: Preparing for potential network failures with disaster recovery plans that outline the steps for restoring network functionality

6. Exam Tips:
   - Understanding these principles and their implementation is vital for the CompTIA Security+ exam. Being able to apply these principles in practical scenarios will be beneficial in both the examination and your future career in IT security.
- Highlighting specific areas of focus regarding network design principles for exam preparation, including understanding the different redundancy protocols, scalability strategies, and security protocols. Providing tips on how to tackle exam questions related to network design.

Network Topologies and Configurations

This section explores various network topologies, their configurations, and how they impact network communication and security, which are vital for your CompTIA Security+ exam preparation and career in IT security.

Certainly, here's a reworded version of the information on various network topologies:

1. Bus Layout:
   - Overview: All nodes are linked to a solitary shared line known as a bus.
   - Pros:
     - Quick to establish.
     - Economical due to minimal cabling.
   - Cons:
     - Central line failure can incapacitate the entire network.
     - Ineffective for extensive networks with numerous nodes.
   - Typical Applications:
     - Basic setups like home or small-scale office networks.
     - Outdated systems where an advanced layout isn't viable.
   - Design Factors:
     - Both ends of the bus line need terminators to avoid signal bounce.
     - Rigorous cable organization is key to averting network outages.

2. Circular Layout:
   - Overview: Every device is linked in a loop, connecting to two adjacent devices.
   - Pros:
     - Allows bidirectional data flow, decreasing collision risk.
   - Cons:
     - A single point of failure can disrupt the entire network.
     - Adding or removing nodes can be intricate and cause downtime.
   - Typical Applications:
     - Environments where dual-direction data flow is essential, such as in specific industrial contexts.
   - Design Factors:
     - The choice between token passing or circulating messages depends on the network needs.
     - Periodic upkeep is mandatory to maintain optimal functionality.

3. Radial Layout:
   - Overview: Each device is directly linked to a core hub or switch.
   - Pros:
     - Simplifies the addition or removal of devices.
     - A single cable malfunction won't incapacitate other devices.
   - Cons:
     - Failure of the core hub can deactivate the entire network.
     - Demands more wiring compared to bus or circular layouts.
   - Typical Applications:
     - Business settings where centralized oversight and easy diagnosis are key.
     - High-reliability networks that necessitate simple scalability.
   - Design Factors:
     - A high-performance central hub is essential for efficient network traffic control.
     - Thorough cable arrangement and tagging are critical for ease of diagnosis and growth.

4. Full-Connectivity Layout:
   - Overview: All devices form multiple connections with every other device in the network. Every device is directly linked to every other device in the system, creating a web of connections.

- Pros:
    - High redundancy ensures network stability.
    - Optimized for data transmission without bottlenecks.
  - Cons:
    - Expensive due to the high number of required cables and connections.
    - Complex to set up and manage.
  - Typical Applications:
    - Data centers where fault tolerance and high-speed data transmission are vital.
    - Environments requiring exceptional reliability, such as emergency services.
  - Design Factors:
    - Rigorous planning is needed to manage the web of connections effectively.
    - Frequent maintenance checks are essential to ensure all links are functional.
- Use Case Scenarios:
  - High-security networks like military or government networks where redundancy and data integrity are crucial.
  - Large data centers with high traffic loads.
- Configuration Considerations:
  - The layout of physical cables and logical connections requires careful planning.
  - Network management systems are crucial for monitoring and maintaining the mesh network

5. Hybrid Topology:
  - Description: A combination of two or more different types of topologies.
  - Advantages:
    - Benefits from the advantages of the combined topologies.
    - Scalable and easy to design.
  - Disadvantages:
    - Can be more complex to set up and manage.
    - Troubleshooting network issues can be challenging.
- Use Case Scenarios:
  - Large enterprises with varied networking requirements across different departments or units.
- Configuration Considerations:
  - Proper planning is required to determine which topologies to combine and how to interconnect them.
  - Network management and troubleshooting can be more complex compared to other topologies.

6. Tree Topology:
  - Description: A combination of star and bus topologies, with a central root node connected to multiple star networks.
  - Advantages:
    - Scalable and easy to manage.
    - Isolation of network issues is possible.
  - Disadvantages:
    - A failure in the central bus will bring down the entire network.
    - The hierarchy can lead to a slower network.
- Use Case Scenarios:
  - Hierarchical organizations where different levels or units require separate network segments.
  - Educational institutions with different departments requiring distinct network segments.
- Configuration Considerations:
  - Careful planning is required to determine the hierarchy and layout of the network.
  - Robust central bus and hubs/switches are crucial for managing network traffic efficiently.

Illustrative Diagrams:

Real-world Applications:
Exploring real-world scenarios where these topologies are employed, and discussing how the choice of topology affects network performance, scalability, and security.

Exam Tips:
Highlighting the importance of understanding network topologies for the CompTIA Security+ exam, offering tips on how to remember the characteristics, advantages, and disadvantages of each topology, and how they apply to real-world network design and security scenarios.

- Being able to differentiate between these topologies, understanding their advantages, disadvantages, and suitable use cases is crucial for the CompTIA Security+ exam.

- Practical knowledge of how to configure these topologies, troubleshoot common issues, and optimize their performance will be beneficial in both the examination and your future career in IT security.

Designing a Secure Corporate Network

1. Understanding Requirements:
   - Business Requirements: Identifying the needs of CorpX such as data privacy, regulatory compliance, and business continuity.
      - Data Privacy: Ensuring the confidentiality of sensitive financial data is paramount. Evaluating the types of data being handled and the privacy requirements surrounding them is the first step.
      - Regulatory Compliance: Financial institutions are subject to various regulations like GLBA, SOX, etc. Understanding these compliance requirements is crucial.
      - Business Continuity: Establishing a business continuity plan to ensure operations continue smoothly in case of network failures or other disruptions.
   - Technical Requirements: Assessing the technical needs like network scalability, redundancy, and security measures.
      - Network Scalability: Assessing future growth and ensuring the network can scale to meet increasing demand.
      - Redundancy: Ensuring that critical network components are redundant to prevent downtime.
      - Security Measures: Identifying the security measures necessary to protect against potential threats

2. Planning and Design:
   - Topology Selection: Opting for a hybrid topology to cater to different departmental needs while ensuring centralized control.
   - Security Measures: Planning for firewalls, intrusion detection systems (IDS), and intrusion prevention systems (IPS) to safeguard the network.
   - Compliance Measures: Ensuring the design complies with financial industry regulations like GLBA and SOX.
   - Topology Selection:
      - Evaluating the pros and cons of different network topologies and selecting the most suitable one for CorpX.
      - Considering a hybrid topology to cater to different departmental needs while ensuring centralized control.
   - Security Measures:
      - Planning for firewalls, intrusion detection systems (IDS), and intrusion prevention systems (IPS) to safeguard the network.
      - Considering additional security measures such as multi-factor authentication (MFA) and encryption to protect sensitive data.
   - Compliance Measures:
      - Working closely with compliance experts to ensure the network design adheres to industry-specific regulations.

- Scheduling routine compliance reviews to promptly detect and address any non-adherence to standards.

3. Execution:
- Infrastructure Deployment: Establishing the network backbone with essential hardware like routers, switches, and firewalls.
- Security Measures: Activating intrusion detection and prevention systems (IDS/IPS), enforcing access management, and initializing encryption methods.
- Validation: Carrying out extensive assessments to validate the network's functionality and its adherence to security benchmarks.
- Infrastructure Details:
- Installing essential network hardware such as routers, switches, and firewalls.
- Fine-tuning the network hardware for secure integration within the network environment.
- Security Protocols:
- Setting up intrusion detection and prevention mechanisms, implementing robust access control measures, and initiating encryption techniques.
- Instituting a secure Virtual Private Network (VPN) for authorized remote access to the business network.
- Testing:
- Conducting rigorous testing to ensure the network operates as designed and meets security standards.
- Identifying any vulnerabilities or weaknesses in the network design and making necessary adjustments

4. Challenges and Solutions:
- Challenge 1 - Security Compliance:
- Solution: Engaging a compliance expert to ensure that the network design adheres to industry-specific regulations.
- Challenge 2 - Scalability:
- Solution: Employing a modular design that allows for easy expansion as CorpX grows.
- Challenge 3 - Threat Management:
- Solution: Implementing a robust threat management system that includes continuous monitoring and regular security audits.

5. Maintenance and Monitoring:
- Network Monitoring: Establishing a network operations center (NOC) for continuous monitoring of network health and security.
- Regular Audits: Conducting regular security audits to identify and rectify vulnerabilities.
- User Training: Educating users on security best practices to minimize the risk of security breaches.

6. Evaluation and Optimization:
- Performance Evaluation: Assessing the network's performance to ensure it meets CorpX's operational and security requirements.
- Optimization: Identifying areas of improvement and implementing optimizations to enhance network security and performance.

7. Future Expansion Plans:
- Cloud Integration: Planning for potential cloud integration to enhance scalability and flexibility.
- Advanced Security Measures: Considering the implementation of advanced security measures like zero-trust security and AI-driven threat detection.

8. Exam Tips:
- Understanding the practical aspects of network design, security implementation, and troubleshooting are critical for the CompTIA Security+ exam.
- Familiarity with real-world challenges and solutions will provide a practical perspective that is invaluable for both the exam and your career in IT security.

Interactive Quizzes: Assess Your Understanding of Network Fundamentals

1. What does TCP stand for?
   - a) Traffic Control Protocol
   - b) Transmission Control Protocol
   - c) Text Communication Protocol
   - d) Terminal Connection Protocol
2. Which port does HTTP use by default?
   - a) 21
   - b) 80
   - c) 443
   - d) 25
3. What is the primary function of a router?
   - a) Data storage
   - b) Network traffic control
   - c) Firewall
   - d) Connecting multiple networks
4. What is DHCP responsible for?
   - a) Encryption
   - b) Assigning IP addresses
   - c) Port Security
   - d) Data filtering
5. What type of IP address is 192.168.1.1?
   - a) Public
   - b) Dynamic
   - c) Static
   - d) Private
6. What does LAN stand for?
   - a) Local Area Network
   - b) Linear Assignment Node
   - c) Large Assessment Network
   - d) Last Arrival Notification
7. What does NAT do?
   - a) Blocks unwanted traffic
   - b) Translates IP addresses
   - c) Encrypts data
   - d) Prioritizes packets
8. What is the primary purpose of VLAN?
   - a) Data Encryption
   - b) Traffic Isolation
   - c) Data Storage
   - d) Load Balancing
9. Which layer of OSI model deals with routing?
   - a) Physical
   - b) Presentation
   - c) Network
   - d) Data link

10. What protocol is commonly used for email retrieval?
   - a) HTTP
   - b) SMTP
   - c) POP3
   - d) FTP
11. What is the size of an IPv4 address?
   - a) 32 bits
   - b) 128 bytes
   - c) 64 bits
   - d) 48 bits
12. What does DNS stand for?
   - a) Data Network Security
   - b) Domain Name System
   - c) Digital Network Service
   - d) Dynamic Name Server
13. What does a switch do?
   - a) Store data
   - b) Assign IP addresses
   - c) Route traffic between networks
   - d) Operate within a LAN to connect devices
14. What is the function of a firewall?
   - a) Data storage
   - b) Control network traffic
   - c) Assigning IP addresses
   - d) Translating web addresses to IP addresses
15. Which port is commonly used for SSH?
   - a) 21
   - b) 22
   - c) 80
   - d) 443
16. What does a VPN provide?
   - a) Increased storage
   - b) A virtual LAN
   - c) Secure network connection
   - d) File sharing capabilities
17. Which protocol operates at the Transport Layer?
   - a) IP
   - b) FTP
   - c) TCP
   - d) ARP
18. What is the function of SNMP?
   - a) Mail Transfer
   - b) File Sharing
   - c) Network Management
   - d) Web Hosting

19. What does ICMP stand for?
- a) Internet Control Management Protocol
- b) Internal Communication Messaging Protocol
- c) Internet Control Message Protocol
- d) Integrated Command Management Protocol

20. What does SSL do?
- a) Assigns IP addresses
- b) Encrypts web traffic
- c) Translates domain names
- d) Manages network devices

21. What is the function of the MAC address?
- a) Network Routing
- b) Data Encryption
- c) Device Identification on a LAN
- d) Bandwidth Management

22. What is the primary purpose of a proxy server?
- a) File Storage
- b) Mail transfer
- c) Web Filtering
- d) Load Balancing

23. What does QoS stand for?
- a) Query of Service
- b) Quality of Service
- c) Quick on Start
- d) Queue of System

24. What is the primary function of ARP?
- a) IP address assignment
- b) Web filtering
- c) Resolving IP to MAC address
- d) Traffic control

25. What does the "P" in VoIP stand for?
- a) Phone
- b) Proxy
- c) Protocol
- d) Port

26. Which protocol uses port 53?
- a) DNS
- b) HTTP
- c) FTP
- d) SMTP

27. What does WAN stand for?
- a) Wide Area Network
- b) Web Access Node
- c) Wireless Application Network
- d) Windows Architecture Network

28. What is the function of an IDS?
- a) Web Hosting
- b) Intrusion Detection

- c) IP Address Assignment
- d) Load Balancing

29. What is the full form of MPLS?
- a) Multi-Port Lan Service
- b) Massive Packet Load System
- c) Multi-Protocol Label Switching
- d) Main-Port Load Server

30. What does SAN stand for?
- a) Storage Area Network
- b) Security Application Node
- c) Simple Assignment Node
- d) Static Area Network

31. What does a NIC do?
- a) Route Traffic
- b) Manage Ports
- c) Connect a device to a network
- d) Data storage

32. What is the purpose of the OSI model?
- a) Data Storage
- b) Traffic Routing
- c) Standardize Network Interactions
- d) Web hosting

33. What is the function of Telnet?
- a) Secure file transfer
- b) Web hosting
- c) Remote access to another computer
- d) Data encryption

34. What does the "F" in FTP stand for?
- a) Frame
- b) File
- c) Forward
- d) Fiber

35. What does APIPA stand for?
- a) Automatic Private IP Addressing
- b) Assigned Public IP Address
- c) Auto-Protocol Internet Port Allocation
- d) Automatic Port Identification and Allocation

36. What does NTP do?
- a) File transfer
- b) Time synchronization
- c) IP address translation
- d) Nothing

37. What does POP3 stand for?
- a) Point of Protocol 3
- b) Post Office Protocol 3
- c) Port over Protocol 3
- d) Packet over Port 3

38. Which of these is an example of unguided media?

- a) Coaxial cable
- b) Fiber optic cable
- c) Microwave
- d) Twisted pair

39. Which protocol uses port 25?
- a) HTTP
- b) DNS
- c) SMTP
- d) FTP

40. What is the primary use of RDP?
- a) Email retrieval
- b) File transfer
- c) Remote desktop access
- d) Time synchronization

ANSWERS

1. What does TCP stand for? Answer: b) Transmission Control Protocol - TCP is responsible for reliable data transmission between devices.

2. Which port does HTTP use by default? Answer: b) 80 - HTTP uses port 80 by default for communication.

3. What is the primary function of a router? Answer: d) Connecting multiple networks - A router's primary function is to connect different networks and route data packets between them.

4. What is DHCP responsible for? Answer: b) Assigning IP addresses - DHCP is responsible for automatically assigning IP addresses to devices on a network.

5. What type of IP address is 192.168.1.1? Answer: d) Private - 192.168.1.1 is an example of a private IP address, typically used within a local network.

6. What does LAN stand for? Answer: a) Local Area Network - LAN stands for Local Area Network, a network that connects computers within a limited area.

7. What does NAT do? Answer: b) Translates IP addresses - NAT allows multiple devices on a local network to use a single public IP address.

8. What is the primary purpose of VLAN? Answer: b) Traffic Isolation - VLANs are used to segment network traffic and isolate it effectively.

9. Which layer of OSI model deals with routing? Answer: c) Network - The Network layer of the OSI model is responsible for routing data packets between devices.

10. What protocol is commonly used for email retrieval? Answer: c) POP3 - POP3 is commonly used for email retrieval.

11. What is the size of an IPv4 address? Answer: a) 32 bits - An IPv4 address is 32 bits in size.

12. What does DNS stand for? Answer: b) Domain Name System - DNS translates domain names to IP addresses.

13. What does a switch do? Answer: d) Operate within a LAN to connect devices - A switch operates within a LAN to connect devices and manage traffic.

14. What is the function of a firewall? Answer: b) Control network traffic - A firewall is designed to control incoming and outgoing network traffic based on predetermined rules.

15. Which port is commonly used for SSH? Answer: b) 22 - SSH commonly uses port 22.

16. What does a VPN provide? Answer: c) Secure network connection - A VPN provides a secure connection over a public network.

17. Which protocol operates at the Transport Layer? Answer: c) TCP - TCP operates at the Transport Layer of the OSI model.

18. What is the function of SNMP? Answer: c) Network Management - SNMP is used for managing devices on IP networks.

19. What does ICMP stand for? Answer: c) Internet Control Message Protocol - ICMP is used by network devices to send error messages and other condition indicators.

20. What does SSL do? Answer: b) Encrypts web traffic - SSL is used for securing data transmission on the internet.

21. What is the function of the MAC address? Answer: c) Device Identification on a LAN - A MAC address uniquely identifies a device on a LAN.

22. What is the primary purpose of a proxy server? Answer: c) Web Filtering - Proxy servers are often used to filter web content.

23. What does QoS stand for? Answer: b) Quality of Service - QoS controls the performance, reliability, and quality of network services.

24. What is the primary function of ARP? Answer: c) Resolving IP to MAC address - ARP is used to find the MAC address of a device from its IP address.

25. What does the "P" in VoIP stand for? Answer: c) Protocol - VoIP stands for Voice over Internet Protocol.

26. Which protocol uses port 53? Answer: a) DNS - DNS uses port 53 for domain name resolution services.

27. What does WAN stand for? Answer: a) Wide Area Network - WAN stands for Wide Area Network, which is a network that extends over a large area.

28. What is the function of an IDS? Answer: b) Intrusion Detection - IDS is used to detect unauthorized access to a network.

29. What is the full form of MPLS? Answer: c) Multi-Protocol Label Switching - MPLS is used to speed up and shape traffic flows across enterprise networks.

30. What does SAN stand for? Answer: a) Storage Area Network - SAN is a dedicated network for data storage.

31. What does a NIC do? Answer: c) Connect a device to a network - NIC is hardware that connects a device to a network.

32. What is the purpose of the OSI model? Answer: c) Standardize Network Interactions - The OSI model is used to standardize how different networking protocols interact.

33. What is the function of Telnet? Answer: c) Remote access to another computer - Telnet provides terminal emulation for accessing remote computers.

34. What does the "F" in FTP stand for? Answer: b) File - FTP stands for File Transfer Protocol.

35. What does APIPA stand for? Answer: a) Automatic Private IP Addressing - APIPA is used for automatic IP address assignment when a DHCP server is not available.

36. What does NTP do? Answer: b) Time synchronization - NTP is used for synchronizing time across network devices.

37. What does POP3 stand for? Answer: b) Post Office Protocol 3 - POP3 is used for retrieving email from a mail server.

38. Which of these is an example of unguided media? Answer: c) Microwave - Microwave is an example of unguided media used in networking.

39. Which protocol uses port 25? Answer: c) SMTP - SMTP uses port 25 for email transmission.

40. What is the primary use of RDP? Answer: c) Remote desktop access - RDP is used to remotely access another computer's desktop.

3) Cryptography

Demystifying Cryptography

1. Grasping Cryptography:
   - Explanation: Cryptography involves the methods and practices to secure data transmission and storage.
   - Objective: Its main goals are to maintain data confidentiality, uphold integrity, and verify authenticity.
2. Essential Elements:
   - Ciphering: Transforming readable text into an unreadable format through a specific algorithm and a cryptographic key.
   - Deciphering: Reversing the ciphering process to convert unreadable text back to its original form.
   - Cryptographic Key: A specific piece of data used for ciphering and deciphering.
3. Varieties of Cryptography:
   - Shared-Key Cryptography: Utilizes a single key for both ciphering and deciphering.
   - Public-Key Cryptography: Employs distinct keys (public and private) for ciphering and deciphering tasks.
   - Hash Algorithms: These produce a constant-size string of characters, usually a numerical sequence, based on variable input data.
4. Historical Progression:
   - Early Encryption Techniques: Examines early cryptographic methods like Scytale and Caesar's cipher.
   - War-Time Role: Evaluates the importance of cryptography in the World Wars, emphasizing devices like the Enigma machine.
   - Contemporary Methods: Investigates the emergence of modern cryptographic standards after the computer age.
   - Early Encryption Techniques:
     - Cryptographic systems have roots in ancient times, with methods like Scytale used by the Spartans and the Caesar's cipher, a basic substitution technique.
     - As time progressed, methods like the Vigenère Cipher emerged, adding more complexity through polyalphabetic substitution.
   - War-Time Role:
     - During the global conflicts of the 20th century, cryptography became pivotal. The Enigma machine was a crucial tool for the Germans, and its eventual cracking had a significant impact on the war.
   - Contemporary Methods:
     - The rise of computers has led to the creation of strong cryptographic algorithms such as AES (Advanced Encryption Standard) and RSA (Rivest-Shamir-Adleman).
5. Utilization of Cryptography:
   - Secure Communications: Protecting various means of communication, like emails and texts.
   - At-Rest Data Protection: Implementing encryption to safeguard stored information.
   - Digital Verification: Confirming the source and unchanged status of digital messages or documents.
   - Secure Communications:
     - Encryption is vital for safeguarding different communication mediums, from emails to instant messaging and VOIP services.
   - At-Rest Data Protection:
     - Encryption is applied to stored data to thwart unauthorized access, be it personal or corporate information.
   - Digital Verification:
     - Digital signatures confirm both the origin and integrity of digital messages or documents.
6. Concerns and Factors:
   - Managing Keys: Explores issues with creating, distributing, and storing cryptographic keys.
   - Code Breaking: Discusses the methods adversaries use to compromise cryptographic systems.
   - Operational Impact: Considers the effect of encryption on system performance.

- Managing Keys:
    - The handling of cryptographic keys is vital and includes their creation, distribution, secure storage, and eventual removal.
- Code Breaking:
    - The goal of code-breaking, or cryptanalysis, is to compromise encryption algorithms, setting up a challenge for cryptographers to stay ahead.
- Operational Impact:
    - Implementing cryptographic solutions may affect system performance, necessitating a trade-off between security and functionality.

7. Future Prospects:
   - Quantum-Based Methods: Introduces the idea of quantum cryptography and its implications for secure communications.
   - Quantum-Resistant Algorithms: Highlights efforts to create cryptographic solutions that can withstand quantum computing attacks.
   - Quantum-Based Methods:
       - Quantum cryptography aims to offer unparalleled security, primarily through techniques like Quantum Key Distribution (QKD).
   - Quantum-Resistant Algorithms:
       - As quantum computing becomes more advanced, there is ongoing work to develop algorithms that can resist quantum-driven attacks.

Encryption Algorithms

1. Symmetric Key Methods:
   - What It Is: Symmetric key encryption uses a single key for both encoding and decoding data. This approach is computationally less demanding, making it well-suited for high-volume data encryption.
   - Real-world Examples:
       - AES: This is a commonly used encryption algorithm, valued for its speed and robust security measures. Its key length can be 128, 192, or 256 bits, allowing for varying levels of security. Ideal for securing sensitive data in sectors like healthcare and finance.
       - DES: Once a forerunner in this space, DES has lost its luster due to its short 56-bit key, making it susceptible to brute-force attacks.
       - 3DES: This is a more secure iteration of DES, as it applies the DES algorithm three times to each data block, but uses different keys.

2. Asymmetric Key Methods:
   - What It Is: In asymmetric encryption, two keys are used: one for encrypting and another for decrypting. While it offers enhanced security, it comes at the cost of being more computationally intensive.
   - Real-world Examples:
       - RSA: A cornerstone in modern security protocols like SSL/TLS. RSA is based on the difficulty of factoring large composite numbers.
       - ECC: Known for its efficiency and shorter key lengths, ECC is especially useful in resource-limited settings.

3. Stream vs Block Algorithms:
   - Stream Algorithms: Ideal for real-time communication, these encrypt data bit-by-bit or byte-by-byte. They offer the advantage of lower latency and are often used in applications like VoIP and video streaming.
   - Block Algorithms: These encrypt data in fixed-size blocks. This makes them suitable for contexts where the total data size is predetermined.

4. Hashing Techniques:
   - What It Is: These algorithms convert input data into a fixed-length string of characters, which appears random.
   - Properties:

- Resistance to Backtracking: It should be virtually impossible to revert to the original data from its hash.
- Collision Safeguard: Two different inputs should not produce the same hash.
- Real-world Examples:
    - SHA-256: Widely used in various security systems.
    - MD5: Now considered insecure and used mainly for non-security purposes.

5. Assessing Cryptographic Strength:
   - Key Size: Longer keys generally mean higher security but can also impact performance.
   - Design Factors: The algorithm should be robust against a variety of attack strategies like differential and linear cryptanalysis.

6. Performance and Constraints:
   - Efficiency: Measured by the computational resources required.
   - Memory Footprint: Algorithms with lower memory requirements are often preferred in resource-limited settings.

7. Adhering to Standards:
   - FIPS 140-2: A U.S. federal standard outlining the security specs for cryptographic modules.
   - Common Criteria: An international framework for evaluating security features of IT products.
   - PCI DSS: Requires strong encryption for transmitting cardholder data over public networks.
   - Regulatory Compliance: Includes GDPR and HIPAA which necessitate strong encryption for sensitive personal data.

8. Future-Proof Encryption:
   - Post-Quantum Algorithms: Research into encryption that can withstand quantum computing attacks.
   - Homomorphic Techniques: Allows computations on encrypted data, which can be decrypted to reveal the result of the operations performed on the original data.

9. Trends and Community Engagement:
   - AI in Cryptography: Emerging trends include using machine learning and AI to enhance encryption.
   - Open-Source Initiatives: The open-source community is instrumental in improving encryption methods through collective scrutiny.

10. Industry Influence:
   - Standardization Bodies: Organizations like the IETF and ISO play a key role in setting and disseminating cryptographic standards.

Public and Private Key Infrastructure

1. Essential Elements of Public Key Infrastructure (PKI):
   - E-Certificates:
     - E-certificates act as the backbone of PKI, serving as digital IDs that verify the legitimacy of participants in a digital activity. A trusted Certificate Issuer (CI) signs these certificates, which contain the public key and additional identification data.
     - Lifecycle Management of Certificates:
       - The complete lifespan of an e-certificate— from its formation to utilization, storage, and ultimate termination or expiration—requires effective administration to uphold the integrity and functionality of the PKI system.
     - Certificate Issuers (CIs):
       - CIs act as the reliable entities within the PKI domain, responsible for distributing, renewing, and canceling e-certificates. They authenticate the participants who apply for a certificate, thereby laying a foundation of trust for secure digital interactions.
     - Primary and Secondary CIs:
       - In a tiered PKI, primary CIs occupy the highest rank, generating their own certificates and providing certificates to secondary CIs. These secondary CIs can then issue certificates to end-users or other secondary CIs, forming a trust hierarchy.
     - Enrollment Authorities (EAs):

- EAs operate as CI assistants, dealing with the initial scrutiny of certificate applications prior to CI processing. They alleviate the CI's verification load, ensuring a smooth certificate allocation process.
- Revocation Checklists (RCLs) and Real-time Certificate Status Checks:
- RCLs and real-time checks are the tools for confirming the termination status of e-certificates, enabling parties to determine if a certificate is still valid and reliable.

2. Working Principles:
- Creation of Key Duos:
- The cornerstone of PKI involves generating a linked pair of cryptographic keys: an open key for public sharing and a restricted key for confidentiality. These keys enable safe data exchange and confirmation.
- Application for and Allotment of Certificates:
- Entities wishing to acquire an e-certificate create a Certificate Application Note (CAN), submitted to a CI or EA for review. Following successful authentication, the CI allocates an e-certificate containing pertinent details and the public key.
- Certificate Confirmation:
- During digital interactions, parties swap and authenticate each other's e-certificates to set up mutual trust before commencing with encrypted exchanges.

3. PKI Use Cases:
- HTTPS for Encrypted Web Navigation:
- PKI serves as the underpinning for HTTPS protocols, critical for encrypting web sessions. PKI enables key swapping and server authentication, guaranteeing data confidentiality and integrity during web transactions.
- High-Trust Certificates:
- These are a specific kind of HTTPS certificate that undergo detailed CI validation for maximum trust and verification.
- Encrypted Email and E-Signatures:
- PKI offers the means to encode emails and attach electronic signatures. This enhances the privacy and reliability of email interactions, particularly for businesses and sensitive communications.
- Encrypted Network Access via VPNs:
- PKI is vital for VPNs, authenticating users and hardware while establishing encrypted pathways for remote corporate network access.
- Mobile Device Trust:
- PKI has a growing role in verifying mobile devices that interact with corporate networks, thereby improving mobile security measures.

4. Hurdles and Future Prospects:
- Expandability:
- Keeping up with the growing digital landscape and the increasing demand for certificates and identities is a key challenge for PKI.
- The Quantum Computing Era:
- The expected arrival of quantum computing could potentially unravel the cryptographic security underpinnings of PKI.
- Distributed Ledger for PKI:
- Blockchain technology could offer a decentralized, immutable ledger for PKI, reducing some of the risks associated with centralized systems.
- AI and ML Enhancements:
- Incorporating AI and ML could improve abnormality detection and security responsiveness in PKI.

5. Compliance and Standardization:
- Regulatory Adherence:
- A strong PKI is essential to comply with laws like GDPR and HIPAA that govern secure digital communications.
- Industry Norms:

- Existing standards like X.509 for e-certificates and ETSI for digital signatures offer a unified blueprint for PKI deployment and governance.

Illustrative Diagram: How Encryption Works

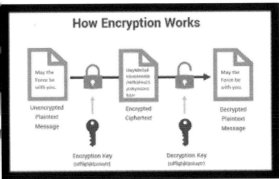

1. Description of Graphic:
   - The visual starts with Alice wanting to dispatch a confidential note to Bob.
   - Alice holds a clear-text message she plans to secure via encryption prior to sending.
   - A cryptographic formula along with a cryptographic key are utilized to morph the clear-text into cipher-text.
   - This cipher-text navigates through the transmission medium, remaining resistant to unauthorized interception and alteration due to its encrypted state.
   - Upon arrival at Bob's end, the cipher-text undergoes decryption through a deciphering formula and key to revert to the original clear-text message.
   - Bob peruses the received clear-text, thus finalizing the cycle of safeguarded correspondence.
2. Elements to Highlight:
   - Clear-Text Note: The initial, legible note that Alice aims to transmit to Bob under secure conditions.
   - Cryptographic Formula: A compilation of mathematical functions that alter the clear-text into an encoded version referred to as cipher-text.
   - Cryptographic Key: A confidential numerical or alphanumeric series employed together with the cryptographic formula to convert the clear-text.
   - Cipher-Text: The uninterpretable outcome derived post-encryption, relayed via the transmission medium.
   - Deciphering Formula: A sequence of mathematical functions designed to undo the encryption, converting the cipher-text back to its clear-text form.
   - Deciphering Key: A confidential numerical or alphanumeric series used together with the deciphering formula to decode the cipher-text.
   - Transmission Medium: The route through which the encrypted note is conveyed from Alice to Bob.
3. Diagram Annotations:
   - Explanatory annotations accompanying each stage of the process to provide readers with a clear understanding of what transpires at each step.
   - A legend denoting the symbols and colors used to represent different components and processes in the diagram.
4. Diagram Flow:
   - The diagram will exhibit a clear flow from left to right, commencing with Alice, traversing the encryption process, the communication channel, the decryption process, and culminating with Bob.
5. Interactive Element:
   - An interactive element allowing readers to click through each stage of the encryption and decryption process, offering a deeper understanding of how encryption works to secure digital communications.

Real World Scenario: Implementing Encryption in a Business Environment

1. Identifying the Need for Encryption:

- As TechCorp Inc. expands its operations, the influx of confidential information like client details, monetary documents, and proprietary assets. of accentuates the imperative of robust data security measures. The leadership recognizes that a robust encryption strategy is quintessential to safeguard this sensitive data and uphold the trust of stakeholders and regulatory bodies.

2. Engaging Expertise:

- To steer the encryption implementation initiative, TechCorp engages a team of seasoned cybersecurity experts. This team is tasked with conducting a thorough assessment of TechCorp's digital infrastructure to pinpoint areas where encryption is crucial and to devise a comprehensive encryption strategy.

3. Selecting Appropriate Encryption Solutions:

- The cybersecurity team meticulously evaluates various encryption algorithms and solutions. Given the sensitive nature of the data, they opt for Advanced Encryption Standard (AES) 256-bit encryption for data at rest and Transport Layer Security (TLS) for data in transit, which are lauded for their robust security features.

4. Implementing Encryption for Data at Rest:

- A phased implementation approach is adopted to encrypt data at rest. The first phase entails encrypting the databases housing customer and financial data. Subsequent phases involve encrypting file systems and other data repositories.

5. Securing Data in Transit:

- Parallelly, measures are taken to secure data in transit. TLS encryption is implemented across all web applications, APIs, and email systems to guarantee the safety of data sent across networks from eavesdropping and man-in-the-middle attacks.

6. Public and Private Key Infrastructure (PKI):

- Recognizing the importance of secure digital identities and communications, TechCorp sets up a Public and Private Key Infrastructure (PKI). This infrastructure facilitates secure email communications, digital signatures, and SSL/TLS implementation for web applications.

7. Employee Training and Awareness:

- TechCorp embarks on a comprehensive training program to educate its workforce on the new encryption protocols. A series of workshops, e-learning modules, and hands-on training sessions are conducted, encompassing topics like secure data handling practices, utilizing encryption tools, and recognizing potential cyber threats. A continuous assessment and feedback mechanism is established to ensure employees remain updated on the evolving encryption practices and cybersecurity landscape.

8. Monitoring and Maintenance:

- A robust monitoring framework is implemented to ensure the ongoing effectiveness of the encryption protocols. This framework encompasses real-time monitoring of encryption/decryption operations, routine security audits, and automated alerts for any unauthorized access attempts or encryption anomalies. Periodic maintenance activities are scheduled, including updates to encryption algorithms, key rotations, and system patches to keep the encryption framework robust against evolving cyber threats.

9. Evaluating and Enhancing Encryption Strategies:

- Post-implementation, a multi-disciplinary team comprising cybersecurity experts, IT personnel, and key stakeholders convenes to evaluate the effectiveness of the encryption strategies. This evaluation hinges on various metrics such as the incidence of data breaches, ease of data recovery, and compliance with regulatory mandates. Insights gleaned from this evaluation are harnessed to enhance the encryption framework continually. This iterative process fosters a culture of continuous improvement, ensuring TechCorp's encryption strategy remains agile and efficient against emerging cybersecurity risks.

10. Engaging with Industry Consortia:

- To ensure its encryption framework remains at the vanguard of cybersecurity best practices, TechCorp engages with industry consortia, cybersecurity communities, and regulatory bodies. By participating in forums, attending cybersecurity conferences, and collaborating with other industry players, TechCorp stays abreast of the latest encryption standards, technologies, and best practices. This engagement also provides a platform for TechCorp to contribute to the broader cybersecurity discourse, sharing its insights and learning from the experiences of others.

11. Leveraging Advanced Technologies:

- TechCorp explores the integration of advanced technologies like Quantum Cryptography and Blockchain to further bolster its encryption framework. These technologies, with their promise of ultra-secure encryption and decentralized security architectures, are evaluated for their potential to enhance data security and privacy in the long term.

Interactive Quizzes: Test your Cryptography Acumen

1. Which of the following is a symmetric encryption algorithm?
   a) RSA
   b) ECC
   c) AES
   d) DH

2. In asymmetric encryption, which key is used to decrypt a message?
   a) Public Key
   b) Private Key
   c) Either Public or Private Key
   d) Symmetric Key

3. What does HMAC stand for?
   a) Hash Message Authentication Code
   b) Hashed Message Authentication Code
   c) Hashing Message Authentication Code
   d) Hashed Message Assurance Code

4. Which of the following is a method to ensure data integrity?
   a) Digital Signatures
   b) Encryption
   c) Decryption
   d) All of the above

5. Which of the following is a cryptographic hash function?
   a) RSA
   b) SHA-256
   c) DES
   d) 3DES

6. What is a nonce in cryptography?
   a) A type of encryption algorithm
   b) A number used once
   c) A type of key
   d) A cryptographic hash function

7. Which of the following attacks is relevant to symmetric cryptography?
   a) Man-in-the-Middle Attack
   b) Birthday Attack
   c) Chosen Ciphertext Attack
   d) All of the above

8. Which cryptographic algorithm is used to secure SSL/TLS protocols?
   a) RSA
   b) AES
   c) DES
   d) MD5

9. What is the length of an MD5 hash value?
   a) 128 bits
   b) 256 bits
   c) 160 bits
   d) 512 bits

10. In a PKI, what does CA stand for?
    a) Certificate Authority
    b) Cryptographic Algorithm
    c) Cryptographic Authentication
    d) Certificate Authentication

11. What is the primary purpose of a digital certificate?
    a) Encryption
    b) Decryption
    c) Authentication
    d) Authorization

12. What does PGP stand for?
    a) Pretty Good Privacy
    b) Pretty Good Protection
    c) Pretty Good Protocol
    d) Pretty Good Password

13. Which of the following is a block cipher mode of operation?
    a) CBC
    b) RSA
    c) ECC
    d) HMAC

14. What is the primary difference between block ciphers and stream ciphers?
    a) The type of keys used
    b) The way they encrypt data

c) The length of the ciphertext

d) The encryption algorithms used

15. Which of the following is NOT a property of a cryptographic hash function?

a) Pre-image resistance

b) Collision resistance

c) Second pre-image resistance

d) Key distribution

16. Which of the following is an asymmetric encryption algorithm?

a) AES

b) DES

c) RSA

d) 3DES

17. In cryptography, what is salting?

a) Adding random data to the key

b) Adding random data to the plaintext

c) Adding random data to the ciphertext

d) Adding random data to the hash

18. What is the process of converting ciphertext back to plaintext called?

a) Encryption

b) Decryption

c) Hashing

d) Signing

19. Which of the following is a type of asymmetric encryption?

a) RSA

b) AES

c) DES

d) CBC

20. What does SSL stand for?

a) Secure Socket Layer

b) Secure Socket Link

c) Secure Security Layer

d) Secure Signature Layer

21. What is the primary function of a cryptographic hash?

a) Encryption

b) Decryption

c) Data integrity verification

d) Key generation

22. Which of the following encryption algorithms is considered the most secure?

a) DES

b) 3DES

c) AES

d) RSA

23. In cryptography, what is a "collision"?

a) Two different plaintexts producing the same ciphertext

b) Two identical plaintexts producing different ciphertexts

c) Two different keys producing the same ciphertext

d) Two identical keys producing different ciphertexts

24. What does TLS stand for?

a) Transport Layer Security

b) Transmission Layer Security

c) Transport Level Security

d) Transmission Level Security

25. Which of the following is a property of a secure hash function?

a) Pre-image resistance

b) Encryption

c) Decryption

d) Key generation

26. In a digital signature, which key is used to sign the document?

a) Public Key

b) Private Key

c) Symmetric Key

d) Either Public or Private Key

27. Which of the following is a method for key exchange?

a) RSA

b) AES

c) Diffie-Hellman

d) HMAC

28. What is the primary purpose of a digital signature?

a) Encryption

b) Decryption

c) Authentication and Integrity

d) Key exchange

29. What is the length of a SHA-256 hash value?

a) 128 bits

b) 256 bits

c) 160 bits

d) 512 bits

30. Which of the following is a stream cipher?

a) RSA

b) AES

c) RC4

d) DES

31. What type of algorithm is used in SSL/TLS for key exchange?

a) Symmetric
b) Asymmetric
c) Either Symmetric or Asymmetric
d) Neither Symmetric nor Asymmetric

32. In which type of encryption is the same key used for both encryption and decryption?
a) Symmetric
b) Asymmetric
c) Either Symmetric or Asymmetric
d) Neither Symmetric nor Asymmetric

33. Which of the following encryption algorithms is no longer considered secure?
a) RSA
b) AES
c) DES
d) ECC

34. What does the "S" in HTTPS stand for?
a) Secure
b) Socket
c) Security
d) Signature

35. Which of the following is NOT a goal of cryptography?
a) Confidentiality
b) Integrity
c) Availability
d) Authentication

36. Which cryptographic protocol is used to secure IP communications?

a) SSL
b) TLS
c) IPSec
d) PGP

37. Which of the following is a common use of public key cryptography?
a) Encrypting data in transit
b) Encrypting data at rest
c) Digital signatures
d) All of the above

38. What is the primary purpose of a Certificate Authority (CA) in a PKI?
a) Issue digital certificates
b) Encrypt data
c) Decrypt data
d) Generate keys

39. What is the main purpose of a cryptographic salt?
a) Enhance the flavor of the ciphertext
b) Prevent rainbow table attacks
c) Encrypt the plaintext
d) Decrypt the ciphertext

40. Which of the following cryptographic attacks aims at finding two different inputs that produce the same hash output?
a) Birthday attack
b) Brute force attack
c) Man-in-the-middle attack
d) Replay attack

ANSWERS

1. Which of the following is a symmetric encryption algorithm? Answer:c) AES Why Correct: The Advanced Encryption Standard (AES) is the go-to symmetric encryption algorithm that's both secure and efficient.

2. In asymmetric encryption, which key is used to decrypt a message? Answer:b) Private Key Why Correct: In asymmetric encryption, the private key is unique to its owner and is used for decryption and signing.

3. What does HMAC stand for? Answer:a) Hash Message Authentication Code (HMAC) Why Correct: HMAC combines a shared secret key with a hash function to provide both integrity and authentication. Exam Pitfall: Don't mix up HMAC with regular hashing, which doesn't involve a secret key.

4. Which of the following is a method to ensure data integrity? Answer: a) Digital Signatures Why Correct: Digital signatures use asymmetric encryption to provide both integrity and non-repudiation.

5. Which of the following is a cryptographic hash function? Answer: b) SHA-256 Why Correct: SHA-256 (Secure Hash Algorithm 256-bit) is a secure hashing function that provides good integrity checks.

6. What is a nonce in cryptography? Answer: b) A number used once Why Correct: This is known as a nonce, which ensures that old communications cannot be reused in replay attacks.

7. Which of the following attacks is relevant to symmetric cryptography? Answer:d) All of the above Why Correct: In most "all of the above" questions, it's essential to consider the comprehensive scope of the subject matter.

8. Which cryptographic algorithm is used to secure SSL/TLS protocols? Answer:a) RSA Why Correct: RSA is a widely-used asymmetric algorithm for encryption and digital signatures.

9. What is the length of an MD5 hash value? Answer:a) 128 bits Why Correct: 128 bits is a common key size for modern encryption algorithms, balancing security and performance.

10. In a PKI, what does CA stand for? Answer:a) Certificate Authority Why Correct: A Certificate Authority (CA) issues digital certificates that validate the ownership of a public key.

11. What is the primary purpose of a digital certificate? Answer:c) Authentication Why Correct: Authentication is the process of validating the credentials of a person, system, or service.

12. What does PGP stand for? Answer:a) Pretty Good Privacy (PGP) Why Correct: PGP is used for encrypting emails and files, leveraging both symmetric and asymmetric encryption.

13. Which of the following is a block cipher mode of operation? Answer:a) CBC Why Correct: Cipher Block Chaining (CBC) is a mode of operation for symmetric encryption algorithms like AES.

14. What is the primary difference between block ciphers and stream ciphers? Answer:b) The way they encrypt data Why Correct: Different encryption algorithms have unique methods for encrypting data.

15. Which of the following is NOT a property of a cryptographic hash function? Answer:d) Key distribution Why Correct: Key distribution is crucial in both symmetric and asymmetric encryption, ensuring that keys are exchanged securely.

16. Which of the following is an asymmetric encryption algorithm? Answer:c) RSA Why Correct: RSA is often used for key exchange in addition to encryption and signing.

17. In cryptography, what is salting? Answer:b) Adding random data to the plaintext Why Correct: This is known as "salting" and is often used in hashing to make dictionary attacks more difficult. Exam Pitfall: Don't confuse salting with padding, which serves to fill out data blocks.

18. What is the process of converting ciphertext back to plaintext called? Answer:b) Decryption Why Correct: Decryption is the process of converting ciphertext back into plaintext.

19. Which of the following is a type of asymmetric encryption? Answer:a) RSA Why Correct: RSA is also used for decrypting ciphertext back into plaintext when asymmetric encryption is involved.

20. What does SSL stand for? Answer:a) Secure Socket Layer (SSL) Why Correct: SSL is a deprecated secure communications protocol but still widely referenced.

21. What is the primary function of a cryptographic hash? Answer:c) Data integrity verification Why Correct: Data integrity verification ensures that the data has not been altered during transmission or storage.

22. Which of the following encryption algorithms is considered the most secure? Answer:c) AES Why Correct: AES (Advanced Encryption Standard) is a strong symmetric encryption algorithm.

23. In cryptography, what is a "collision"? Answer:a) Two different plaintexts producing the same ciphertext Why Correct: This describes a cryptographic collision, a situation to be avoided as it undermines data integrity and confidentiality. Exam Pitfall: Collisions are generally considered a weakness in a cryptographic algorithm.

24. What does TLS stand for? Answer:a) Transport Layer Security (TLS) Why Correct: TLS is the successor to SSL and is used for securing communications over a network.

25. Which of the following is a property of a secure hash function? Answer:a) Pre-image resistance Why Correct: This is a property of a good cryptographic hash function, making it computationally infeasible to reverse-engineer the original input.

26. In a digital signature, which key is used to sign the document? Answer:b) Private Key Why Correct: In asymmetric cryptography, the private key is used for decryption and must be kept secure.

27. Which of the following is a method for key exchange? Answer:c) Diffie-Hellman Why Correct: Diffie-Hellman is a key exchange protocol allowing two parties to securely share a cryptographic key over an insecure network.

28. What is the primary purpose of a digital signature? Answer:c) Authentication and Integrity Why Correct: These are two of the primary goals of cryptography, ensuring that data is both genuine and unchanged.

29. What is the length of a SHA-256 hash value? Answer:b) 256 bits Why Correct: 256-bit keys offer a higher level of security than smaller key sizes like 128-bit or 192-bit.

30. Which of the following is a stream cipher? Answer:c) RC4 Why Correct: RC4 is an older symmetric encryption algorithm that has fallen out of favor due to security vulnerabilities.

31. What type of algorithm is used in SSL/TLS for key exchange? Answer:b) Asymmetric Why Correct: Asymmetric cryptography involves a pair of keys: a public key for encryption and a private key for decryption.

32. In which type of encryption is the same key used for both encryption and decryption? Answer:a) Symmetric Why Correct: Symmetric encryption uses a single key for both encryption and decryption.

33. Which of the following encryption algorithms is no longer considered secure? Answer:c) DES Why Correct: Data Encryption Standard (DES) is an older symmetric key algorithm largely considered to be insecure today.

34. What does the "S" in HTTPS stand for? Answer:a) Secure Why Correct: In the context of cryptography, "secure" typically refers to algorithms or protocols considered resistant to various forms of attack.

35. Which of the following is NOT a goal of cryptography? Answer:c) Availability Why Correct: Availability ensures that authorized users have timely and uninterrupted access to resources.

36. Which cryptographic protocol is used to secure IP communications? Answer:c) IPSec Why Correct: IPSec (Internet Protocol Security) is a suite of protocols for securing Internet Protocol (IP) communications.

37. Which of the following is a common use of public key cryptography? Answer:d) All of the above Why Correct: These types of questions test your overall understanding and knowledge of the subject matter.

38. What is the primary purpose of a Certificate Authority (CA) in a PKI? Answer:a) Issue digital certificates Why Correct: Certificate Authorities (CAs) are responsible for issuing digital certificates that validate the ownership of a public key.

39. What does VPN stand for? Answer:b) Prevent rainbow table attacks Why Correct: Salting a hash before storing it can protect against rainbow table attacks by making each hash unique.

40. What is the difference between a block cipher and a stream cipher? Answer:a) Birthday attack Why Correct: This is a type of attack that applies to cryptographic hash functions and is based on the probability of two distinct inputs having the same output.

Hands-on Exercise: Encrypting and Decrypting Messages

Objective:
This exercise aims to provide hands-on experience with encryption and decryption processes, emphasizing the practical application of symmetric and asymmetric encryption techniques.

Part 1: Symmetric Encryption
Introduction:
Symmetric encryption, also known as private-key cryptography, uses the same key for both encryption and decryption processes. Common symmetric encryption algorithms include AES, DES, and 3DES. In this part of the exercise, we'll use the AES algorithm to encrypt and decrypt a message.

Task 1.1: Setting Up Your Environment
Download and install a cryptography toolkit like OpenSSL from the official website.
Browse through the documentation to familiarize yourself with the basic functions and capabilities of OpenSSL.
Explore the command line interface of OpenSSL by executing openssl help.

Task 1.2: Encrypting a Message
Create a plaintext message file named message.txt with a text editor.
Open a command line terminal and navigate to the directory containing message.txt.
Execute the following command to encrypt the message using the AES algorithm with a 256-bit key in CBC mode:
openssl enc -aes-256-cbc -in message.txt -out message.enc
You will be prompted to enter a passphrase. Note down this passphrase as it will be needed for decryption.

Task 1.3: Decrypting the Message
In the command line terminal, execute the following command to decrypt the message back to plaintext:

openssl enc -aes-256-cbc -d -in message.enc -out decrypted_message.txt

You will be prompted to enter the passphrase from the previous step

Once decrypted, open decrypted_message.txt and compare it with the original message to ensure they match.

Reflection:

Reflect on the importance of the passphrase in symmetric encryption. Discuss what would happen if the passphrase was lost or compromised. Explore other symmetric encryption algorithms and compare their strengths and weaknesses against AES.

Part 2: Asymmetric Encryption

Introduction:

Asymmetric encryption, or public-key cryptography, uses a pair of keys for encryption and decryption. The public key is used for encryption, while the private key is used for decryption. In this part, we'll use the RSA algorithm for our exercise.

Task 2.1: Generating Key Pair

In the command line terminal, execute the following command to generate a private key using the RSA algorithm:

openssl genpkey -algorithm RSA -out private_key.pem

Next, generate the corresponding public key with the following command:

openssl rsa -pubout -in private_key.pem -out public_key.pem

Task 2.2: Encrypting a Message

With the keys generated, let's move on to encrypting a message. First, ensure you have a plaintext message file named message.txt.

Execute the following command to encrypt the message using the public key:

openssl rsautl -encrypt -pubin -inkey public_key.pem -in message.txt -out message.enc

This command reads the plaintext message from message.txt, encrypts it using the public key contained in public_key.pem, and writes the encrypted message to message.enc.

Task 2.3: Decrypting the Message

Now, let's decrypt the encrypted message back to plaintext using the private key:

openssl rsautl -decrypt -inkey private_key.pem -in message.enc -out decrypted_message.txt

Open decrypted_message.txt and compare it with the original message to ensure they match.

Reflection:

Reflect on the differences between symmetric and asymmetric encryption, discussing the benefits and drawbacks of each.

Discuss scenarios where one type of encryption might be preferred over the other.

Explore other asymmetric encryption algorithms such as ECC and discuss how they compare to RSA.

Discussion:

Engage in a discussion with your peers about the importance of encryption in modern communication. Discuss how encryption can protect data integrity and confidentiality or forum to share experiences, challenges, and insights gained from this exercise. Reflect on the following points:

1. Key Management:
    - Discuss the importance of secure key management and the challenges associated with it.
    - Explore solutions and best practices for key storage, distribution, and rotation.
2. Algorithm Choices:
    - Discuss why RSA was chosen for this exercise and explore other asymmetric algorithms like Elliptic Curve Cryptography (ECC) and Diffie-Hellman.
    - Compare and contrast the security, performance, and use case scenarios for these algorithms.
3. Real-World Applications:
    - Discuss real-world scenarios where symmetric and asymmetric encryption are applied.

- Explore how these encryption methods contribute to data privacy and security in industries like finance, healthcare, and e-commerce.

Advanced Tasks:

Explore the concept of message digests and how they ensure data integrity.

- Generate a SHA-256 hash of your original message and discuss its properties.

2. Digital Signatures:
- Delve into digital signatures, understanding their role in verifying the authenticity and integrity of data.
- Create and verify a digital signature for your original message using the RSA key pair generated earlier.

3. Public Key Infrastructure (PKI):
- Investigate the role of Public Key Infrastructure in managing digital keys and certificates.
- Set up a simple PKI and issue a digital certificate for your public key.

4. Hybrid Encryption:
- Understand the concept of hybrid encryption, where both symmetric and asymmetric encryption are used together.
- Implement a hybrid encryption scheme to securely transmit a message to a peer.

5. Exploring Other Cryptographic Tools:
- Explore other cryptographic tools and libraries such as GnuPG and Bouncy Castle.
- Perform the encryption and decryption tasks using one of these alternative tools.

4) Identity and Access Management

Controlling Access

1. Basics of Permission Management:
   - What it is: Permission management involves selectively limiting access to particular locations or digital assets.
   - Aim: Its main objective is to regulate how individuals can interact with resources.
2. Foundational Concepts:
   - User Recognition: The action of providing a recognizable identity (e.g., a username).
   - Identity Confirmation: Validating the provided identity (e.g., through a password).
   - Access Clearance: Deciding if the validated identity has permissions.
   - User Oversight: Monitoring and logging activities conducted by users.
3. Rules for Permission:
   - User-Defined Access Control (UDAC): Permissions are set based on individual choices.
   - Rule-Governed Access Control (RGAC): Permissions are decided by data labeling and user credentials.
   - Position-Based Access Control (PBAC): Access is determined by job roles within an organization.
4. Permission Handling Tools:
   - Permission Lists (PLs): Records that indicate which users or processes have access to certain resources.
   - Permission Grids: Charts that align users on one axis and resources on another, showing access levels.
   - Access Tokens: Digital keys that allow a user specified kinds of access to a resource.
5. Guidelines for Implementation:
   - Minimal Access: Only provide the least amount of access needed for users to complete their tasks.
   - Task Distribution: Allocate different parts of a task to different individuals to minimize errors and fraud.
   - Time-Based Limits: Restricting resource access by time.
6. Permission-Related Technologies:
   - ID Cards: Physical cards containing user credentials.
   - Physical Identification: Utilizing unique physical features for identity verification and access.
   - Security Devices: Physical gadgets used for secure access.
7. Oversight and Inspection:
   - Ongoing Surveillance: Continuously monitor permissions to ensure their ongoing effectiveness.
   - Periodic Review: Random checks to validate the functionality of permission systems.
8. Cutting-Edge Permission Techniques:
   - Attribute-Governed Access Control (AGAC):
      - Unlike PBAC, AGAC uses various attributes (user, resource, environment) for a nuanced control of access, useful for large organizations with intricate needs.
   - Rule-Driven Access Control:
      - This model employs preset guidelines outlined by the system admin to dictate access.
      - The model can adapt to real-time changes, offering a flexible control mechanism.
   - Situation-Dependent Access Control:
      - This model takes into account conditions like geographic location or time, for determining access.
      - Particularly useful when resource sensitivity varies by location or time.
9. Obstacles in Permission Management:
   - Expandability: With organizational growth, the complexity in managing permissions can increase.
   - Consistent Rule Application: Making sure that access rules are uniformly applied across different systems.
   - Regulatory Adherence: Conforming to laws and standards like GDPR or HIPAA, which have explicit rules regarding access control.
10. Recommended Actions:
   - Frequent Checks: Undertake regular inspections to confirm the effectiveness and enforcement of permission rules.

- Staff Awareness: Educating staff about the significance of permission systems can lower the probability of breaches.
- Emergency Protocols: Preparing a response strategy for unexpected situations like data breaches is vital.
11. Upcoming Developments:
   - Trust-Nothing Architecture:
      - This framework follows the "verify, then trust" mantra, requiring rigorous identity checks for all individuals and devices trying to access a private network.
   - AI & Predictive Analytics:
      - Emerging technologies like AI and machine learning offer the possibility of enhancing permission systems by monitoring user behavior and detecting irregularities.

Authentication and Authorization Mechanisms

1. Grasping the Concept of Verification:
   - What it is: Verification is the process of confirming a user's or system's identity.
   - The Goal: To ensure that only those who are who they say they are can interact with a system.
2. Ways to Verify Identity:
   - Knowledge-Based: Includes elements like passwords, PIN codes, or security questions.
   - Possession-Based: Involves items like mobile devices, security tokens, or smart cards.
   - Biometrics: Utilizes unique physical attributes like fingerprints or facial scans.
   - Multi-Level Verification: Uses a combination of the methods above for enhanced security.
3. Widely Used Verification Protocols:
   - LDAP (Lightweight Directory Access Protocol)
   - The Kerberos Protocol
   - SSL/TLS (Secure Sockets Layer/Transport Layer Security)
   - OAuth Standard
4. Grasping the Concept of Permission Assignment:
   - What it is: Permission assignment allows specific actions for verified users.
   - The Goal: To guarantee that verified users can only access and modify what they are permitted to.
5. Methods to Assign Permissions:
   - Role-Oriented Permissions: Based on an individual's role in an organization.
   - Attribute-Oriented Permissions: Determined by specific attributes related to the user, resources, or situational factors.
   - Rule-Oriented Permissions: Permissions are dictated by preset organizational policies.
6. Widely Used Permission Protocols:
   - RBAC (Role-Based Access Control)
   - ABAC (Attribute-Based Access Control)
   - OAuth 2.0 and OIDC (OpenID Connect)
7. Real-World Applications of Verification and Permission:
   - Unified Login (Single Sign-On): Enables one-time verification for multiple services.
   - Cross-Organizational Identity: Extending verification and permissions across different organizations.
   - Secure API Interactions: Safeguarding the communication between various software components.
8. Obstacles and Effective Strategies:
   - Security vs. User Experience: Finding the optimum between robust security and ease of use.
   - Periodic Reviews and Oversight: Confirming that verification and permission systems work as expected.
   - User Awareness: Educating end-users about best practices to avoid common security errors like reusing passwords.
9. Future Directions:
   - Distributed Identity Models: Investigating the impact of blockchain and similar technologies on identity management.

- Trustless Systems: Exploring the "verify first, trust later" principle and its effects on verification and permission systems.

10. Cutting-Edge Verification Approaches:
  - Beyond Passwords:
    - Examining advanced methods like mobile or biometric verification that eliminate the need for passwords.
    - Discussing the advantages, such as improved user experience and less reliance on easily-compromised passwords.
    - Adaptive Verification (Risk-Based):
    - Discussing verification methods that adapt to the risk profile of a login attempt, based on factors like geographic location and user behavior.
    - Exploring how these methods offer an extra layer of security for unusual or suspicious login activities.

11. Innovative Permission Systems:
  - Adaptive Permission Assignment:
    - Investigating real-time permission adjustments that offer nuanced control over resource accessibility.
    - Discussing how dynamic policies meet the complex requirements of large organizations.
  - Centralized Policy Decision Points:
    - Discussing platforms that make centralized decisions about permissions based on set policies.
    - Investigating how such platforms simplify the management of permissions.

12. Exploring SAML (Security Assertion Markup Language):
  - What it is: SAML is a standard for the exchange of verification and permission data among parties.
  - Its Role: Discussing how SAML enables unified login systems and simplifies the verification and permission processes across different platforms.

13. Identity and Access Management (IAM) Platforms:
  - Delving into modern IAM platforms that centralize authentication and authorization processes.
  - Discussing the benefits of utilizing IAM platforms including improved security, compliance, and operational efficiency.

14. Regulatory Compliance:
  - Discussing the importance of compliance with regulatory standards like GDPR, HIPAA in the context of authentication and authorization.
  - Exploring the challenges and best practices in ensuring compliance while maintaining operational efficiency.

15. Case Studies:
  - Presenting real-world case studies to illustrate the impact of robust authentication and authorization mechanisms in preventing security breaches.
  - Discussing lessons learned from these case studies and how they can be applied to improve authentication and authorization processes.

Identity Management Systems

1. Core Components of Identity Management:
  - Identity Repository:
    - The identity repository is where an organization stores identity information such as usernames, passwords, and user attributes. This repository can be a database, directory, or other types of data stores.
  - Identity Provisioning:
    - Identity provisioning involves creating, managing, and de-provisioning identities. This includes processes like onboarding new users, managing user lifecycles, and ensuring that obsolete user accounts are promptly deactivated.
  - Identity Governance:
    - This part focuses on controlling how resources are accessed within an organization. It covers the formulation and execution of strategies to competently handle digital identities.

2. The Cycle of Identity Handling:
- Joining the Organization:
- Initial setup of digital identities for newcomers.
- Ongoing Management:
- Periodic updates and oversight of existing digital identities.
- Exiting the Organization:
- Procedures for safely removing digital identities when individuals depart.

3. Controlling Resource Accessibility:
- This area is concerned with regulating access to organizational assets. It involves generating and applying rules to make sure individuals can only access what they are supposed to, based on their job roles.

4. Unified Authentication & Cross-Organization Trust:
- One-Time Authentication (Single Sign-On):
- Allows a single authentication action to provide access to multiple systems.
- Trusted Partnerships (Federation):
- Enables the secure interchange of identity data across different organizations.

5. Identity Consistency and Data Aggregation:
- Discusses the techniques and technologies to keep identity data harmonized across different platforms and applications.

6. Analytics in Identity and Access Oversight:
- Observing and evaluating identity and access metrics for compliance, issue detection, and process enhancement.

7. Compliance Standards and Review Processes:
- Discusses the importance of meeting different regulatory frameworks and how audits contribute to improved security and compliance.

8. Cutting-Edge Developments:
- Self-Managed Digital Identities:
- Investigates emerging methods like blockchain for granting more control to individuals over their identity information.
- Role of AI & ML:
- Explores how artificial intelligence and machine learning contribute to better, more secure identity management systems.

9. Specialized Identity Control Mechanisms:
- Elevated Access Control (Privileged Access Management):
- Examines the governance of accounts with special access rights and why it's crucial to secure them.
- Assurance in Identity Validation:
- Discusses the varying assurance levels associated with different authentication methods and their significance in confirming an individual's identity.

10. Guidelines and Communication Standards for Identity Management:
- Directory Information Services Protocol (LDAP):
- Examines LDAP's role in providing a method for retrieving and managing distributed identity information.
- Assertion Protocols (SAML):
- Investigates SAML's role in the interchange of identity and permission-related data.
- OAuth-Based Identity Framework (OpenID Connect):
- Reviews OIDC as a basic identity layer that functions in conjunction with the OAuth 2.0 protocol.

11. Identity Management Challenges:
- Scalability:
- Discussing the challenges of scaling identity management solutions as organizations grow and the user base expands.
- Privacy and Data Protection:

- Delving into the challenges of protecting user privacy and data in identity management systems.
12. Best Practices:
   - Regular Audits and Monitoring:
      - Discussing the importance of conducting regular audits and monitoring to ensure that identity management systems are functioning as intended.
   - User Education and Training:
      - Exploring the role of user education and training in ensuring the success of identity management initiatives.
13. Case Studies:
   - Presenting real-world case studies to illustrate the impact of robust identity management systems in preventing security breaches and ensuring compliance.
   - Discussing lessons learned from these case studies and how they can be applied to improve identity management processes.
14. Future of Identity Management:
   - Discussing the evolving landscape of identity management with the advent of new technologies like blockchain, artificial intelligence, and machine learning.
   - Exploring how these technologies are poised to reshape the identity management domain.

Illustrative Diagram: Access Control Models

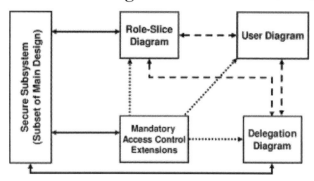

1. User-Defined Access Control (DAC):
   - Figure 1: A basic visualization of a User-Defined Access Control model, highlighting user-controlled permissions.
   - Overview: In this model, the resource or data owner decides the access permissions. The figure will outline how such permissions can be set or removed by the owner.
2. System-Mandated Access Control (MAC):
   - Figure 2: A graphic display of a System-Mandated Access Control model, focusing on compulsory restrictions based on data classifications.
   - Overview: MAC categorizes both users and data with specific classification levels. The figure will clarify how access decisions are made based on these categorizations.
3. Function-Based Access Control (RBAC):
   - Figure 3: An illustration representing a Function-Based Access Control model, emphasizing role-centric permissions.
   - Overview: RBAC permissions are connected to roles rather than individual users. The figure will show how roles are formulated, designated, and how they influence access to assets.
4. In-Depth on User-Defined Access Control (DAC):
   - Detailed Permissions:
      - DAC allows for a nuanced approach to permissions, such as the ability to specify read, write, execute, and delete functions.
   - Associated Risks:

- Analysis of the potential downsides of DAC, including the risk of unintentionally assigning excessive access rights.

5. In-Depth on System-Mandated Access Control (MAC):
    - Categorization and Labeling:
      - Examines the various classification tiers and their relation to differing sensitivity levels.
    - Enforced by the System:
      - Discusses how MAC enforces restrictions directly at the system layer, barring users from sidestepping the rules.

6. In-Depth on Function-Based Access Control (RBAC):
    - Hierarchical Roles:
      - Explores the concept of a role hierarchy, where elevated roles adopt permissions from roles lower in the hierarchy.
    - Role Limitations:
      - Investigates how conditions can be set to govern the activation or use of specific roles.

7. Comparative Evaluation of Models:
    - An analytical comparison of User-Defined, System-Mandated, and Function-Based Access Control, underlining their distinct capabilities, advantages, and disadvantages.
    - Scenario Analysis:
      - Evaluation of cases where one model could be more suitable than others, depending on organizational demands and security criteria.

8. Composite Access Control Approaches:
    - Introduction to blended models that integrate elements from multiple access control frameworks to address multifaceted organizational needs.
    - Evaluation of how such composite models can offer a balanced mix of adaptability and security.

9. Access Control Models: The Road Ahead:
    - Examination of the future trajectory of access control frameworks, considering innovations in areas like machine learning, AI, and blockchain technology.
 - Exploring how these technologies might shape the future of access control, leading to more dynamic and adaptive access control models.

Real-world Scenario: Managing Access in a Growing Enterprise

1. The Challenge:
    - TechX Corp, with a modest beginning of 15 employees, has witnessed exponential growth over the years, now boasting a workforce of over 500. With growth came an explosion of digital resources and a myriad of access control challenges. The once manageable manual processes became a behemoth, prone to errors and security lapses.

2. Initial Setup:
    - Initially, access control was handled manually. New hires would wait for days to get the necessary access, while departing employees' access often lingered, posing a security risk.

3. The Shift to Automated Identity and Access Management (IAM):
    - Realizing the imminent need for a robust IAM solution, TechX Corp adopted an automated IAM platform. This platform facilitated streamlined onboarding and offboarding processes, ensuring timely access provision and revocation.

4. Implementing Role-Centric Access Control (RBAC):
    - The shift to RBAC marked a pivotal moment in streamlining access control. By associating permissions with specific roles instead of individual users, the organization improved its security posture and simplified compliance and auditing processes.

5. Overseeing Elevated Access via Privileged Access Management (PAM):
    - As more personnel were granted access to confidential data, the deployment of PAM became imperative. This strategy kept privileged access tightly supervised, minimizing the likelihood of unauthorized data exposure.

6. Ongoing Surveillance and Periodic Examinations:
   - TechX Corp installed a continuous oversight mechanism to identify and counter any unusual access activities in real-time. In addition, periodic assessments were carried out to validate adherence to diverse regulatory standards and to pinpoint possible enhancements.
7. Educating Users and Heightening Awareness:
   - Consistent instructional sessions were arranged to enlighten staff about safe cyber practices, including the significance of robust password selection and how to spot phishing endeavors.
8. Challenges Encountered:
   - The journey wasn't without challenges. From resistance to change, to ensuring a smooth transition to new systems, TechX Corp navigated through a sea of challenges to establish a robust access control framework.
9. The Outcomes:
   - The transition to an automated IAM system, coupled with RBAC and PAM, led to a significant reduction in security incidents, streamlined operations, and improved compliance posture.
10. Lessons Learned:
    - The case of TechX Corp underscores the importance of proactive access management, continuous monitoring, and educating users to foster a security-conscious culture.
11. Detailed Transition to RBAC:
    - The transition to RBAC wasn't overnight. It required meticulous planning, role definitions, and mapping of employees to their respective roles. The company also had to ensure minimal disruption during the transition.
12. Engagement with Vendors:
    - TechX Corp engaged with IAM solution vendors to ensure the system implemented was scalable and met the organization's unique needs. This engagement also involved continuous support and updates to the IAM solution to meet evolving security and compliance requirements.
13. Customized Educational Modules:
    - Specialized learning courses were designed so that every staff member, regardless of their job description, grasped the revamped access control systems. These lessons covered procedures for requesting access, protocols for dealing with confidential information, and the proper channels for flagging suspicious behavior.
14. Iterative Feedback Mechanisms:
    - The implementation of recurring feedback cycles with various workforce groups and departments was vital for ongoing enhancements. Such regular input aided in fine-tuning the Identity and Access Management (IAM) platform to better align with organizational demands and elevate the user interface.
15. Emergency Response Strategy:
    - A comprehensive plan for responding to unauthorized access or additional security breaches was formulated. This blueprint was consistently evaluated and modified to accommodate shifts in the company's organizational makeup and operational methods.
16. Collaboration with Legal and Compliance Teams:
    - Ensuring compliance with various regulations required close collaboration with legal and compliance teams. This collaboration ensured that the IAM solution met all legal requirements and was prepared for external audits.
17. Technology Stack Evaluation:
    - As the organization grew, so did the technology stack. Regular evaluations were conducted to ensure that the IAM solution remained compatible with other technologies deployed within the organization.
18. Cost Management:
    - Managing the costs associated with transitioning to and maintaining the new IAM solution was a challenge. Budgeting and cost management strategies were developed to ensure cost-effectiveness while not compromising on security.
19. Vendor Lock-in Concerns:
    - TechX Corp was mindful of vendor lock-in concerns and ensured that the IAM solution chosen allowed for flexibility and integration with other systems.

20. Future-proofing Access Management:
   - Looking ahead, TechX Corp is exploring advanced technologies like AI and Machine Learning to further enhance access control, ensuring the IAM solution remains robust amidst the rapidly evolving cyber threat landscape.

Interactive Quizzes: Evaluate your grasp on Identity and Access Management

1. What is the primary purpose of Multi-Factor Authentication (MFA)?
a) Increasing complexity
b) Reducing costs
c) Enhancing security
d) Simplifying user experience

2. Which of the following is NOT a method of authentication?
a) Something you are
b) Something you do
c) Something you know
d) Something you forget

3. What is the main advantage of using Role-Based Access Control (RBAC)?
a) Complexity
b) Scalability
c) Usability
d) Flexibility

4. Which protocol is commonly used for Single Sign-On (SSO)?
a) HTTP
b) SAML
c) DNS
d) FTP

5. In a Mandatory Access Control (MAC) model, what property must an object have for a subject to access it?
a) Username and Password
b) Same security level
c) Group Membership
d) Digital Certificate

6. What is the purpose of identity federation?
a) Increase security risks
b) Provide Single Sign-On across organizational boundaries
c) Enable multi-cloud support
d) Enhance user experience on a single domain

7. Which of the following is a biometric form of authentication?
a) Token
b) Fingerprint scan
c) Smart card
d) Password

8. What is the primary drawback of using a smart card for authentication?
a) High Cost
b) Scalability
c) Complexity
d) Phishing susceptibility

9. In the context of IAM, what does IaaS stand for?
a) Identity as a Service
b) Infrastructure as a Script
c) Identity and Access Solution
d) Infrastructure as a Service

10. What does the principle of "least privilege" mean?
a) Giving users the minimum levels of access — or permissions — needed to perform their duties
b) Assigning users to the most privileged roles available
c) Always allowing administrative access
d) None of the above

11. What type of authentication does a smart card provide?
a) Two-factor authentication
b) Single-factor authentication
c) Three-factor authentication
d) None of the above

12. What does AAA stand for in the context of IAM?
a) Authorization, Application, Authentication
b) Authentication, Authorization, Accounting
c) Application, Access, Architecture
d) None of the above

13. What is the purpose of Single Sign-On (SSO)?
a) To improve security
b) To reduce password fatigue
c) To enhance complexity
d) To improve scalability

14. Which IAM technology is primarily associated with Windows-based systems?
a) LDAP
b) Active Directory
c) OpenID
d) OAuth

15. Which of the following terms is associated with the unauthorized creation of user IDs?
a) User Provisioning

b) Rogue Account Creation
c) Identity Harvesting
d) Identity Federation

16. In which of the following IAM models does the system administrator define the roles?
a) MAC
b) DAC
c) RBAC
d) ABAC

17. What is the primary benefit of federated IAM?
a) Reducing Costs
b) Enhancing Security
c) User Convenience
d) Simplifying Complexity

18. In IAM, what is the purpose of the "deny all, permit by exception" principle?
a) To reduce security
b) To reduce complexity
c) To enhance security
d) To enhance user experience

19. What is OAuth primarily used for?
a) Password Management
b) Token-based Authorization
c) Access Control
d) Biometric Authentication

20. What does the "access" in IAM stand for?
a) Accessibility
b) Access Control
c) Acccss Points
d) Access Tokens

21. What is the disadvantage of using passwords as a single form of authentication?
a) They are hard to remember
b) They are susceptible to being forgotten
c) They are susceptible to attacks like phishing and brute force
d) They are complex to implement

22. What does Just-In-Time (JIT) provisioning enable in IAM?
a) Instant account creation when needed
b) Delayed account deletion
c) Temporary access to privileged accounts
d) Real-time accounting of access

23. What does "NIST" stand for?
a) National Institute of Software Technology
b) National Institute of Standards and Technology
c) Non-Interfering Set of Tasks
d) None of the above

24. Which algorithm is considered the most secure for password hashing?
a) MD5
b) SHA-1
c) bcrypt
d) SHA-256

25. Which of the following is considered the strongest type of multi-factor authentication?
a) Two things you know
b) Something you know and something you have
c) Something you have and something you are
d) Two things you have

26. What is the main purpose of using CAPTCHA in an authentication process?
a) To verify if the user is a human
b) To provide additional security layers
c) To simplify the user experience
d) To collect user data

27. What is the process of confirming that a digital certificate is valid?
a) Encryption
b) Certification
c) Validation
d) Authentication

28. What does "BYOD" stand for in the context of IAM?
a) Build Your Own Device
b) Buy Your Own Domain
c) Bring Your Own Device
d) Build Your Own Domain

29. What is "context-aware" authentication?
a) Authentication based on device, location, and other factors
b) Authentication solely based on passwords
c) Authentication without considering environmental factors
d) None of the above

30. Which of the following is NOT a benefit of IAM?
a) Increased security
b) Enhanced user experience
c) Decreased compliance
d) Improved efficiency

31. In IAM, what does PAM stand for?
a) Process Access Management
b) Privileged Access Management
c) Protected Access Model
d) Public Access Management

32. What does the principle of "separation of duties" in IAM aim to prevent?
a) Efficiency
b) Collaboration
c) Fraud
d) Redundancy

33. Which of the following best describes the "Chain of Trust" in digital certificates?
a) Series of trusted third parties
b) Encryption algorithm sequence
c) Backup recovery sequence
d) None of the above

34. What is the process of matching one's live scan to a stored template?
a) Fingerprinting
b) Scanning
c) Validation
d) Verification

35. Which of the following best describes "password salting"?
a) The process of adding random data to each password before hashing
b) The process of encrypting a password
c) The process of adding complexity to a password
d) The process of storing multiple passwords

36. What is a common disadvantage of biometric authentication methods?
a) High False Positive Rate
b) Low Security
c) Complexity
d) Expense

37. What is an advantage of using a Time-Based One-Time Password (TOTP)?
a) It is valid for a long time
b) It is valid for a short time
c) It can be easily guessed
d) None of the above

38. What does the "implicit deny" principle mean?
a) Permitting all unless explicitly denied
b) Denying all unless explicitly permitted
c) Permitting all unless implicitly denied
d) None of the above

39. Which IAM protocol allows you to authorize one application to interact with another on your behalf without giving away your password?
a) OAuth
b) SAML
c) OpenID
d) HTTP

40. In the context of IAM, what is the primary purpose of access review?
a) To revoke outdated or unnecessary permissions
b) To grant new permissions
c) To overlook the current system
d) To add new users to the system

ANSWER

1. What is the primary purpose of Multi-Factor Authentication (MFA)? Answer: c) Enhancing security. Explanation: MFA uses multiple methods to confirm the identity of a user, thereby providing an additional layer of security.

2. Which of the following is NOT a method of authentication? Answer: d) Something you forget. Explanation: Authentication factors are generally categorized into something you are (biometric), something you do (behavioral), and something you know (passwords, PINs). "Something you forget" does not fit into these categories.

3. What is the main advantage of using Role-Based Access Control (RBAC)? Answer: b) Scalability. Explanation: RBAC simplifies administration and scales easily, allowing administrators to manage users in groups based on their role rather than individually.

4. Which protocol is commonly used for Single Sign-On (SSO)? Answer: b) SAML. Explanation: Security Assertion Markup Language (SAML) is often used to enable Single Sign-On, allowing users to authenticate once and gain access to multiple systems.

5. In a Mandatory Access Control (MAC) model, what property must an object have for a subject to access it? Answer: b) Same security level. Explanation: In MAC, a subject can only access an object if they have the same or higher security level. This ensures data integrity and confidentiality.

6. What is the purpose of identity federation? Answer: b) Provide Single Sign-On across organizational boundaries. Explanation: Identity federation enables SSO capabilities across different organizations and systems, allowing for a seamless user experience without compromising security.

7. Which of the following is a biometric form of authentication? Answer: b) Fingerprint scan. Explanation: A fingerprint scan is a form of biometric authentication, which involves recognizing unique physical characteristics.

8. What is the primary drawback of using a smart card for authentication? Answer: a) High Cost. Explanation: Smart cards, while secure, often incur higher costs for implementation and maintenance.

9. In the context of IAM, what does IaaS stand for? Answer: a) Identity as a Service. Explanation: In the context of IAM, IaaS stands for Identity as a Service, providing identity and access management capabilities through a cloud-based solution.

10. What does the principle of "least privilege" mean? Answer: a) Giving users the minimum levels of access — or permissions — needed to perform their duties. Explanation: The principle of "least privilege" suggests only giving users the permissions they absolutely need to perform their roles, thereby reducing the risk of unauthorized access.

11. What type of authentication does a smart card provide? Answer: a) Two-factor authentication. Explanation: A smart card is often used in conjunction with a PIN, offering two-factor authentication (something you have + something you know).

12. What does AAA stand for in the context of IAM? Answer: b) Authentication, Authorization, Accounting. Explanation: AAA stands for Authentication, Authorization, and Accounting. These are the core principles involved in access control and IAM.

13. What is the purpose of Single Sign-On (SSO)? Answer: b) To reduce password fatigue. Explanation: SSO aims to simplify the user experience by reducing the need for multiple passwords, thereby reducing "password fatigue."

14. Which IAM technology is primarily associated with Windows-based systems? Answer: b) Active Directory. Explanation: Active Directory is commonly associated with Windows-based systems and is widely used for identity services on such platforms.

15. Which of the following terms is associated with the unauthorized creation of user IDs? Answer: b) Rogue Account Creation. Explanation: Rogue Account Creation refers to the unauthorized creation of user IDs, often by attackers for malicious purposes.

16. In which of the following IAM models does the system administrator define the roles? Answer: c) RBAC. Explanation: In Role-Based Access Control (RBAC), the system administrator defines roles and attaches policies to these roles.

17. What is the primary benefit of federated IAM? Answer: c) User Convenience. Explanation: Federated IAM primarily enhances user convenience by allowing users to use the same credentials across multiple services.

18. In IAM, what is the purpose of the "deny all, permit by exception" principle? Answer: c) To enhance security. Explanation: "Deny all, permit by exception" is a security principle that enhances system security by only allowing necessary actions and denying all others by default.

19. What is OAuth primarily used for? Answer: b) Token-based Authorization. Explanation: OAuth is commonly used for token-based authorization, allowing secure API access without transmitting passwords.

20. What does the "access" in IAM stand for? Answer: b) Access Control. Explanation: The "access" in IAM primarily refers to "Access Control," which governs the permissible interactions a user can have with a system.

21. What is the disadvantage of using passwords as a single form of authentication? Answer: c) They are susceptible to attacks like phishing and brute force. Explanation: Passwords are vulnerable to a variety of attacks, including phishing and brute force, which is why they are often not considered sufficient as a sole form of authentication.

22. What does Just-In-Time (JIT) provisioning enable in IAM? Answer: a) Instant account creation when needed. Explanation: Just-In-Time (JIT) provisioning enables the immediate creation of accounts as they are needed, improving efficiency and resource allocation.

23. What does "NIST" stand for? Answer: b) National Institute of Standards and Technology. Explanation: NIST stands for the National Institute of Standards and Technology, a federal agency that sets standards, including those for cybersecurity and IAM.

24. Which algorithm is considered the most secure for password hashing? Answer: c) bcrypt. Explanation: bcrypt is currently considered one of the most secure algorithms for password hashing because of its resistance to brute-force attacks.

25. Which of the following is considered the strongest type of multi-factor authentication? Answer: c) Something you have and something you are. Explanation: The strongest type of multi-factor authentication includes something you have (like a security token) and something you are (like a fingerprint).

26. What is the main purpose of using CAPTCHA in an authentication process? Answer: a) To verify if the user is a human. Explanation: CAPTCHA is primarily used to determine whether the user is human or a bot, adding an additional layer of security to authentication processes.

27. What is the process of confirming that a digital certificate is valid? Answer: d) Authentication. Explanation: Confirming the validity of a digital certificate is part of the authentication process, ensuring that a message or document has been signed by a private key corresponding to the listed public key. |

28. What does "BYOD" stand for in the context of IAM? Answer: c) Bring Your Own Device. Explanation: BYOD stands for "Bring Your Own Device," a policy allowing employees to bring their own devices to work and use them for job-related tasks.

29. What is "context-aware" authentication? Answer: a) Authentication based on device, location, and other factors. Explanation: Context-aware authentication evaluates multiple factors, such as device, location, and time, to make more accurate authentication decisions.

30. Which of the following is NOT a benefit of IAM? Answer: c) Decreased compliance. Explanation: Decreasing compliance is not a benefit of IAM. In fact, a well-implemented IAM system should improve regulatory compliance.

31. In IAM, what does PAM stand for? Answer: b) Privileged Access Management. Explanation: PAM stands for Privileged Access Management, focusing on the special requirements of powerful accounts within an organization.

32. What does the principle of "separation of duties" in IAM aim to prevent? Answer: c) Fraud. Explanation: The principle of "separation of duties" aims to prevent fraud by ensuring that no single individual has control over all aspects of any critical financial transaction.

33. Which of the following best describes the "Chain of Trust" in digital certificates? Answer: a) Series of trusted third parties. Explanation: A Chain of Trust refers to a series of trusted entities, systems, or components that work together to ensure the integrity of some process or data.

34. What is the process of matching one's live scan to a stored template? Answer: d) Verification. Explanation: Matching a live scan to a stored template for biometric authentication is called verification.

35. Which of the following best describes "password salting"? Answer: a) The process of adding random data to each password before hashing. Explanation: Password salting involves adding random data, known as a "salt," to each password before hashing it. This makes it more difficult for attackers to use pre-computed tables to crack the passwords.

36. What does "SSO" stand for in the context of IAM? Answer: d) Expense. Explanation: Biometric authentication methods often require specialized hardware, making them more expensive to implement than other types of authentication.

37. What is "tokenization" in the context of IAM? Answer: b) It is valid for a short time. Explanation: A Time-Based One-Time Password (TOTP) is valid for only a short period of time, usually 30 seconds to a minute, making it secure against replay attacks.

38. What are "orphaned accounts"? Answer: b) Denying all unless explicitly permitted. Explanation: The "implicit deny" principle means that everything is denied by default and permissions must be explicitly granted.

39. In IAM, what is the purpose of "time-based" access control? Answer: a) OAuth. Explanation: OAuth Explanation: OAuth allows one application to interact with another on your behalf without the need for you to share your password, thus enhancing security.

40. What does "RBAC" stand for? Answer: c) RADIUS. Explanation: RADIUS (Remote Authentication Dial-In User Service) is a networking protocol that provides centralized authentication, authorization, and accounting for users.

Hands-on Exercise: Setting up a Basic Access Control System

1. Understanding the Requirements:
   - Situation: You've recently been designated as the IT Security Specialist at XYZ Corporation. Your initial assignment is to establish a foundational access control mechanism for the organization's data server.
   - Goal: Guarantee that solely approved staff members have the ability to reach the data server, while maintaining a configuration that is both straightforward and capable of expansion.
2. Choosing the Right Access Control Model:
   - Evaluate the pros and cons of different access control models (DAC, MAC, RBAC) and choose one that fits the requirements of ABC Corp.
   - Outcome: Choose RBAC for its simplicity, scalability, and ease of management.
3. Defining Roles and Permissions:
   - Identify the different roles within ABC Corp (e.g., Admin, HR, Finance, etc.) and define the access permissions for each role.
   - Outcome: A table of roles and their corresponding access permissions.
4. Setting Up the Access Control System:
   - Install and configure an access control software (e.g., Microsoft Active Directory).
   - Create the defined roles and assign the necessary permissions.
   - Outcome: A functioning access control system reflecting the defined roles and permissions.
5. Testing the Setup:
   - Create test user accounts for each role and verify if the access permissions work as intended.
   - Outcome: Verification that the access control system operates as per the defined roles and permissions.
6. Documentation:
   - Document the setup process, the roles and permissions defined, and any other relevant information.
   - Outcome: A comprehensive documentation for future reference and auditing purposes.
7. Training and Communication:
   - Conduct training sessions for employees to educate them on how to interact with the new access control system.
   - Communicate the change to all stakeholders and provide channels for reporting any issues or concerns.
   - Outcome: Well-informed employees and a channel for continuous feedback and improvement.
8. Monitoring and Review:
   - Set up monitoring tools to keep track of who accesses what and when.
   - Regularly review the setup to ensure it meets the evolving needs of ABC Corp.
   - Outcome: A monitored and regularly reviewed access control system.
9. Future Expansion Plans:
   - Envision future expansion plans to incorporate more advanced access control features such as biometric authentication or integration with other systems.
   - Outcome: A plan for advancing the access control system to meet future needs.
10. Setting Up the Access Control System (Part 2):
    - After creating the roles, set up the access control rules and policies ensuring they align with the requirements of ABC Corp.
    - Set up a few test user accounts, each assigned to a different role, to validate the access control setup.
11. Testing the Setup:
    - Design a testing plan to validate the setup. The plan should include various test cases to ensure that the access control system is functioning as intended.
    - Execute the testing plan by logging in with the test user accounts created earlier and verifying if the access permissions work as intended.
12. Documentation:

- Document the entire setup process in a step-by-step manner, including screenshots and configurations settings where necessary.

- Create a troubleshooting guide to address common issues that may arise while interacting with the access control system.

13. Training and Communication:

- Design a training program to educate the employees about the new access control system. Include practical demonstrations to show how the system works.

- Schedule training sessions and ensure to cover all departments within ABC Corp. Collect feedback to understand if any part of the training needs to be improved.

14. Monitoring and Review:

- Implement monitoring tools to log and review all access control events. This includes successful logins, unsuccessful sign-in efforts and modifications to the authorization configurations.

- Set up regular review meetings with department heads to ensure that the access control setup still aligns with the operational requirements of ABC Corp.

15. Future Expansion Plans:

- Evaluate the scalability of the current setup and envision how it can be expanded or improved to cater to the growing needs of ABC Corp.

- Research on advanced access control features and technologies that could be integrated into the current setup to enhance security and efficiency.

16. Reflection and Improvement:

- Reflect on the entire process, identify any challenges faced, and how they were overcome.

- Seek feedback from the users and identify areas for improvement in the access control setup. Plan for implementing the necessary improvements in a phased manner.

5) Risk Management

Navigating the Seas of Risk

Understanding Risk:
Risk is characterized as the possibility of encountering setbacks or harm when a threat takes advantage of a weakness. In the field of information technology, such risks could encompass unauthorized data access, system unavailability, and challenges in legal or regulatory compliance. The structure of risk includes threats, susceptibilities, and the prospective ramifications for the enterprise.

Significance of Managing Risks:
Managing risks acts as the pivot between operational effectiveness and organizational security. It involves the recognition, evaluation, and governance of threats to a company's assets and revenues. These threats could come from numerous directions, including financial volatility, legal obligations, errors in strategic management, unforeseen incidents, and environmental catastrophes.

1. Uninterrupted Operations: One of the main objectives of risk management is to maintain operational continuity even in the face of difficulties. By pinpointing likely risks and formulating ways to lessen or control them, companies can minimize operational interruptions.

2. Adherence to Legal and Regulatory Guidelines: In the growing arena of legal and regulatory stipulations, particularly in areas like data security and privacy, effective risk management ensures that the company's procedures are in compliance, thus avoiding legal complications.

3. Economic Resilience: Through the proactive control of risks, companies can avert financial downturns. resulting from data breaches, system failures, or other adverse events.

4. Reputation Management: In a world where reputation is a significant asset, managing risks to prevent incidents that could tarnish an organization's image is crucial.

5. Strategic Decision Making: Armed with a robust risk management framework, decision-makers can make informed choices that consider the organizational risk posture.

Roles of Risk Management in IT:
The landscape of IT embodies a fertile ground for various risks, courtesy of its inherent complexity and rapid evolution. Risk management in IT entails:

1. Security Posture Assessment: Assessing the organization's security stance to pinpoint weaknesses and potential dangers.

2. Policy and Procedure Development: Crafting policies and procedures that encapsulate best practices in managing identified risks.

3. Incident Response Planning: Preparing for adverse events by developing and testing incident response plans.

4. Training and Awareness: Fostering a culture of awareness and education to ensure that every stakeholder understands the significance of risk management and adheres to the established policies and procedures.

5. Technology Investment: Guiding investments in security technologies based on the risk assessment, ensuring that resources are utilized optimally to mitigate and manage risks.

6. Continuous Monitoring and Improvement: Establishing a regime of continuous monitoring to detect and respond to risks timely, coupled with a culture of continuous improvement to evolve the risk management strategies as the organizational and threat landscape changes.

7. Asset Identification: Before diving into risk assessment, it's pivotal to identify and catalog all assets within an organization. Every piece of hardware, software, and data is an asset that could be at risk. An accurate asset inventory lays the foundation for effective risk management.

8. Vulnerability Assessment: Identifying the weaknesses within the system that could be exploited by threats is a critical step. Vulnerability assessments should be a regular activity, employing tools like vulnerability scanners and penetration testing to uncover weaknesses.

9. Threat Analysis: Understanding the myriad of threats that could exploit the vulnerabilities is essential. Threat analysis involves studying different threat actors, their motivations, and the methods they might use.

6. Resource Optimization: Effective risk management ensures that resources, both human and financial, are deployed optimally. By understanding the risk landscape, organizations can allocate resources more efficiently.

7. Investor and Stakeholder Confidence: Demonstrating a robust risk management framework instills confidence in investors and stakeholders, reassuring them about the organization's ability to navigate through challenges.

8. Competitive Advantage: In a competitive market, having a strong risk management framework can provide a significant advantage. It not only ensures operational continuity but also fosters an environment of trust with customers and partners.

7. Compliance Auditing: Regular audits to ensure compliance with the established policies, procedures, and regulatory requirements are a crucial aspect of IT risk management. Audits help in identifying areas of non-compliance and improving the processes.

8. Risk Reporting and Communication: Effective communication of the risks to all stakeholders, including the board of directors, management, and employees, is essential for informed decision-making.

9. Supplier and External Service Provider Risk Mitigation: In our highly networked environment, it's essential to manage risks tied to suppliers and third-party services. This includes evaluating their security standing and making sure they meet the organization's security criteria.

10. Crisis Recovery and Ongoing Business Plans: Crafting and trialing plans for crisis recovery and long-term business resilience to guarantee swift organizational recuperation from unfavorable events.

11. Change Oversight: Overseeing changes in an organized and planned way to confirm that modifications do not bring new risks or harm the security condition.

12. Feedback Mechanism: Creating a system for ongoing enhancement in risk management, which entails gathering input from different participants, post-incident scrutiny, and using lessons learned to refine the risk management structure.

Risk Assessment and Mitigation

Grasping Risk Evaluation:
Risk evaluation is a methodical procedure to discover and examine possible dangers that could negatively influence an organization's assets or operations. This serves as the basis for formulating an effective risk management plan.
1. Spot Potential Dangers: Start by spotting various types of dangers, such as cyber threats, data leaks, or system outages, especially in the IT sector.
2. Examine Weak Points: Study the potential weak spots that the detected dangers could exploit.
3. Gauge Impact and Probability: For each risk (a mix of danger and vulnerability), approximate the possible impact on the organization and how likely it is to happen.
4. Rank Risks: Based on impact and probability, rank risks to allocate resources optimally for risk alleviation.
Approaches to Reducing Risks:
Once the risks are evaluated and ranked, the subsequent step is to create approaches to alleviate or manage them.
1. Prevention: Introduce safeguards to stop risks from occurring, such as implementing strong security measures, consistent system upkeep, and staff training.
2. Mitigation: If prevention isn't possible, focus on diminishing the impact or the chance of those risks happening. This might involve additional security features or bolstering system resilience.
3. Risk Sharing: Offload risks to third parties, often done via insurance or subcontracting specific functions.
4. Acceptance: In certain cases, it might be most viable to simply accept the risks and prepare backup plans.
Instruments and Procedures:
1. Risk Evaluation Frameworks:
   - NIST SP 800-30: Offers guidelines for risk evaluations.
   - FAIR: A quantitative model for interpreting and examining risks.
2. Automated Risk Evaluation Tools:

- Nessus or Qualys can help spot weak points and evaluate risks.

3. Risk Management Software:

   - Software like SpiraPlan or RiskWatch assists organizations in supervising their risk evaluation and alleviation methods.

4. Frequent Checks and Security Tests:

   - Carry out routine checks and security tests to gauge the effectiveness of risk alleviation plans.

5. Operational Impact Analysis:

   - Perform an analysis to comprehend how varied risks could influence the organization's functions and financial status.

Practical Applications:

1. Cybersecurity Risk Evaluation:

   - Perform risk evaluations to discover potential threats and vulnerabilities, then formulate risk alleviation plans.

2. Project Risk Handling:

   - Examine and manage project risks to ensure completion within scope, time, and budget.

3. Compliance Risk Assessment:

   - Ascertain compliance with legal requirements by recognizing and managing associated risks.

Focusing on Risk Alleviation Techniques:

1. Incident Response Preparations:

   - Planning your organizational reaction to potential incidents is an essential part of risk alleviation. This encompasses establishing an Incident Response Team and conducting training sessions.

2. Ongoing Surveillance:

   - Utilize continuous monitoring systems to keep track of network and system performance, identifying and responding to risks as they arise.

3. Data Encryption and Access Restrictions:

   - Employ encryption methods for sensitive data protection and enforce strict access controls.

4. Education and Awareness Initiatives:

   - Regularly run programs to educate employees about risks and how best to prevent them.

Deep Dive into Tools and Software:

1. GRC Platforms:

   - Software like Archer or ServiceNow GRC offer comprehensive tools to manage governance, risk, and compliance.

2. Weak Point Scanners and Security Checks:

   - Utilize tools like Nessus, Qualys, or OpenVAS for scanning vulnerabilities, and conduct security audits for policy adherence.

3. Threat Intelligence Software:

   - Software like Recorded Future or ThreatConnect deliver valuable threat intelligence to understand emerging threats and act accordingly.

Extended Practical Scenario:

Imagine a mid-sized financial institution looking to enhance its risk management practices. They begin with an all-encompassing risk evaluation using a hybrid model. The internal team identifies a variety of risks, including potential data leaks, compliance issues, and system failures. They use a GRC platform for efficient risk management. The organization frequently performs penetration tests and vulnerability scans to spot weaknesses and proactively tackle them. They also create and test an incident response plan, establish continuous monitoring for real-time risk identification and response, and continuously train employees on security best practices and the evolving threat landscape. By dedicating resources to comprehensive risk evaluation and mitigation, the institution notably diminishes its vulnerability to financial and reputational harms, ensuring a secure and compliant operational framework.

Security Guidelines and Protocols

Defining Security Guidelines and Protocols:
Security policies are formalized statements that define how an organization manages, protects, and aligns its IT infrastructure with business objectives. Procedures, on the other hand, are the sequential guidelines required for the regular performance of tasks.
1. Policy Development:
   - Identifying Stakeholders: Engage stakeholders from across the organization to ensure that the policies are comprehensive and aligned with business objectives.
   - Regulatory Compliance: Ensure that the policies comply with legal and regulatory requirements relevant to the organization's industry.
   - Alignment with Best Practices: Adopt industry best practices such as those outlined in frameworks like ISO 27001 or NIST SP 800-53.
2. Procedure Development:
   - Operational Efficiency: Procedures should be designed to enhance operational efficiency while ensuring security.
   - Documentation: Document procedures in a clear, concise manner, ensuring they are easily understandable to all relevant personnel.
Implementing Security Policies and Procedures:
Effective implementation is crucial for the success of security policies and procedures.
1. Communication:
   - Make sure every staff member is informed about and comprehends the rules and guidelines.
   - Conduct training sessions and provide resources for employees to learn more about compliance requirements
2. Enforcement:
   - Implement technical controls to enforce policies.
   - Regularly audit compliance with policies and procedures, taking corrective action when necessary.
3. Automation:
   - Utilize automation tools to enforce procedural compliance and reduce the scope of human error.
Maintaining Security Policies and Procedures:
Security is a moving target, and as such, policies and procedures must evolve to stay effective.
1. Regular Review:
   - Policies and procedures ought to be examined periodically to confirm their ongoing relevance and efficacy.
   - Engage stakeholders in the review process to gather feedback and make necessary adjustments.
2. Continuous Improvement:
   - Adopt a culture of continuous improvement, learning from incidents, and making iterative improvements to policies and procedures.
3. Updating Training Materials:
   - Update training materials and resources to reflect any changes in policies or procedures.
Real-world Scenario:
Consider a healthcare provider that must comply with HIPAA regulations. The organization develops stringent security policies to protect patient data and implements procedures for managing data access. Frequent training sessions are held to keep all employees up-to-date on rules and guidelines, while automated tools help maintain adherence to these procedures. Routine audits are performed to verify sustained compliance, and the insights gained from these audits contribute to ongoing enhancements in the security protocols and practices.
In our healthcare provider scenario, post the initial implementation of security policies, an incident occurs where sensitive patient data is accidentally sent to a third-party due to a misconfiguration. The incident response team swings into action, the issue is rectified, and a root cause analysis is conducted. It's discovered that the existing procedures did not adequately cover data handling during system upgrades. The procedures are then updated to include additional checks and balances during system changes. Moreover, a lesson-learned session is conducted organization-wide to

share knowledge and prevent such incidents in the future. This scenario exemplifies the dynamic nature of maintaining security policies and procedures, highlighting the importance of continuous improvement and learning from incidents

Expanding on Policy and Procedure Development:

1. Policy Development:

   - Risk Assessment: Conduct a thorough risk assessment to understand the threats and vulnerabilities facing the organization. This will help in developing policies that are tailored to mitigate these risks.

   - Benchmarking: Benchmark against industry standards and competitors to understand where your organization stands in terms of security maturity.

   - Legal Consultation: Engage legal experts to ensure that the policies are in compliance with all applicable laws and regulations.

2. Procedure Development:

   - Task Analysis: Conduct a task analysis to understand the step-by-step processes involved in various operational activities. This will help in developing procedures that are both efficient and secure.

   - Feedback Loops: Establish feedback loops with the operational teams to ensure that the procedures are practical and do not hinder productivity.

Deep Dive into Implementation Strategies:

1. Change Management:

   - Employ change management principles to ensure smooth implementation of new policies and procedures. This includes communicating the changes effectively, providing training, and managing resistance.

2. Technology Alignment:

   - Ensure that the organization's technology infrastructure is aligned with the new policies and procedures. This may involve upgrading systems, implementing new security controls, or even changing vendors to ensure compliance.

3. Performance Metrics:

   - Develop performance metrics to measure the effectiveness of the policies and procedures. This could include metrics like the number of security incidents, compliance audit scores, or employee adherence to procedures.

In-depth on Maintenance Strategies:

1. Incident Learning:

   - Learn from security incidents to identify weaknesses in the current policies and procedures, and make necessary amendments to prevent reoccurrence.

2. Industry Evolution:

   - Stay updated on the evolution of industry best practices and regulatory requirements. Revise policies and procedures accordingly to ensure ongoing compliance.

3. Employee Feedback:

   - Collect feedback from employees to understand the practicality and effectiveness of the policies and procedures. Use this feedback to make improvements.

The Risk Management Lifecycle

1. Identify:

   - Asset Identification: Document all assets and resources crucial to the organization.

   - Threat Identification: Identify potential threats facing the organization.

   - Vulnerability Identification: Pinpoint vulnerabilities within the system that could be exploited.

2. Assess:

   - Risk Evaluation: Assess the recognized risks according to their probability and potential impact.

   - Risk Ranking: Arrange risks in order of their potential repercussions on the organization.

3. Take Action:

   - Risk Response: Decide whether to lessen, shift, accept, or sidestep each risk.

   - Apply Safeguards: Put into place protective measures to lessen the pinpointed risks.

4. Observe:

- Ongoing Surveillance: Utilize tracking tools to identify and act on security occurrences.
- Success Indicators: Evaluate how well the risk management plan is functioning.

5. Examine:
   - Periodic Assessments: Perform frequent evaluations of the risk management procedure to confirm its efficacy.
   - Stakeholder Input: Solicit opinions from relevant parties and implement needed changes to the risk management plan.

Real-world Application:

For instance, a financial institution embarks on a new project to launch a mobile banking app. During the Identify phase, they document all assets related to the project and identify potential threats like cyber-attacks, and vulnerabilities like software bugs. In the Assess phase, they analyze and prioritize these risks. During the Mitigate phase, they decide to employ robust encryption and conduct rigorous testing to address the identified risks. In the Monitor phase, they employ security monitoring tools to detect any suspicious activities. Finally, in the Review phase, they gather feedback from various stakeholders, including customers and internal security teams, to assess the efficacy of their risk management initiatives and implement required enhancements for future projects.

Extending the scenario of the financial institution launching a mobile banking app, during the Review phase, they also conduct a comparative analysis with industry benchmarks to understand how their risk management practices measure up against peers. They engage external auditors to validate their risk management process, and based on the findings, they refine their risk management framework to better align with industry best practices. This iterative process of reviewing and refining the risk management structure contributes to the advancement of the organization's risk maturity management practices over time

1. Identify:
   - Asset Classification: Beyond just identifying assets, classifying them based on their importance and sensitivity is crucial. It involves defining the value and the role of assets in the organization.
   - Threat Modeling: Employ threat modeling techniques to understand the adversaries, their capabilities, and the tactics they might use.
   - Vulnerability Scanning: Use automated tools to perform regular vulnerability scanning and identify weaknesses in the system.

2. Assess:
   - Risk Scenarios: Develop scenarios to understand the potential impact of risks. Scenario analysis helps in visualizing the consequences and preparing for potential issues.
   - Stakeholder Engagement: Engage stakeholders in risk assessment to understand the business impact from various perspectives.

3. Mitigate:
   - Control Selection: Selecting the right controls based on the nature of risks and compliance requirements.
   - Cost-Benefit Analysis: Conduct a cost-benefit analysis to ensure that the cost of mitigation does not outweigh the benefits.

4. Monitor:
   - Incident Detection: Establish incident detection mechanisms to identify and respond to security incidents promptly.
   - Reporting and Alerting: Set up reporting and alerting mechanisms to ensure the right people are informed about potential risks or ongoing incidents.

5. Review:
   - Lessons Learned: After the occurrence of incidents or near misses, conduct a lessons-learned session to understand what mistakes were made and how to avert similar incidents going forward.
   - Benchmarking: Benchmark the organization's risk management practices against industry standards to identify areas of improvement.

Conducting a Risk Assessment in a Tech Startup

Scenario Setting:

Consider a tech startup, TechNova, specializing in developing AI-powered solutions for healthcare. With a small yet dynamic team, TechNova secured a project to develop a predictive analytics platform for a mid-sized hospital. Before diving into development, the leadership decided to perform a risk evaluation to ensure the security and compliance of the upcoming project.

Phase 1: Identification

1. Asset Identification:
   - Challenges: With limited resources, identifying and documenting all assets was a challenge.
   - Solutions: Utilized automated asset discovery tools to streamline the process.
2. Threat and Vulnerability Identification:
   - Challenges: Being in a niche field, identifying relevant threats required specialized knowledge.
   - Solutions: Engaged external cybersecurity consultants to assist in threat modeling.

Phase 2: Assessment

1. Risk Analysis:
   - Challenges: Quantifying the impact and likelihood of risks was challenging due to the lack of historical data.
   - Solutions: Adopted an approach to risk evaluation based on qualitative methods, leveraging the insights of experts for risk assessment
2. Risk Prioritization:
   - Challenges: Balancing business objectives with risk mitigation was challenging.
   - Solutions: Established a risk committee to ensure a balanced perspective in risk prioritization.

Phase 3: Mitigation

1. Control Selection and Implementation:
   - Challenges: Limited budget constrained the implementation of desired controls.
   - Solutions: Prioritized implementation of critical controls, and planned for phased implementation of others.
2. Cost-Benefit Analysis:
   - Challenges: Demonstrating the return on investment (ROI) of risk mitigation efforts.
   - Solutions: Developed a risk mitigation ROI model to justify the investments.

Phase 4: Monitoring and Review

1. Continuous Monitoring:
   - Challenges: Limited in-house expertise in security monitoring.
   - Solutions: Outsourced security monitoring to a managed security service provider (MSSP).
2. Regular Reviews:
   - Challenges: Engaging busy stakeholders for regular risk reviews.
   - Solutions: Scheduled quarterly risk review meetings, ensuring stakeholder engagement through clear communication of the value derived from these reviews.

Interactive Quizzes: Check your Proficiency in Managing Risks

1. What is the primary objective of risk management?
a) Eliminate all risks
b) Mitigate risks
c) Identify risks
d) Transfer risks

2. What does SLE stand for in risk management?
a) Single Loss Exposure
b) Single Loss Expectancy
c) Security Loss Exposure
d) System Loss Expectancy

3. What does ALE stand for?
a) Average Loss Exposure
b) Asset Loss Expectancy
c) Average Loss Expectancy
d) Annual Loss Expectancy

4. What is the most common method for risk calculation?

a) SLE x ALE
b) ALE / SLE
c) ARO x SLE
d) SLE / ARO

5. What is "residual risk"?
a) The risk that remains after all mitigations
b) The initial risk before any mitigations
c) The average risk over time
d) The risk transferred to a third party

6. What is the concept of "risk appetite"?
a) The level of risk an organization is willing to take
b) The process of eating up risks
c) The maximum allowable risk
d) The process of identifying risks

7. What does a "risk matrix" help with?
a) Identifying risks
b) Quantifying risks
c) Visualizing risks
d) Mitigating risks

8. What does a "Threat Landscape" refer to?
a) A software tool for risk assessment
b) The collection of potential threats faced by an organization
c) A physical area affected by a particular threat
d) A map showing the locations of all threats

9. What is a Common Vulnerability Scoring System (CVSS)?
a) A type of firewall
b) A methodology for ranking vulnerabilities
c) A database of all known threats
d) A type of antivirus software

10. What is the main purpose of a Business Impact Analysis (BIA)?
a) To identify the potential effects of interruption to business processes
b) To estimate the budget for a project
c) To analyze the threats facing a business
d) To investigate the impact of a particular threat

11. What does the RTO (Recovery Time Objective) represent?
a) The time it takes to recover data
b) The time it takes to respond to an incident
c) The time within which a process must be restored
d) The time it takes to identify an incident

12. What is a Disaster Recovery Plan primarily focused on?
a) Identifying risks
b) Business continuity

c) Restoring IT systems
d) Preventing risks

13. What is a hot site in disaster recovery?
a) A website that's gone viral
b) A fully operational offsite data center
c) A place where data backups are stored
d) A site suffering from an ongoing attack

14. What is the purpose of a cold site in disaster recovery?
a) To provide instant switch-over
b) To act as a decoy for attackers
c) To provide physical space where the backup systems are stored
d) To store frozen samples of sensitive data

15. What does RPO (Recovery Point Objective) represent?
a) The time between data backups
b) The oldest data that needs to be recovered
c) The point where risk is zero
d) The point to restore service to minimum capabilities

16. What does a SWOT analysis stand for?
a) Software, Workflow, Options, Tactics
b) Strengths, Weaknesses, Opportunities, Threats
c) Systems, Windows, Operations, Tactics
d) Security, Web, Operations, Threats

17. What is due diligence in the context of risk management?
a) The care that a reasonable person exercises to avoid harm
b) A type of insurance against risks
c) An audit performed annually
d) A backup strategy for data

18. What does ISO 27001 primarily focus on?
a) Web security
b) Information security management
c) Physical security
d) Network security

19. What is the purpose of a risk register?
a) To record all the risks identified
b) To list all previous risk assessments
c) To register the impact of each risk
d) To list all security controls

20. Which one of these is not a type of control in risk management?
a) Preventive
b) Detective
c) Corrective
d) Infective

21. What does a "False Positive" mean in the context of risk management?
a) A real threat that is ignored
b) A perceived risk that is actually not a risk
c) An accurate prediction of a risk
d) A risk that has been mitigated but still occurs

22. What is the first step in the risk management process?
a) Risk assessment
b) Risk identification
c) Risk mitigation
d) Risk transfer

23. What is "risk transference"?
a) Eliminating the risk
b) Passing the risk to another party
c) Reducing the risk
d) Accepting the risk

24. Which of the following is NOT a type of risk?
a) Strategic
b) Operational
c) Financial
d) Imaginary

25. What is a risk assessment primarily used for?
a) To identify vulnerabilities and threats
b) To calculate the budget for a project
c) To audit the financial aspects of a project
d) To define project scope

26. What does a vulnerability assessment focus on?
a) Calculating the impact of potential risks
b) Identifying weaknesses in a system
c) Evaluating the likelihood of a risk occurring
d) Assessing the financial impact of a risk

27. What is a penetration test aimed at?
a) Finding holes in the organization's firewall
b) Simulating cyber attacks to assess security posture
c) Measuring the organization's risk appetite
d) Calculating the potential loss from an attack

28. What is "Inherent Risk"?
a) The risk before any type of action is taken
b) The risk that can't be avoided
c) The risk after mitigation efforts
d) The risk that is transferred

29. What is the opposite of "Qualitative Risk Analysis"?
a) Inherent Risk Analysis
b) Quantitative Risk Analysis
c) Descriptive Risk Analysis
d) Subjective Risk Analysis

30. What does VAR (Value at Risk) indicate?
a) The value of the assets at risk
b) The maximum potential loss an investment portfolio could face
c) The minimum amount to invest to mitigate a risk
d) The value of the business as a whole

31. What does ERM stand for?
a) Emergency Risk Management
b) Effective Risk Management
c) Enterprise Risk Management
d) Early Risk Management

32. What does FAIR stand for in risk management?
a) Financially Adjusted Risk
b) Factor Analysis of Information Risk
c) Focused Analysis of Internal Risks
d) Federal Approval of Internal Risks

33. What is "Loss Magnitude"?
a) The financial impact of a risk event
b) The emotional impact of a loss
c) The estimated loss in terms of project time
d) The duration of a loss event

34. What is risk avoidance?
a) Choosing not to engage in an activity that could carry risk
b) Ignoring a known risk
c) Transferring the risk to another party
d) Minimizing the impact of a risk

35. What is COSO framework mainly used for?
a) Cybersecurity risk management
b) Internal organizational governance
c) Financial risk assessment
d) Legal compliance

36. What does a "heat map" in risk management visually display?
a) The hottest issues the organization is facing
b) The likelihood vs impact of identified risks
c) The geographical locations of risks
d) The speed at which risks are being mitigated

37. What does the term "tail risk" refer to?
a) A risk that is about to happen
b) A risk that is being ignored
c) A risk that has a low likelihood but high impact
d) A risk related to physical security

38. What does "Black Swan" refer to in the context of risk?
a) An easily predicted event
b) An extremely rare event with severe consequences
c) A manageable risk

d) A type of cyber attack

39. What is "risk tolerance"?

a) The highest risk that an organization is willing to take

b) The lowest risk that is acceptable

c) The medium level of risk that an organization can bear

d) The risk that is transferred to a third party

40. What is the main goal of incident response in the context of risk management?

a) To identify the attacker

b) To assess the damage

c) To restore normal operations as quickly as possible

d) To find vulnerabilities

ANSWERS

1. What is the primary objective of risk management? Answer: c) The time within which a process must be restored - Explanation: RTO stands for Recovery Time Objective and refers to the maximum amount of time that a process can be down before there's a significant impact on the business.

2. What does SLE stand for in risk management? Answer: c) Restoring IT systems - Explanation: A Disaster Recovery Plan is primarily focused on restoring IT systems after a disruptive event.

3. What does ALE stand for? Answer: b) A fully operational offsite data center - Explanation: A hot site is a fully operational offsite data center, ready to take over operations in the case of a disaster.

4. What is the most common method for risk calculation? Answer: c) To provide physical space where the backup systems are stored - Explanation: A cold site is a physical location where an organization can move to continue its operations in case of a disaster. It doesn't have immediately available technology infrastructure.

5. What is "residual risk"? Answer: b) The oldest data that needs to be recovered - Explanation: RPO, or Recovery Point Objective, indicates the age of the data that must be recovered from backup storage for normal operations to resume.

6. What is the concept of "risk appetite"? Answer: b) Strengths, Weaknesses, Opportunities, Threats - Explanation: SWOT analysis helps in identifying the Strengths, Weaknesses, Opportunities, and Threats related to business competition or project planning.

7. What does a "risk matrix" help with? Answer: a) The care that a reasonable person exercises to avoid harm - Explanation: Due diligence refers to the care that a reasonable person exercises to avoid harm to other persons or their property.

8. What does a "Threat Landscape" refer to? Answer: b) Information security management - Explanation: ISO 27001 focuses on information security management systems (ISMS).

9. What is a Common Vulnerability Scoring System (CVSS)? Answer: a) To record all the risks identified - Explanation: A risk register is used to identify, assess, and prioritize the risks.

10. What is the main purpose of a Business Impact Analysis (BIA)? Answer: d) Infective - Explanation: Preventive, Detective, and Corrective are types of controls in risk management. "Infective" is not a type of control.

11. What does the RTO (Recovery Time Objective) represent? Answer: b) A perceived risk that is actually not a risk - Explanation: A False Positive refers to an event that is flagged as a risk or issue but is actually non-harmful.

12. What is a Disaster Recovery Plan primarily focused on? Answer: b) Risk identification - Explanation: The first step in the risk management process is usually identifying the risks that exist.

13. What is a hot site in disaster recovery? Answer: b) Passing the risk to another party - Explanation: Risk transference means shifting the risk from one party to another, often using insurance or outsourcing.

14. What is the purpose of a cold site in disaster recovery? Answer: d) Imaginary - Explanation: Strategic, Operational, and Financial are types of risk. "Imaginary" is not a recognized type of risk.

15. What does RPO (Recovery Point Objective) represent? Answer: a) To identify vulnerabilities and threats - Explanation: Risk assessments are mainly used for identifying vulnerabilities and threats to understand the risks an organization faces.

16. What does a SWOT analysis stand for? Answer: b) Increasing impact while reducing likelihood - Explanation: Risk Magnification refers to making a risk more impactful but less likely. This is not a standard risk management term but is used here to test understanding.

17. What is due diligence in the context of risk management? Answer: d) Quantitative and qualitative - Explanation: Risk assessments can be both quantitative and qualitative. Quantitative assessments are numerical; qualitative are descriptive.

18. What does "Least Privilege" mean in Identity and Access Management? Answer: a) To reduce the risk to an acceptable level - Explanation: Risk mitigation aims to reduce the negative impact of risks as well as the likelihood that they will occur.

19. What is Multi-Factor Authentication (MFA)? Answer: d) All of the above - Explanation: BCP should include objectives, responsibilities, and emergency response procedures, among other elements.

20. What is the primary purpose of a firewall? Answer: c) Taking advantage of an opportunity - Explanation: Risk exploitation involves taking steps to ensure an opportunity is realized.

21. What does the term "social engineering" refer to? Answer: b) Something that can exploit a vulnerability - Explanation: A threat is something that has the potential to exploit a vulnerability and cause harm.

22. What is the key purpose of encryption? Answer: a) Identifying the cost of different risk strategies - Explanation: Cost-benefit analysis is used for calculating and comparing the benefits and costs of a project, decision or strategy, including different risk strategies.

23. What is a Zero-Day Vulnerability? Answer: b) The likelihood and impact of a risk occurring - Explanation: Risk magnitude is calculated by assessing both the likelihood and the impact of a particular risk.

24. What does VPN stand for? Answer: a) It is a document detailing the procedures to follow in case of a disaster - Explanation: A Disaster Recovery Plan (DRP) outlines the procedures to follow to recover and protect a business IT infrastructure in the event of a disaster.

25. What is "Data Loss Prevention" (DLP)? Answer: b) The value of a risk based on its impact and likelihood - Explanation: Risk exposure calculates the potential impact of a risk by multiplying its probability of occurring by the cost to the project if it does occur.

26. What is the main difference between hashing and encryption? Answer: c) Accept the risk and continue operating as usual - Explanation: Risk acceptance means acknowledging a risk but taking no special measures to address it.

27. What is the purpose of an Intrusion Detection System (IDS)? Answer: a) The risk of loss due to a penetration tester's actions - Explanation: Risk of exploit specifically refers to the likelihood of an attacker leveraging a vulnerability, not a penetration tester.

28. Which of the following best describes the term "air gap"? Answer: c) A group of risks that have the potential to drastically impact an organization - Explanation: Risk Portfolio is the aggregation of all risks affecting an organization.

29. What does Business Continuity Planning (BCP) involve? Answer: d) Managing the risk from an organization-wide perspective - Explanation: Enterprise Risk Management (ERM) involves identifying and handling risks on an organizational level.

30. What does the principle of "Non-Repudiation" guarantee? Answer: a) A list of potential risks and their attributes - Explanation: A risk register is a document where all details about potential risks are recorded.

31. What is the primary function of a Web Application Firewall (WAF)? Answer: c) Risk of loss from an unknown source - Explanation: Inherent risk refers to the risk involved in a process or business that exists naturally.

32. What is a Zero-Day Vulnerability? Answer: b) A risk that remains after all risk responses have been implemented - Explanation: Residual risk is the amount of risk remaining after protective measures have been implemented.

33. What is the primary purpose of a Digital Certificate? Answer: a) Costs more than the benefit of mitigating a risk - Explanation: If the cost of mitigation exceeds the benefit, it is often considered not worth mitigating.

34. What does "Phishing" most commonly refer to? Answer: b) Identifies the triggers of risks - Explanation: A risk breakdown structure is a hierarchical depiction of the identified project risks arranged by risk category.

35. What is the principle of "Least Privilege"? Answer: c) Man-made risks - Explanation: These risks are due to human actions, such as terrorism or fraud.

36. Which security concept involves separating a network into various parts to manage traffic and restrict access? Answer: b) The likelihood of a risk occurring - Explanation: Risk probability refers to the likelihood of a specific risk occurring.

37. In which type of attack does an attacker secretly relay or alter the communication between two parties? Answer: a) Loss of reputation or competitive advantage - Explanation: Strategic risk is related to factors that affect an organization's ability to compete.

38. Which encryption algorithm is considered the most secure? Answer: c) Comprehensive evaluation of an organization's IT systems - Explanation: An IT audit is a comprehensive evaluation of an organization's information technology infrastructure, policies and operations.

39. What is the main purpose of a VPN? Answer: a) Standardized guidelines for risk management - Explanation: The NIST Special Publication 800-37 provides guidelines for risk management within federal agencies and by contractors working on behalf of those agencies.

40. What does the term "Air Gap" refer to in a network context? Answer: b) Risk reduction - Explanation: Risk mitigation is synonymous with risk reduction. It involves actions taken to reduce the severity of a risk.

Hands-on Exercise: Setting up a Basic Access Control System

Exercise Overview
1. Identifying Resources and Users:
   - List all the resources you want to protect (e.g., files, databases, applications).
   - Identify the users who will need access to these resources and categorize them based on their roles within the organization.
2. Defining Access Permissions:
   - Determine the level of access each user category should have for each resource.
   - Create an Access Control Matrix to visualize the access permissions.
3. Selecting an Access Control Software:
   - Research and select a basic access control software that suits the needs of your scenario.
   - Install the software following the vendor's guidelines.
Implementation:
1. Configuring the Access Control System:
   - Input the resources, users, and access permissions into the access control software.
   - Set up authentication methods for users (e.g., passwords, biometric authentication).
   - Resource and User Configuration: Begin by inputting the resources and users into the access control software. Make sure to input the details meticulously to ensure accurate configuration.
   - Permission Configuration: Implement the access permissions as defined in the Access Control Matrix. Test each permission setting to ensure it corresponds accurately to the defined access levels.
   - Authentication Setup: Establish authentication methods for users. This could include setting up username and password authentication, biometric authentication, or multi-factor authentication. Configure password policies to enforce strong password practices
2. Testing the Access Control System:
   - Conduct evaluations to confirm that the access restrictions are functioning correctly.
   - Spot any anomalies or unanticipated actions and make required modifications.
   - Access Verification: Execute comprehensive evaluations to confirm that the access restrictions operate as intended. Examine various user types to ensure they possess the correct degree of access to specific resources.
   - Unauthorized Access Testing: Attempt to access the resources with unauthorized user accounts to test the effectiveness of the access controls. Document any anomalies and address them accordingly.
3. Documenting the Access Control Setup:
   - Document the setup process, configurations, and any issues encountered and how they were resolved.
   - Create a user guide for end-users to understand how to access the resources and whom to contact for access issues.

   - Documentation: Create detailed documentation of the setup process, configurations, and any issues encountered along with their solutions. This documentation will serve as a valuable reference for future troubleshooting and audits.
   - User Guide: Develop a user guide to help end-users understand how to access the resources, how to manage their credentials, and whom to contact for access issues.

Review and Monitoring:

1. Reviewing the Access Control Setup:
   - Have a third party or another team member review the setup to ensure it meets the access control requirements.
   - Obtain feedback and make any necessary adjustments.
   - Peer Review: Have a third party or another team member review the setup to ensure it meets the access control requirements. Collect feedback for any improvements.
   - Feedback Implementation: Incorporate the feedback received to enhance the access control setup. Make necessary adjustments to ensure a secure and user-friendly access control system.

2. Monitoring and Adjusting the Access Control System:
   - Set up monitoring to detect unauthorized access attempts.
   - Review logs regularly and adjust the access control settings as necessary based on the monitoring feedback.
   - Monitoring Setup: Establish monitoring mechanisms to detect unauthorized access attempts and other security incidents related to access control.
   - Regular Review: Conduct regular reviews of the access control settings and the monitoring logs to identify any patterns or issues that may arise. Adjust the access control settings as necessary based on the findings.

6) Security Technologies and Tools

Overview of Security Technologies

Firewall Systems:

Firewall systems serve as the initial security barrier in controlling network data flow based on pre-established criteria. These can either be software or hardware solutions, crucial for restricting unauthorized network access. Firewalls are designed to filter out data originating from specific locations or apps, while permitting essential data. Advanced firewalls have expanded their capabilities to include stateful inspection that monitors active sessions and deep packet scrutiny to check for harmful content within data packets. Next-Generation Firewalls (NGFWs) add extra features like intrusion prevention and application-level controls, making them even more effective at combatting cyber threats.

Intrusion Monitoring Tools:

These tools are specialized in surveying networks for unauthorized activities or malicious actions. They can be either network or host-focused, and upon detecting irregularities, notify administrators for additional examination.

Data Scrambling Solutions:

Crucial for ensuring data privacy and integrity, these solutions transform readable data into a coded version using specific algorithms. Various standards like AES and RSA are used for securing data both in transit and at rest. Additional features like digital signatures and hash functions can also validate the source and integrity of data.

Malware Defense Software:

Essential for the detection and removal of malicious software types like viruses and trojans, these tools use signature matching, heuristic evaluation, and behavioral assessment to neutralize threats before they inflict harm.

Private Network Tunnels (VPNs):

VPNs establish an encrypted path between a user's device and a network, ensuring data confidentiality and integrity, offering a secure method for remote network access.

Permission Control Systems:

Vital for governing access within an organization, these systems implement policies that specify which users or processes have rights to particular resources. Understanding different access control models is key to ensuring that only authorized personnel gain access to restricted data.

Security Event and Log Management (SELM) Platforms:

Integral for sophisticated threat discovery and incident response, these platforms gather and analyze log data from multiple organizational sources. By matching events from different logs, SELM platforms can detect abnormal patterns and offer immediate security alert analysis.

Remote Device Security Solutions:

These solutions secure an organization's network when accessed by remote devices like mobile phones or laptops, ensuring that such endpoints do not compromise network security, especially in a BYOD policy setting.

Internet Safety Barriers:

These barriers operate at the internet entry point to mitigate online security threats. They can prevent harmful traffic and ensure policy adherence, essential for warding off web-based risks.

Device Governance Solutions (MDM):

With the growing use of mobile devices, it's crucial to govern and secure these devices within the corporate setting. MDM solutions can impose security measures, verify device compliance, and offer remote management features.

Information Leakage Prevention (ILP) Systems:

ILP systems aid in identifying and preventing the unauthorized distribution or destruction of sensitive data. These systems are critical for safeguarding data at all stages, ensuring it remains within controlled boundaries.

Active Threat Prevention Systems (IPS):

Extending the capabilities of intrusion monitoring tools, these systems detect and also take predetermined steps to prevent malicious activities, offering proactive security measures.

Identity and Role Verification Systems (IAM):

IAM systems confirm that only approved users have specified information access. They are a foundational element of an organization's security framework.

Web Safety Shields (SWGs):

Web Safety Shields offer real-time web reputation evaluation and malware scanning, ensuring hazardous content is filtered prior to reaching the user network.

All-in-One Security Solutions (UTM):

UTM systems amalgamate multiple security technologies into one centralized platform, providing a streamlined and comprehensive security strategy suitable for organizations of all sizes.

Monitoring and Analysis Tools

Network Monitoring Tools:

Network monitoring tools provide real-time insights into an organization's network traffic, enabling the identification of unusual activity that could signify a security threat. Tools such as Wireshark, SolarWinds, and PRTG Network Monitor are instrumental in capturing and analyzing network packets, providing a granular view of network activities. Understanding the features and capabilities of network monitoring tools is crucial for maintaining network health and security. Utilizing network monitoring tools effectively requires a solid understanding of networking principles and the ability to interpret the data these tools provide. For instance, Wireshark, a packet analyzer, can provide a treasure trove of information about network traffic, but understanding the significance of this data and how to act upon it is crucial. This includes identifying patterns of malicious traffic, understanding the protocols being used, and the ability to pinpoint issues that could be affecting network performance or security.

Vulnerability Assessment Tools:

Vulnerability assessment tools like Nessus, OpenVAS, and Qualys help in identifying weaknesses in an organization's systems and network. By conducting regular scans, these tools provide valuable insights into potential vulnerabilities, allowing for timely remediation before they can be exploited by malicious actors. Delving into the functionality of vulnerability assessment tools will equip you with the knowledge to establish a proactive security posture. The effectiveness of vulnerability assessment tools also hinges on a well-configured setup and timely analysis. These tools can generate a voluminous amount of data, and sifting through this data to identify the most critical vulnerabilities requires a solid understanding of the system being protected and the potential threats it faces. Furthermore, these tools are only as good as their latest update; keeping them updated with the latest vulnerability definitions is paramount

Security Information and Event Management (SIEM) Systems:

SIEM systems, such as Splunk and ArcSight, aggregate and analyze log data from various sources across the organization. They provide a centralized view for monitoring, analysis, and reporting, enabling timely detection and response to security incidents. Exploring SIEM systems' capabilities will elucidate how they play a pivotal role in enhancing organizational security through real-time analysis and historical data review. SIEM systems are at the heart of many organization's security infrastructure. They provide a centralized point for collecting and analyzing data from across the network, turning a flood of information into actionable intelligence. A well-configured SIEM can provide early warning of an ongoing attack, provide the data necessary for investigating incidents, and ensure compliance with various regulatory requirements.

Performance Assessment Tools:

Performance assessment tools like Nagios and Zabbix provide comprehensive monitoring of system performance, ensuring that all components are functioning optimally. They can alert administrators to issues such as system overload, network latency, or failure of critical services, allowing for prompt resolution to maintain system integrity and availability.Performance assessment tools are not traditionally seen as security tools, yet they play a vital role in maintaining a secure and reliable network. A sudden drop in system performance could be indicative of a security incident. These tools can also play a critical role in ensuring that security controls do not adversely affect system performance, helping to strike a balance between security and usability.

Utilizing Security Tools in an Enterprise Environment

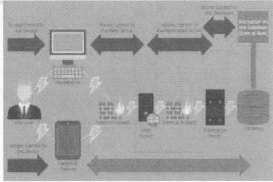

Layered Security Approach:

The diagram illustrates a layered security approach, showing how various tools like firewalls, intrusion detection systems, and encryption tools work together to create multiple layers of defense. This strategy, often referred to as defense in depth, is crucial for ensuring that there are multiple barriers to potential security threats. The layered security approach, as illustrated, adopts multiple security measures at various levels within the organization's infrastructure. For instance, at the network perimeter, firewalls act as the first line of defense against external threats. The diagram showcases how the next layer might incorporate intrusion detection systems (IDS) to monitor traffic for suspicious activities. Further in, anti-malware tools and encryption technologies protect the organization's data at rest and in transit. Each layer is designed to halt or slow down threat actors, ensuring that even if one layer is breached, subsequent layers continue to provide protection.

Monitoring and Analysis:

Illustrated are the monitoring and analysis tools in action, capturing and analyzing network traffic, identifying vulnerabilities, and assessing system performance. The visual representation helps in understanding the flow of information and how these tools provide the insights necessary for timely response to security incidents. The diagram visually portrays how monitoring and analysis tools play a critical role in real-time detection and response. It shows how tools like SIEM systems collect and correlate data from various sources, providing a centralized view of the organization's security posture. Additionally, it illustrates the flow of information from network monitoring tools to vulnerability assessment platforms, showcasing how these tools complement each other in identifying and responding to potential threats

Integration and Automation:

The diagram also depicts how modern security tools can be integrated and automated, providing a seamless security management experience. Automation plays a key role in responding to security incidents swiftly, and integration ensures that all tools are working together harmoniously.Integration and automation, as depicted in the diagram, are the linchpins of modern security operations. The diagram demonstrates how integrating security tools creates a cohesive system that can respond to threats in a coordinated manner. It also emphasizes the importance of automation in accelerating incident response, showing how automated workflows can be triggered by specific security events, allowing for quicker mitigation and reducing the window of opportunity for attackers.

Selecting and Implementing the Right Security Tools for Organizational Security

Understanding the Security Needs:

Mr. Adams embarks on a meticulous journey to unravel TechGuard's security needs. The endeavor commences with a comprehensive assessment of the existing infrastructure, scrutinizing network configurations, server setups, and data handling practices. A thorough inventory of critical assets is compiled to ascertain the crown jewels requiring heightened protection. Mr. Adams also orchestrates a series of interviews with department heads to fathom operational requisites and regulatory compliance mandates, ensuring alignment with business objectives and legal frameworks. The narrative transitions into the meticulous realms of Mr. Adams' endeavors as he embarks on a quest to unravel the security enigma that TechGuard faces. His first order of business is a comprehensive reconnaissance of the existing security infrastructure. The networks are scrutinized, server setups are audited, and data handling practices are put under a magnifying glass. The essence of this venture is to establish a baseline, a security datum against which the efficacy of future initiatives can be measured.Mr. Adams compiles a meticulous inventory of critical assets, identifying the crown jewels of TechGuard that require an impenetrable security aegis. This inventory is the cornerstone upon which the edifice of their security strategy would be erected.He also orchestrates a series of interviews with department heads, delving into the operational requisites, and regulatory compliance mandates. The dialogues are a confluence of technical jargons and business lexicons, as Mr. Adams strives to ensure an alignment between business objectives and legal frameworks.

Market Research and Vendor Evaluation:

Mr. Adams and his team delve into an extensive exploration of the security solutions market, evaluating a plethora of security tools. The evaluation matrix extends beyond functionalities; it encapsulates scalability, reliability, and the support ecosystem offered by vendors. The narrative elucidates how Mr. Adams orchestrates sessions with various vendors, diving into detailed demonstrations to gauge the efficacy and fitment of the tools in TechGuard's environment. With a clearer understanding of the security needs, Mr. Adams and his team delve into the vast expanse of the security solutions market. They sift through a plethora of security tools, each with its unique proposition and a promise of a fortress-like defense. But Mr. Adams is well-versed in the art of discerning the chaff from the grain. His evaluation matrix extends beyond mere functionalities; it delves into the realms of scalability, reliability, and the support ecosystem that accompanies these tools.The narrative draws the readers into sessions with various vendors, each a tableau of hopes and promises. Mr. Adams dives into detailed demonstrations, evaluating the efficacy and fitment of the tools in TechGuard's dynamic environment. The narrative elucidates how Mr. Adams meticulously scores each tool against a well-crafted evaluation matrix, ensuring a comprehensive assessment that leaves no stone unturned.

Testing and Piloting:

Mr. Adams orchestrates a rigorous testing regime for shortlisted tools in a controlled, simulated environment reflective of TechGuard's operational ecosystem. Different attack scenarios are simulated to evaluate the resilience and efficacy of these tools in detecting and mitigating threats. The ease of use and learning curve associated with each tool are also evaluated, as these factors significantly impact the adoption rate among the IT staff.

Training and Implementation:

Upon conclusion of the testing phase, a meticulous plan for training and implementation is charted out. Mr. Adams collaborates with vendors to arrange comprehensive training sessions for the IT staff. The implementation phase is systematically phased to mitigate any potential disruptions, with a gradual rollout from less critical to more critical environments. The dawn of implementation brings along a buzz of activity within TechGuard. Mr. Adams, with a team of seasoned security experts, oversees the rollout. They navigate through the initial hiccups, configuring the tools to align with the organizational policies and security requirements.Training sessions are orchestrated for the staff, ensuring a seamless transition to the new security infrastructure. The narrative delves into the importance of a well-informed staff, elucidating how human error is often the weakest link in cybersecurity.

Review and Continuous Improvement:

Post-implementation, a robust review mechanism is established to evaluate the effectiveness of the new security tools. Feedback is gathered from users, performance data is analyzed, and regular review meetings are conducted to identify areas for improvement, fostering a culture of continuous learning and improvement.Post-implementation, Mr. Adams institutes a review mechanism to gauge the effectiveness of the new security infrastructure. Metrics are tracked, incidents are logged and analyzed, and performance against pre-defined benchmarks is evaluated.The narrative underscores the importance of a continuous improvement approach in cybersecurity. It delves into how feedback from these reviews fuels enhancements in the security policies, processes, and the tools, fortifying TechGuard's security posture against evolving threats.

Interactive Quiz: Technologies and Tools Proficiency

1. What does IDS stand for?
   - a) Internet Delivery System
   - b) Intrusion Detection System
   - c) Identity Denial Service
   - d) Internal Data Stream
2. Which tool is used for network mapping?
   - a) Nessus
   - b) Nmap
   - c) Wireshark
   - d) Aircrack-ng
3. What is the primary function of a firewall?
   - a) Data backup
   - b) Monitoring bandwidth
   - c) Network security
   - d) File encryption
4. What does HIDS stand for?
   - a) Host-based Intrusion Detection System
   - b) Hardware Inspection Delivery Service
   - c) Human Identity Discovery System
   - d) Host Interface Drive Socket
5. What is a honeypot?
   - a) A storage solution
   - b) A decryption algorithm
   - c) A network decoy
   - d) An encryption tool
6. What does DLP stand for?
   - a) Data Loss Prevention
   - b) Data Link Protocol
   - c) Dynamic Load Processing
   - d) Digital Light Processing
7. Which of these is a port scanner?
   - a) Airodump-ng
   - b) John the Ripper
   - c) OpenVAS
   - d) Nmap
8. What is the purpose of a VPN?
   - a) Data analytics
   - b) Secure communication
   - c) Performance monitoring
   - d) File sharing
9. What does MDM stand for?
   - a) Master Data Management
   - b) Mobile Device Management
   - c) Memory Dump Manager
   - d) Media Delivery Mechanism
10. What is a rootkit?
   - a) Malware
   - b) Data backup software
   - c) Firewall
   - d) VPN
11. Which technology is primarily used for web content filtering?
   - a) Antivirus
   - b) DNS filtering
   - c) IDS
   - d) DLP
12. What is the primary function of a SIEM?
   - a) File encryption
   - b) Data backup
   - c) Security information and event management
   - d) VPN
13. What is Snort?
   - a) VPN
   - b) IDS
   - c) Firewall
   - d) Antivirus
14. What is the primary function of a UTM?
   - a) Unified Threat Management
   - b) Data analytics
   - c) File storage
   - d) VPN
15. What does SAML stand for?
   - a) Simple Access Markup Language
   - b) Security Assertion Markup Language
   - c) Secure Application Management Layer
   - d) Simple Application Management Language
16. What is a vulnerability scanner?
   - a) A firewall
   - b) A type of malware
   - c) A tool to detect weaknesses in systems
   - d) A network monitoring tool
17. What does IPS stand for?
   - a) Intrusion Prevention System
   - b) Internet Protocol Security
   - c) Intelligent Port Scanner
   - d) Internal Processing System
18. Which of these is an example of a password cracker?
   - a) Wireshark
   - b) John the Ripper
   - c) Snort
   - d) Airodump-ng

19. What does TLS stand for?
 - a) Transport Layer Security
 - b) Trusted Link System
 - c) Tethered Load Services
 - d) Terminal Line Services
20. What is the primary function of a proxy server?
 - a) Data backup
 - b) Network security
 - c) Content filtering and caching
 - d) Storage
21. What is a PKI?
 - a) Public Key Interface
 - b) Public Key Infrastructure
 - c) Private Key Interface
 - d) Password Key Identifier
22. What does RADIUS stand for?
 - a) Remote Authentication Dial-In User Service
 - b) Radio Authentication Dialing and Internet User System
 - c) Real-time Adaptive Data Input Unified System
 - d) Random Access Dial-in User Service
23. What is the purpose of BitLocker?
 - a) Firewall
 - b) Data encryption
 - c) VPN
 - d) Bandwidth monitoring
24. What is OpenVAS used for?
 - a) Network mapping
 - b) Vulnerability scanning
 - c) Packet capturing
 - d) Firewall
25. What does NAT stand for?
 - a) Network Access Technology
 - b) Network Address Translation
 - c) Next Application Tunneling
 - d) None of the above
26. What is the primary function of Aircrack-ng?
 - a) Network mapping
 - b) Cracking Wi-Fi encryption
 - c) Vulnerability scanning
 - d) Data encryption
27. What does WAF stand for?
 - a) Web Application Firewall
 - b) Wireless Access Firewall
 - c) Wide-Angle Format
 - d) Web Authentication Format
28. What does PAM stand for?
 - a) Public Access Module
 - b) Pluggable Authentication Module
 - c) Public Address Mechanism
 - d) Proxy Access Method
29. What does SMB stand for?
 - a) Simple Mail Bridge
 - b) Server Message Block
 - c) Secure Memory Bank
 - d) System Monitoring Backend
30. What does AV stand for?
 - a) Advanced Virus
 - b) Audio Visual
 - c) Antivirus
 - d) Application Versioning
31. What does EDR stand for?
 - a) Event Data Recorder
 - b) Endpoint Detection and Response
 - c) Encrypted Data Retrieval
 - d) External Drive Reader
32. What is a WIPS designed to prevent?
 - a) Water leaks in data centers
 - b) Unauthorized wireless access
 - c) Internet outages
 - d) Data corruption
33. What is Zero Trust Architecture primarily focused on?
 - a) Trust all network devices
 - b) Trust no one, verify everything
 - c) Trust but verify
 - d) Trust external networks
34. Which technology is used to secure communication over a public network?
 - a) Firewall
 - b) VPN
 - c) Intrusion Detection System
 - d) Load balancer
35. What does API security protect?
 - a) Application Program Interface
 - b) Advanced Personal Identity
 - c) Application Process Isolation
 - d) All Ports Internal
36. What does a network topology map represent?
 - a) The current data flow
 - b) The layout of the network
 - c) The list of authorized users
 - d) The latest security patches
37. What does PAM control?
 - a) Privilege Access Management
 - b) Public Access to Media

- c) Protocol Analysis and Monitoring
- d) Port Assignment Methodology

38. What do IAM systems primarily manage?
- a) Intrusion Analysis and Monitoring
- b) Identity and Access Management
- c) Internet Allocation Mechanism
- d) Internal Archive Management

39. What does SIEM stand for?
- a) Software Identity Encryption Manager
- b) Security Information and Event Management
- c) System Isolation Execution Mode
- d) Secure Internal Email Manager

40. What does MFA add to the authentication process?
- a) Mainframe Access
- b) Manual File Access
- c) Multi-Factor Authentication
- d) Message Format Approval

ANSWERS

1. What does IDS stand for? Answer: b) Intrusion Detection System - Explanation: IDS is used to detect and alert on network intrusions.

2. Which tool is used for network mapping? Answer: b) Nmap - Explanation: Nmap is primarily used for network discovery and security auditing.

3. What is the primary function of a firewall? Answer: c) Network security - Explanation: Firewalls are used to filter incoming and outgoing traffic based on predetermined rules.

4. What does HIDS stand for? Answer: a) Host-based Intrusion Detection System - Explanation: HIDS monitors activities on the host it's installed on, providing a layer of security against unauthorized activities.

5. What is a honeypot? Answer: c) A network decoy - Explanation: Honeypots act as traps to lure attackers away from legitimate network resources.

6. What does DLP stand for? Answer: a) Data Loss Prevention - Explanation: DLP systems prevent unauthorized data access and sharing.

7. Which of these is a port scanner? Answer: d) Nmap - Explanation: Nmap also includes capabilities for port scanning.

8. What is the purpose of a VPN? Answer: b) Secure communication - Explanation: VPNs encrypt internet communication, making it secure.

9. What does MDM stand for? Answer: b) Mobile Device Management - Explanation: MDM solutions allow administrators to control mobile devices across an organization.

10. What is a rootkit? Answer: a) Malware - Explanation: A rootkit provides root-level, unauthorized access to a computer.

11. Which technology is primarily used for web content filtering? Answer: b) DNS filtering - Explanation: DNS filtering blocks access to certain websites by intercepting DNS requests.

12. What is the primary function of a SIEM? Answer: c) Security information and event management - Explanation: SIEM collects and analyzes security alerts from various network devices.

13. What is Snort? Answer: b) IDS - Explanation: Snort is an open-source IDS.

14. What is the primary function of a UTM? Answer: a) Unified Threat Management - Explanation: UTM is a security solution that combines multiple security features into one appliance.

15. What does SAML stand for? Answer: b) Security Assertion Markup Language - Explanation: SAML is an XML-based standard for exchanging authentication and authorization data.

16. What is a vulnerability scanner? Answer: c) A tool to detect weaknesses in systems - Explanation: Vulnerability scanners assess computers, networks, or applications for security weaknesses.

17. What does IPS stand for? Answer: a) Intrusion Prevention System - Explanation: IPS is similar to IDS but can also block or prevent identified intrusions.

18. Which of these is an example of a password cracker? Answer: b) John the Ripper - Explanation: This tool is used for cracking password hashes.

19. What does TLS stand for? Answer: a) Transport Layer Security - Explanation: TLS is used to secure communication over a network.

20. What is the primary function of a proxy server? Answer: c) Content filtering and caching - Explanation: Proxy servers act as intermediaries that filter content and can cache data to improve performance.

21. What is a PKI? Answer: b) Public Key Infrastructure - Explanation: PKI is used to manage digital keys and certificates.

22. What does RADIUS stand for? Answer: a) Remote Authentication Dial-In User Service - Explanation: RADIUS is a client/server protocol for centralized authentication.

23. What is the purpose of BitLocker? Answer: b) Data encryption - Explanation: BitLocker is a disk encryption program.

24. What is OpenVAS used for? Answer: b) Vulnerability scanning - Explanation: OpenVAS is used for scanning vulnerabilities.

25. What does NAT stand for? Answer: b) Network Address Translation - Explanation: NAT modifies IP address information in packet headers.

26. What is the primary function of Aircrack-ng? Answer: b) Cracking Wi-Fi encryption - Explanation: Aircrack-ng is primarily used for cracking wireless networks.

27. What does WAF stand for? Answer: a) Web Application Firewall - Explanation: WAFs are used to protect web applications by filtering and monitoring HTTP traffic between a web app and the Internet.

28. What does PAM stand for? Answer: b) Pluggable Authentication Module - Explanation: PAM is used for authentication within Unix systems.

29. What does SMB stand for? Answer: b) Server Message Block - Explanation: SMB is a network protocol mainly used for providing shared access to files.

30. What does AV stand for? Answer: c) Antivirus - Explanation: AV stands for antivirus software, designed to detect and remove malware.

31. What does EDR stand for? Answer: b) Endpoint Detection and Response - Explanation: EDR platforms monitor endpoints and can automatically respond to security incidents.

32. What is a WIPS designed to prevent? Answer: b) Unauthorized wireless access - Explanation: WIPS (Wireless Intrusion Prevention Systems) protect against unauthorized network access over wireless networks.

33. What is Zero Trust Architecture primarily focused on? Answer: b) Trust no one, verify everything - Explanation: Zero Trust Architecture requires strict identity verification for every person and device trying to access resources.

34. Which technology is used to secure communication over a public network? Answer: b) VPN - Explanation: VPNs are used to secure communication over untrusted networks.

35. What does API security protect? Answer: a) Application Program Interface - Explanation: API security aims to secure Application Program Interfaces from potential threats.

36. What does a network topology map represent? Answer: b) The layout of the network - Explanation: A network topology map outlines how different elements within a network interact with each other.

37. What does PAM control? Answer: a) Privilege Access Management - Explanation: PAM solutions help control privileged access within an organization.

38. What do IAM systems primarily manage? Answer: b) Identity and Access Management - Explanation: IAM systems are used for identifying, authenticating, and authorizing individuals or groups.

39. What does SIEM stand for? Answer: b) Security Information and Event Management - Explanation: SIEM provides real-time analysis of security alerts generated by hardware and software infrastructure.

40. What does MFA add to the authentication process? Answer: c) Multi-Factor Authentication - Explanation: MFA involves two or more independent credentials for enhanced security during the authentication process.

7) Security Architecture and Design

Principles of Security Architecture

The modern digital environment is a complex ecosystem with an ever-evolving set of challenges and threats. A robust security architecture is crucial to address these challenges in an efficient and effective manner. This chapter will unravel the core principles of security architecture, shedding light on concepts like defense in depth, least privilege, and fail-safe stance. These principles are the building blocks that will help in devising a secure infrastructure to protect an organization's critical assets.

Defense in Depth

Defense in depth, often compared to layers of an onion, is a security strategy that employs a series of protective barriers to prevent unauthorized access to valuable data and resources. It's about having multiple layers of security measures so that if one layer fails, others are in place to thwart an attack. The layers could include physical security, network security, application security, and more. Each layer adds an additional level of protection, making it increasingly difficult for attackers to gain unauthorized access.
- Physical Security: Ensuring the physical premises are secure, with measures like surveillance cameras, biometric access, etc.
- Network Security: Employing firewalls, intrusion detection systems, and other technologies to protect the network perimeter.
- Application Security: Implementing security measures within applications like secure coding practices, application firewalls, etc.
In the contemporary digital landscape, a single layer of security is often insufficient to thwart sophisticated threats. Here's a more comprehensive look at the layers involved in a Defense in Depth strategy:
- Endpoint Security: Protecting endpoints like computers, mobile devices from threats.
- Identity and Access Management: Ensuring only authorized individuals can access certain information.
- Data Encryption: Encrypting data both at rest and in transit to prevent unauthorized access.
- Regular Audits and Monitoring: Conducting security audits and monitoring systems to detect and respond to threats promptly
Real-world Example: A bank employing security guards, CCTV cameras, secure vaults (Physical Security), network firewalls, and intrusion detection systems (Network Security), and secure coding practices for its online banking application (Application Security).

Least Privilege

The principle of least privilege (PoLP) dictates that individuals or systems should have only the minimum levels of access — or permissions — they need to accomplish their tasks. This minimizes the potential damage in the event that an account is compromised.
 Expanding on the principle of Least Privilege, it's imperative to understand the implications of over-privileged access and how to implement PoLP effectively.
- Role-Based Access Control (RBAC): Assigning access based on roles within the organization.
- Temporary Elevated Access: Granting higher-level access temporarily when necessary and revoking it as soon as the task is completed.
Scenario: In a healthcare setting, a receptionist might have access to appointment schedules but not to medical records, which are accessible only by medical personnel.

Fail-Safe Stance

The fail-safe stance is about ensuring that if a system fails, it fails securely. In other words, if an error occurs, the system defaults to a secure state that doesn't expose sensitive information or grant unauthorized access.
Scenario: An e-commerce website encountering a system error that logs users out instead of potentially exposing sensitive account information.

As we delve deeper into these principles, we'll explore how they form the backbone of security architecture, fostering a culture of security awareness and proactive defense strategies. The application of these principles, tailored to an organization's unique needs and challenges, lays the groundwork for a robust security posture capable of adapting to the dynamic threat landscape.

Delving further into the fail-safe stance, it's crucial to understand the mechanisms that ensure a system defaults to a secure state during failures.

- Secure Error Handling: Implementing error handling that doesn't leak sensitive information.
- Session Timeouts: Ensuring sessions expire after a period of inactivity to prevent unauthorized access.

Security Models and Frameworks

Security models and frameworks form the theoretical and practical foundation upon which secure systems and networks are built and maintained. Let's explore some of the fundamental models and frameworks that have been instrumental in shaping the domain of cybersecurity.

Bell-LaPadula Model:

The Bell-LaPadula Model focuses on maintaining the confidentiality of information. It introduces two primary rules:

1. Simple Security Property: A subject at a specific clearance level cannot read an object at a higher clearance level.
2. -Property (Star Property): A subject at a specific clearance level cannot write to an object at a lower clearance level.

These rules help in preventing data leakage and ensuring that sensitive information remains confined to authorized personnel.

The Bell-LaPadula Model is a cornerstone in the field of security models. Its focus on confidentiality has made it a go-to model for military and government applications. There are additional principles within the Bell-LaPadula Model that are worth noting:

3. Strong Star Property: A subject with both read and write access can only write to an object if and only if the subject and object have the same classification level.
4. Discretionary Security Property: It permits the specification of access control at an individual user level, allowing a fine-grain control over who has access to what.

Clark-Wilson Model:

On the other hand, the Clark-Wilson Model is oriented towards ensuring data integrity through well-formed transaction and separation of duties principles:

1. Well-formed Transactions: Every transaction must transform the system from one consistent state to another.
2. Separation of Duties: Access and authority are divided among multiple users or systems to prevent fraud and errors.

This model is particularly useful in financial systems where data integrity is of paramount importance.

Common Security Frameworks:

ISO 27001:

ISO 27001 is a globally recognized standard for the establishment, implementation, operation, monitoring, review, maintenance, and improvement of an Information Security Management System (ISMS). It helps organizations manage and protect their information assets so that they remain safe and secure.

NIST Cybersecurity Framework:

Developed by the National Institute of Standards and Technology, this framework is designed to help organizations manage and reduce cybersecurity risk. It comprises five core functions: Identify, Protect, Detect, Respond, and Recover.

CIS Controls:

The Center for Internet Security Controls is a prioritized set of actions that collectively form a defense-in-depth set of best practices to mitigate the most common attacks against systems and networks.

Biba Model:

The Biba Model is another classic model focused on data integrity as opposed to confidentiality in the Bell-LaPadula Model. It operates on three fundamental principles:

1. Simple Integrity Property: A subject at a specific level cannot read an object at a lower level.

2. -Integrity (Star Integrity) Property: A subject at a specific level cannot write to an object at a higher level.

3. Invocation Property: A subject at a lower integrity level cannot request services from a subject at a higher integrity level.

Brewer-Nash Model:

Often referred to as the "Cinderella Model," the Brewer-Nash Model is designed to prevent conflicts of interest by restricting access to information for individuals who have accessed other particular information.

Common Criteria (CC):

The Common Criteria for Information Technology Security Evaluation is a framework used internationally for evaluating and certifying the security attributes of information technology products and systems.

PCI DSS:

The Payment Card Industry Data Security Standard is a widely adopted security standard for organizations that handle branded credit cards from major card schemes.

HIPAA and HITECH:

For healthcare organizations in the United States, compliance with the Health Insurance Portability and Accountability Act (HIPAA) and the Health Information Technology for Economic and Clinical Health Act (HITECH) is critical for ensuring the confidentiality, integrity, and availability of health information.

GDPR:

The General Data Protection Regulation is a regulation that demands businesses to protect the personal data and privacy of EU citizens for transactions that occur within EU member states.

Security Frameworks Summary:

These frameworks provide a structured approach to managing various security aspects, offering organizations a blueprint for building robust security architectures. By adhering to these frameworks, organizations can ensure they are compliant with legal and regulatory requirements, which in turn helps in building trust with stakeholders and customers.

ISO 27001:

The ISO 27001 standard is part of the broader ISO/IEC 27000 family of standards, designed to help organizations keep information assets secure. It provides a framework for an Information Security Management System (ISMS) to provide a systematic approach to managing sensitive company information.

1. Scope Definition: Defining the scope of the ISMS is a critical first step. It includes identifying the information to be protected, the systems and hardware involved, and the locations from where the system is accessed.

2. Risk Assessment: Identifying and evaluating risks to the confidentiality, integrity, and availability of information.

3. Selection of Controls: Based on the risk assessment, appropriate controls are selected to mitigate the identified risks.

4. Implementation: Implementing the selected controls and documenting the processes.

5. Monitoring and Review: Regular monitoring and review of the ISMS to ensure its effectiveness and to identify any improvements that may be necessary.

6. Continuous Improvement: Continually refining and improving the ISMS based on regular reviews and monitoring.

NIST Cybersecurity Framework:

The National Institute of Standards and Technology (NIST) Cybersecurity Framework provides guidelines on how organizations can assess and improve their ability to prevent, detect, and respond to cyber incidents.

1. Identify: Identifying the assets, systems, and data that need protection.

2. Protect: Implementing safeguards to ensure the delivery of critical infrastructure services.

3. Detect: Developing the necessary activities to identify the occurrence of a cybersecurity event.

4. Respond: Developing and implementing appropriate activities to take action regarding a detected cybersecurity event.

5. Recover: Developing and implementing appropriate activities to restore any capabilities or services that were impaired due to a cybersecurity event.

CIS Controls:

The Center for Internet Security (CIS) Controls are a set of actionable controls that provide a prioritized approach to securing your organization from known cyber-attack vectors.

1. Basic Controls: Key controls that should be implemented in every organization for essential cyber defense readiness.
2. Foundational Controls: These are the next step up from basic controls, providing a solid foundation of cybersecurity readiness.
3. Organizational Controls: These are more complex and are often tailored to specific types of organizations or companies with more sophisticated security needs.

Elements of a Secure Network Architecture

When designing a secure network architecture, various security principles and models must be taken into consideration to ensure that the network is robust against potential threats while still meeting the operational needs of the organization.

Layered Security (Defense in Depth):
A layered security approach, often referred to as Defense in Depth, involves implementing multiple security measures at various layers of the network to create a comprehensive security solution. This includes:
1. Perimeter Security: Firewalls, Intrusion Prevention Systems (IPS), and border routers are deployed to protect the network perimeter.
2. Network Security: Internally, network segmentation, Network Access Control (NAC), and secure network protocols help to maintain network security.
3. Host Security: At the host level, antivirus software, host-based firewalls, and host intrusion prevention systems (HIPS) are implemented.
4. Application Security: Security measures are implemented within applications to prevent application-level attacks.
Least Privilege:
The principle of least privilege (PoLP) entails granting only the minimum levels of access — or permissions — needed for users (or systems) to accomplish their tasks.
Zero Trust Architecture:
Zero Trust Architecture (ZTA) operates on the assumption that threats can come from anywhere — even inside your network. Therefore, trust is never assumed and verification is required from anyone trying to access resources in your network.
Secure Network Design Principles:
1. Segmentation: Network segmentation divides a network into smaller parts to minimize the attack surface and to contain potential damages in case of a security incident.
2. Encryption: Implementing encryption protects data in transit and at rest.
3. Monitoring and Anomaly Detection: Employing monitoring solutions and anomaly detection helps in identifying suspicious activities early.

Security Policies and Procedures:
Security policies and procedures form the backbone of a secure network architecture. These documents define how the organization manages and protects its assets. They encompass:
1. Access Control Policies: Who has access to what within the network.
2. Incident Response Procedures: Steps to follow when a security incident occurs.
3. Change Management Policies: Procedures for making changes to the network architecture.
4. Disaster Recovery and Business Continuity Plans: Preparations and plans for recovering from disasters and business interruptions.
 Compliance and Standards:
Adhering to industry standards and compliance requirements is crucial in ensuring a secure network architecture. Some of the common standards include:

1. ISO 27001: An international standard for information security management systems.
2. PCI DSS: A standard for organizations that handle credit card transactions.
3. HIPAA: Compliance requirement for protecting sensitive patient data.

Intrusion Detection and Prevention Systems (IDPS):

IDPS are crucial tools in identifying and preventing potential security threats on the network. They monitor network traffic, detect malicious activities, and can take predefined actions to mitigate the threat.

Regular Audits and Assessments:

Conducting regular security audits and assessments is essential to ensure that the security measures in place are effective and up to date. It involves:
1. Vulnerability Assessments: Identifying weaknesses in the network architecture.
2. Penetration Testing: Simulated cyber-attacks to test the defense mechanisms.
3. Security Audits: Regular reviews of security policies, procedures, and systems.

Employee Training and Awareness:

Employees play a crucial role in network security. Training and creating awareness among employees about security best practices and the current threat landscape is essential.

Real-world Scenario: Architecting a Secure E-commerce Platform

Stage 1: Requirements Gathering and Analysis

Before diving into the technical aspects of security architecture, it's imperative to understand the business objectives, the nature of the data handled by the platform, and the potential threats that could impact the business.

Challenges Encountered:
1. Understanding Business Objectives: Aligning security measures with business goals.
2. Identifying Sensitive Data: Pinpointing the data that needs to be protected.
3. Assessing Potential Threats: Understanding the threats the platform could face.

Solutions Implemented:
1. Stakeholder Meetings: Conducting meetings with stakeholders to understand business objectives.
2. Data Classification: Classifying data based on its sensitivity and importance to the business.
3. Threat Modeling: Employing threat modeling techniques to assess potential threats.

Stage 2: Designing the Security Architecture

With a clear understanding of the requirements, the next step is designing the security architecture. This involves creating a blueprint that outlines how security controls will be implemented to protect the platform.

Challenges Encountered:
1. Selecting Appropriate Security Controls: Choosing the right mix of security controls that provide robust protection while aligning with budget constraints.
2. Compliance Requirements: Ensuring the architecture complies with legal and regulatory requirements.
3. Scalability and Flexibility: Designing an architecture that can scale and adapt to changing business needs.

Solutions Implemented:
1. Security Control Assessment: Evaluating and selecting security controls that provide the required level of protection.
2. Compliance Review: Reviewing the design with compliance experts to ensure it meets all legal and regulatory requirements.
3. Modular Design: Adopting a modular design approach to allow for scalability and flexibility.

Stage 3: Implementing Security Controls

With the security requirements and architecture blueprint in place, the next step is implementing security controls. This involves setting up firewalls, intrusion detection systems, and encryption mechanisms to protect data in transit and at rest.

Challenges Encountered:
1. Cost Constraints: High costs associated with purchasing and implementing premium security solutions.

2. Technical Challenges: Difficulty in configuring security controls and ensuring they work harmoniously without affecting the platform's performance.

3. Vendor Lock-in: Relying heavily on a particular vendor's security solutions could lead to vendor lock-in and less flexibility in the future.

Solutions Implemented:

1. Cost-effective Solutions: Researching and selecting cost-effective yet robust security solutions, and considering open-source alternatives.

2. Expert Consultation: Engaging security consultants to ensure the correct configuration of security controls.

3. Vendor Diversification: Utilizing a mix of security solutions from different vendors to avoid dependency on a single vendor.

Stage 4: Testing and Validation

After implementing security controls, it's crucial to validate their effectiveness. This involves conducting vulnerability assessments and penetration testing to identify any weaknesses.

Challenges Encountered:

1. Identifying All Vulnerabilities: It's challenging to identify all vulnerabilities in a complex e-commerce platform.

2. Mitigating Identified Risks: Some risks might require substantial effort and resources to mitigate.

Solutions Implemented:

1. Regular Testing: Conducting regular security testing to identify and mitigate vulnerabilities.

2. Continuous Monitoring: Establishing a continuous monitoring process to identify and address security issues in real-time.

Stage 5: Maintenance and Continuous Improvement

Security is not a one-time effort but a continuous process. It requires regular updates, monitoring, and improvements to ensure the e-commerce platform remains secure as new threats emerge.

Challenges Encountered:

1. Keeping Up with Emerging Threats: The constantly evolving threat landscape.

2. Resource Constraints: Limited resources for continuous monitoring and improvement.

Solutions Implemented:

1. Threat Intelligence: Subscribing to threat intelligence feeds to stay updated on emerging threats.

2. Automated Monitoring: Implementing automated monitoring solutions to optimize resource usage.

Interactive Quiz: Security Architecture Comprehension

1. What is the primary purpose of a DMZ in network architecture?
   - a) Data backup
   - b) Threat detection
   - c) Isolate servers from internal network
   - d) Load balancing

2. What is the OSI model's first layer?
   - a) Application
   - b) Physical
   - c) Network
   - d) Transport

3. What is a HIDS?
   - a) Hardware Intrusion Detection System
   - b) Host-based Intrusion Detection System
   - c) Hardware Identification Security
   - d) Human Interaction Design System

4. Which protocol is responsible for web security?
   - a) FTP
   - b) HTTP
   - c) HTTPS
   - d) DNS

5. What does a firewall primarily protect against?
   - a) Data loss
   - b) Unauthorized access
   - c) Malware
   - d) Phishing

6. What is a secure method for remote access?
   - a) Telnet
   - b) SSH
   - c) FTP
   - d) HTTP

7. What does VPN stand for?
   - a) Variable Protocol Network
   - b) Very Private Navigation

- c) Virtual Private Network
- d) Verified Protection Node

8. Which technology isolates a system to run multiple OS instances?
  - a) Firewall
  - b) VPN
  - c) Virtualization
  - d) Tokenization

9. What does a WAF protect?
  - a) Windows Activation Framework
  - b) Wide Area Frequencies
  - c) Web Application Firewall
  - d) Web Access Features

10. What does UTM stand for?
  - a) Unified Threat Management
  - b) Unmetered Traffic Meter
  - c) Universal Transfer Mode
  - d) User Time Management

11. What is SSO?
  - a) Single Sign-Off
  - b) Secure Socket Output
  - c) Single Sign-On
  - d) System Security Operations

12. What is the primary function of a proxy server?
  - a) Load balancing
  - b) Network isolation
  - c) Data caching
  - d) User authentication

13. What is the purpose of a bastion host?
  - a) Remote user access
  - b) File storage
  - c) Intrusion detection
  - d) Exposure to external network

14. What does SDN stand for?
  - a) System Defined Networking
  - b) Secure Data Node
  - c) Software Defined Networking
  - d) Standard Deviation Networking

15. What is the function of a SIEM system?
  - a) Event management and monitoring
  - b) Data backup
  - c) VPN tunneling
  - d) Network routing

16. What does NAC enforce?
  - a) Naming conventions
  - b) File storage limits
  - c) Security compliance
  - d) Data encryption

17. Which device filters traffic between networks?
  - a) Router
  - b) Switch
  - c) Firewall
  - d) Hub

18. What is the purpose of an IPS?
  - a) Intrusion Prevention System
  - b) Internal Processing System
  - c) Information Protection Service
  - d) Internet Protocol Security

19. What is an air gap?
  - a) Network segmentation technique
  - b) Physical isolation of a computer
  - c) Secure wireless network
  - d) Firewall setup

20. What does VDI stand for?
  - a) Virtual Desktop Infrastructure
  - b) Validated Data Inputs
  - c) Variable Digital Interface
  - d) Verified Disk Image

21. What type of architecture uses a centralized approach to manage security?
  - a) Declarative
  - b) Monolithic
  - c) Service-oriented
  - d) Hub-and-Spoke

22. What does a VLAN primarily help with?
  - a) Performance improvement
  - b) Virtualization
  - c) Network segmentation
  - d) Encryption

23. What is the primary use of a honeypot?
  - a) Data storage
  - b) To attract attackers
  - c) To encrypt data
  - d) To distribute load

24. Which of the following is an example of a network security control?
  - a) Firewall rules
  - b) Password policy
  - c) Encryption algorithms
  - d) Anti-virus software

25. What is the function of a DLP system?
  - a) Network optimization
  - b) Data backup
  - c) Prevent data leakage
  - d) File compression

26. What type of architecture supports scalability and modularity?
- a) Peer-to-peer
- b) Microservices
- c) Monolithic
- d) Grid

27. What does PKI stand for?
- a) Public Key Infrastructure
- b) Private Kernel Interface
- c) Protected Key Input
- d) Personal Key Issuance

28. What is the purpose of IAM?
- a) Internet Access Management
- b) Identity and Access Management
- c) Instant Application Mapping
- d) Internal Audit Mechanism

29. Which protocol is used for secure email communication?
- a) SNMP
- b) SMTP
- c) S/MIME
- d) IMAP

30. What does a CASB provide?
- a) Cloud Access Security Broker
- b) Centralized Application Server Base
- c) Continuous Authentication Security Base
- d) Content Aggregation Service Broker

31. What does EDR stand for?
- a) Event Data Recorder
- b) Endpoint Detection and Response
- c) Encrypted Data Retrieval
- d) External Drive Reader

32. What is a WIPS designed to prevent?
- a) Water leaks in data centers
- b) Unauthorized wireless access
- c) Internet outages
- d) Data corruption

33. What is Zero Trust Architecture primarily focused on?
- a) Trust all network devices
- b) Trust no one, verify everything
- c) Trust but verify
- d) Trust external networks

34. Which technology is used to secure communication over a public network?
- a) Firewall
- b) VPN
- c) Intrusion Detection System
- d) Load balancer

35. What does API security protect?
- a) Application Program Interface
- b) Advanced Personal Identity
- c) Application Process Isolation
- d) Advanced Password Integrity

36. What does a network topology map represent?
- a) The geography of the network
- b) The layout of the network
- c) The list of network protocols
- d) The data flow on the network

37. What does PAM stand for?
- a) Privilege Access Management
- b) Public Access Management
- c) Protocol Analysis Module
- d) Password Authentication Mechanism

38. What is the role of an IAM system?
- a) Intrusion Analysis and Monitoring
- b) Identity and Access Management
- c) Internal Archive Management
- d) Internet Allocation and Mapping

39. What is the main function of a SIEM?
- a) Software Identity Encryption Module
- b) Security Information and Event Management
- c) Secure Intrusion Evasion Method
- d) System Isolation and Encryption Method

40. What is MFA?
- a) Mainframe Authentication
- b) Manual File Access
- c) Multi-Factor Authentication
- d) Message Format Algorithm

ANSWERS

1. What is the primary purpose of a DMZ in network architecture? Answer: c) Single Sign-On - Explanation: SSO stands for Single Sign-On, which allows a user to log in once and gain access to multiple systems without being prompted to log in again.

2. What is the OSI model's first layer? Answer: d) User authentication - Explanation: A proxy server primarily serves as an intermediary for requests from clients to access resources. It can provide user authentication.

3. What is a HIDS? Answer: d) Exposure to external network - Explanation: A bastion host is designed to be the point of exposure to external networks and is expected to be highly secure.

4. Which protocol is responsible for web security? Answer: c) Software Defined Networking - Explanation: SDN stands for Software Defined Networking, which enables dynamic management of network resources.

5. What does a firewall primarily protect against? Answer: a) Event management and monitoring - Explanation: SIEM stands for Security Information and Event Management. It is designed for real-time monitoring, event correlation, and notifications.

6. What is a secure method for remote access? Answer: c) Security compliance - Explanation: NAC (Network Access Control) enforces security compliance before allowing a device onto the network.

7. What does VPN stand for? Answer: c) Firewall - Explanation: Firewalls filter traffic between networks based on an organization's previously configured rules.

8. Which technology isolates a system to run multiple OS instances? Answer: a) Intrusion Prevention System - Explanation: IPS stands for Intrusion Prevention System. Its purpose is to identify and prevent known and unknown threats.

9. What does a WAF protect? Answer: b) Physical isolation of a computer - Explanation: An air gap is the physical isolation of a computer or network, disconnecting it from the internet and other unsecured networks.

10. What does UTM stand for? Answer: a) Virtual Desktop Infrastructure - Explanation: VDI stands for Virtual Desktop Infrastructure, allowing the remote operation of desktop operating systems within a virtual machine on a centralized server.

11. What is SSO? Answer: b) Monolithic - Explanation: Monolithic architecture uses a centralized approach, where all the components are interconnected and interdependent.

12. What is the primary function of a proxy server? Answer: c) Network segmentation - Explanation: VLANs are used to segment networks, thus improving security and reducing broadcast domains.

13. What is the purpose of a bastion host? Answer: b) To attract attackers - Explanation: A honeypot is a decoy system used to attract attackers and keep them away from actual network resources.

14. What does SDN stand for? Answer: a) Firewall rules - Explanation: Firewall rules are explicitly designed to control network traffic and are thus considered network security controls.

15. What is the function of a SIEM system? Answer: c) Prevent data leakage - Explanation: DLP (Data Loss Prevention) systems monitor data transfer to prevent data leakage and protect sensitive information.

16. What does NAC enforce? Answer: b) Microservices - Explanation: Microservices architecture promotes scalability and modularity, allowing individual components to be developed, deployed, and scaled independently.

17. Which device filters traffic between networks? Answer: a) Public Key Infrastructure - Explanation: PKI stands for Public Key Infrastructure, which is used to manage digital keys and certificates for secure communications.

18. What is the purpose of an IPS? Answer: b) Identity and Access Management - Explanation: IAM stands for Identity and Access Management, aimed at identifying, authenticating, and authorizing users.

19. What is an air gap? Answer: c) S/MIME - Explanation: S/MIME (Secure/Multipurpose Internet Mail Extensions) is a standard used for public key encryption and signing of email.

20. What does VDI stand for? Answer: a) Cloud Access Security Broker - Explanation: CASB stands for Cloud Access Security Broker, providing visibility and control over cloud services.

21. What type of architecture uses a centralized approach to manage security? Answer: b) Endpoint Detection and Response - Explanation: EDR stands for Endpoint Detection and Response, focusing on detecting, investigating, and mitigating suspicious activities on endpoints.

22. What does a VLAN primarily help with? Answer: b) Unauthorized wireless access - Explanation: WIPS (Wireless Intrusion Prevention System) is designed to monitor and prevent unauthorized wireless access.

23. What is the primary use of a honeypot? Answer: b) Trust no one, verify everything - Explanation: Zero Trust Architecture follows the principle of "never trust, always verify", meaning no entity should be trusted by default.

24. Which of the following is an example of a network security control? Answer: b) VPN - Explanation: VPN (Virtual Private Network) is used to secure communication over public networks by creating a private tunnel.

25. What is the function of a DLP system? Answer: a) Application Program Interface - Explanation: API security protects the Application Program Interface, which is how different software applications communicate with each other.

26. What type of architecture supports scalability and modularity? Answer: b) The layout of the network - Explanation: A network topology map outlines how different elements of a network are connected.

27. What does PKI stand for? Answer: a) Privilege Access Management - Explanation: PAM stands for Privilege Access Management, a solution that helps organizations restrict and monitor privileged access within their environments.

28. What is the purpose of IAM? Answer: b) Identity and Access Management - Explanation: IAM (Identity and Access Management) focuses on identifying, authenticating, and authorizing individuals or groups to have access to applications, systems or networks.

29. Which protocol is used for secure email communication? Answer: b) Security Information and Event Management - Explanation: SIEM stands for Security Information and Event Management. It provides real-time analysis of security alerts generated by hardware and software infrastructure.

30. What does a CASB provide? Answer: c) Multi-Factor Authentication - Explanation: MFA stands for Multi-Factor Authentication, which uses multiple methods to confirm the users' identity for a login or transaction.

31. What does EDR stand for? Answer: b) Endpoint Detection and Response - Explanation: EDR is designed to continuously monitor and respond to threats on endpoints. It doesn't merely record events or retrieve encrypted data.

32. What is a WIPS designed to prevent? Answer: b) Unauthorized wireless access - Explanation: WIPS (Wireless Intrusion Prevention System) is designed to monitor and prevent unauthorized wireless access to a network, not water leaks, internet outages, or data corruption.

33. What is Zero Trust Architecture primarily focused on? Answer: b) Trust no one, verify everything - Explanation: The principle of Zero Trust Architecture is to never implicitly trust any entity and to rigorously verify credentials and permissions for all.

34. Which technology is used to secure communication over a public network? Answer: b) VPN - Explanation: VPN (Virtual Private Network) creates a secure communication channel over a public network. It is not the primary role of firewalls, intrusion detection systems, or load balancers to do this.

35. What does API security protect? Answer: a) Application Program Interface - Explanation: API security protects the Application Program Interfaces that enable software applications to communicate and interact with each other.

36. What does a network topology map represent? Answer: b) The layout of the network - Explanation: A network topology map illustrates the layout and design of the network, showing how nodes are connected.

37. What does PAM stand for? Answer: a) Privilege Access Management - Explanation: PAM controls and monitors privileged access within an organization. It doesn't deal with public access or protocol analysis.

38. What is the role of an IAM system? Answer: b) Identity and Access Management - Explanation: IAM systems manage the identification and authentication of users, not intrusions, archives, or internet allocations.

39. What is the main function of a SIEM? Answer: b) Security Information and Event Management - Explanation: SIEM solutions provide real-time analysis of security alerts and events, not software identity encryption or system isolation.

40. What is MFA? Answer: c) Multi-Factor Authentication - Explanation: MFA enhances security by requiring multiple forms of authentication before granting access. It doesn't pertain to mainframes, manual file access, or message formats.

8) Threats, Attacks, and Vulnerabilities

Understanding Threat Landscape

In the modern digital era, the threat landscape is constantly evolving as new technologies emerge and become integrated into daily operations within organizations. Understanding this landscape is crucial for anyone looking to secure a network or system against potential threats. This section aims to provide an insight into the various threats prevalent in the cybersecurity landscape, highlighting malware, phishing, and social engineering attacks, among others, and discussing how these threats evolve over time.

Malware:

Malware, short for malicious software, refers to any software designed to cause harm to a computer, server, client, or computer network. There are various types of malware, including viruses, worms, Trojans, spyware, adware, and ransomware. Each of these malware types has unique characteristics and behaviors. For instance, viruses attach themselves to clean files and spread throughout a computer system, corrupting files and system functionalities. On the other hand, ransomware encrypts files and demands a ransom for the decryption key.

Phishing:

Phishing is a type of social engineering attack where attackers disguise themselves as trustworthy entities to steal sensitive information such as login credentials, credit card numbers, and personal identification numbers. Typically, phishing attacks are carried out via email or text messages, luring the victim into clicking a malicious link that leads to a fake website designed to trick the individual into providing personal information.

Social Engineering:

Social engineering attacks exploit human psychology rather than technical hacking techniques to gain unauthorized access to systems or information. Besides phishing, other common social engineering attacks include pretexting, baiting, quid pro quo, and tailgating. Each of these attacks manipulates individuals into revealing confidential information or performing specific actions that compromise security.

Evolution of Threats:

The evolution of cyber threats is closely tied to the advancement of technology. As new technologies are developed, they often introduce new vulnerabilities that can be exploited by adversaries. Additionally, attackers are continually refining their techniques and developing new methods to bypass security measures. For instance, malware has evolved from simple viruses to sophisticated, multi-functional malware like Advanced Persistent Threats (APTs), which can remain undetected in a network for a prolonged period while exfiltrating data or causing damage.

The proliferation of mobile devices, cloud computing, and Internet of Things (IoT) devices has also expanded the threat landscape, introducing new attack vectors and vulnerabilities. Moreover, the rise of cybercriminal marketplaces and forums has facilitated the sharing of malicious tools and techniques among attackers, further accelerating the evolution of threats.

Understanding the threat landscape is a continuous process that requires staying updated on the latest threats and vulnerabilities, as well as adopting a proactive approach to cybersecurity, which includes regular training, updating and patching systems, and implementing a robust cybersecurity policy.

Malware Cont'd:

Rootkits: A rootkit is a type of malware that provides administrative access to unauthorized users. Once installed, it hides its presence and the presence of other malware.

Spyware: This malware spies on the user's activity without their knowledge. It can collect a variety of data, including keystrokes, browsing history, and personal information.

Botnets: Botnets are networks of compromised computers that attackers control remotely, often used for DDoS attacks, spamming, and fraudulent activities.

Phishing Variants:

Spear Phishing: Unlike generic phishing attacks, spear phishing targets specific individuals or organizations. It's often more sophisticated and may involve extensive research to make the attack more convincing.

Whaling: Whaling attacks are a form of spear phishing but target high-profile individuals like CEOs or CFOs, aiming to manipulate them into revealing sensitive company information.

Pharming: Pharming redirects users from legitimate websites to fraudulent ones, which then collect the users' information.

The Human Element:

The human element remains the weakest link in cybersecurity. Educating employees about the risks and how to recognize suspicious activities is crucial. Regular training programs can significantly reduce the risk posed by human error.

Emerging Threats

AI-Driven Threats: The use of artificial intelligence by attackers is on the rise. AI can automate the discovery of new vulnerabilities and develop malware that can change its behavior to evade detection.

5G Threats: The rollout of 5G networks introduces new threats. With increased speeds and connectivity, attackers have more opportunities to infiltrate networks.

Smart Device Vulnerabilities: The proliferation of smart devices creates new opportunities for attackers. Many of these devices lack robust security features, making them an easy target.

Threat Intelligence

Threat intelligence involves collecting and analyzing information about current and potential threats to predict and prevent attacks. By understanding the tactics, techniques, and procedures (TTPs) used by attackers, organizations can better prepare and defend against potential threats.

Threat Mitigation Strategies

Regular Patching: Keeping software and systems up to date is crucial for mitigating vulnerabilities.

Use of Security Software: Employing a range of security software including anti-malware tools, firewalls, and intrusion detection and prevention systems can provide a solid defense against various threats.

Multi-Factor Authentication (MFA): Implementing MFA can significantly reduce the risk of unauthorized access.

Incident Response Plan: Having a well-thought-out incident response plan in place is crucial for effectively dealing with any security incidents that do occur.

Attack Mechanisms and Vulnerabilities

Distributed Denial of Service (DDoS) Attacks:

Definition and Mechanism:

DDoS attacks flood networks, systems, or applications with traffic to exhaust resources and bandwidth, thereby denying access to legitimate users. Attackers often employ botnets to generate the overwhelming traffic.

Mitigation Strategies:

Employing anti-DDoS tools and services, maintaining a backup internet connection, and utilizing content delivery networks are common mitigation strategies.

SQL Injection (SQLi):

Definition and Mechanism:

SQLi is a code injection technique that might destroy your database. It's one of the most common web hacking techniques. It can also bypass login algorithms, extract, erase, or modify data in the database.

Mitigation Strategies:

Using prepared statements, input validation, and least privilege principle can help mitigate SQLi attacks.

Cross-Site Scripting (XSS):

Definition and Mechanism:

XSS attacks inject malicious scripts into content viewed by other users. These scripts could steal information such as cookies or credentials.

Mitigation Strategies:

Input validation, output encoding, and utilizing security headers like Content Security Policy (CSP) are effective mitigation strategies.

Network Vulnerabilities:

Misconfigurations:

Improperly configured networks can expose sensitive information, provide entry points for attackers, or lead to service disruptions.

Unpatched Systems:

Failing to apply patches in a timely manner can leave systems vulnerable to known exploits.

Insecure Protocols:

Usage of outdated or insecure network protocols can lead to data interception and unauthorized access.

System Vulnerabilities:

Software Bugs:

Bugs in software can create vulnerabilities that attackers might exploit to gain unauthorized access, disrupt services, or steal data.

Lack of Encryption:

Failure to encrypt sensitive data can lead to data breaches.

Insufficient Access Controls:

Improper access controls can allow unauthorized users to access sensitive areas of systems.

Vulnerability Management:

Regular Scanning:

Conducting regular vulnerability scans can help identify weaknesses before attackers do.

Patch Management:

A robust patch management process can ensure that identified vulnerabilities are remedied in a timely manner.

Penetration Testing:

Simulating cyber-attacks can help identify vulnerabilities and test the effectiveness of security measures.

Real-world Example: Equifax Data Breach:

The 2017 Equifax data breach, which exposed the personal information of 147 million people, was the result of a known vulnerability in the Apache Struts web application framework that the company failed to patch in time. This breach emphasizes the importance of timely patch management and vulnerability scanning in preventing cyber attacks.

Man-In-The-Middle (MITM) Attacks:

Definition and Mechanism:

MITM attacks occur when attackers intercept and potentially alter the communication between two parties without them knowing. This can lead to eavesdropping or data tampering.

Mitigation Strategies:

Employing strong encryption for data in transit, utilizing secure protocols like HTTPS, and employing certificate pinning are effective mitigation strategies.

Phishing and Spear Phishing:

Definition and Mechanism:

Phishing involves tricking individuals into revealing sensitive information, like passwords or credit card numbers, by masquerading as a trustworthy entity. Spear phishing is a more targeted form of phishing.

Mitigation Strategies:

Education and awareness training, email filtering, and verification procedures can help mitigate phishing threats.

Zero-Day Vulnerabilities:

Definition and Mechanism:

Zero-day vulnerabilities are flaws that are unknown to the vendor at the time they are exploited by attackers. They are extremely dangerous as there are no available fixes at the time of exploitation.

Mitigation Strategies:

Employing a robust patch management strategy, utilizing intrusion detection systems, and conducting regular security audits can help mitigate the risks associated with zero-day vulnerabilities.

Password Attacks:

Definition and Mechanism:

Password attacks involve attempting to obtain or crack user passwords. Techniques might include brute force, dictionary attacks, or credential stuffing.

Mitigation Strategies:

Implementing strong password policies, employing multi-factor authentication, and educating users on the importance of password security are effective mitigation strategies.

Malware

Definition and Mechanism:

Malware is malicious software designed to infiltrate or damage computer systems. Common types include viruses, worms, trojan horses, spyware, and ransomware.

Mitigation Strategies:

Utilizing updated antivirus software, employing firewalls, and educating users about the risks of downloading from suspicious sources can help mitigate malware threats.

Advanced Persistent Threats (APTs):

Definition and Mechanism:

APTs are long-term targeted attacks where attackers infiltrate networks to steal data over an extended period.

Mitigation Strategies:

Continuous monitoring, intrusion detection systems, and employing a defense-in-depth strategy are effective against APTs.

Insider Threats:

Definition and Mechanism:

Insider threats originate from within the organization, typically by employees or contractors who have access to sensitive systems and data. They might misuse this access for malicious purposes or personal gain.

Mitigation Strategies:

Employing the principle of least privilege, monitoring user activities, and conducting regular audits can help in mitigating insider threats.

Rootkits:

Definition and Mechanism:

Rootkits are malicious software tools that provide unauthorized access to a computer. They are designed to remain hidden and can be very hard to detect.

Mitigation Strategies:

Utilizing anti-rootkit tools, keeping systems updated, and employing integrity checking mechanisms can help in detecting and removing rootkits.

Drive-By Downloads:

Definition and Mechanism:

Drive-by downloads refer to the unintentional download of malicious software onto a user's system when visiting a compromised or malicious website.

Mitigation Strategies:

Keeping browsers and plugins updated, employing browser security settings, and educating users about the risks associated with visiting unknown websites can help mitigate this threat.

Eavesdropping and Shoulder Surfing:

Definition and Mechanism:

Eavesdropping involves intercepting private communications, while shoulder surfing involves directly observing or capturing sensitive information by looking over someone's shoulder.

Mitigation Strategies:

Using privacy screens, being aware of one's surroundings, and employing encryption for data in transit can help mitigate these threats.

Social Engineering Attacks:

Definition and Mechanism:

Social engineering attacks manipulate individuals into divulging confidential information. Techniques include pretexting, quid pro quo, baiting, and tailgating.

Mitigation Strategies:

Education and awareness training can help individuals recognize and resist social engineering attacks.

Buffer Overflow Attacks:

Definition and Mechanism:

Buffer overflow attacks occur when data exceeds the buffer's capacity, leading to system crashes or the execution of malicious code.

Mitigation Strategies:

Employing secure coding practices, input validation, and code analysis tools can help prevent buffer overflow attacks.

Security Misconfigurations:

Definition and Mechanism:

Security misconfigurations occur when security settings are not properly configured, leaving systems vulnerable to attacks.

Mitigation Strategies:

Regular security reviews, automated scanning for misconfigurations, and following best practices for configuration management can help mitigate these threats.

Insecure Deserialization:

Definition and Mechanism:

Insecure deserialization occurs when untrusted data is used to exploit the logic of an application, leading to remote code execution.

Mitigation Strategies:

Input validation, employing allow-lists, and understanding the deserialization process can help prevent insecure deserialization attacks.

Real-world Scenario: Mitigating a Ransomware Attack

Stage 1: Identifying the Ransomware Attack

As the IT administrator at TechCorp sifted through the network logs, they discovered that the ransomware, identified as Ryuk, had been propagating through the network using a combination of hard-coded credentials and exploiting known vulnerabilities in the Windows SMB protocol. The encryption process had started to affect critical business applications, causing disruptions in the operations.

Detailed Analysis:

- Network Traffic Analysis: The initial hint was an abnormal spike in network traffic, especially traffic associated with known malicious IP addresses. This necessitated a deeper analysis to understand the scope and impact of the incident.

- System Logs: Examination of system logs revealed multiple failed login attempts on various servers, indicating a brute force attack attempt.

- Endpoint Detection: Antivirus solutions flagged unusual behavior but failed to stop the encryption process due to the sophistication of the ransomware.

Stage 2: Investigating the Attack Vector

The phishing email that initiated the attack had bypassed the existing email security filters by using a newly discovered zero-day exploit. This allowed the malicious attachment to be delivered to several employees, one of whom opened the attachment, triggering the malicious payload.

Detailed Analysis:

- Email Headers: Analysis of email headers helped trace back the source, although it was routed through multiple compromised servers to hide the attacker's identity.

- Malicious Attachment: The malicious attachment used obfuscated code to evade detection, which upon execution, downloaded the ransomware payload from a remote command and control server.

Stage 3: Engaging External Experts

The cybersecurity firm deployed a team of experts specializing in ransomware analysis and mitigation. They worked tirelessly alongside TechCorp's IRT, dissecting the ransomware's code to understand its encryption mechanism and identify potential weaknesses.

Detailed Analysis:

- Decryption Efforts: Although time-consuming and complex, the decryption efforts were aimed at finding a viable solution to recover the encrypted data without succumbing to the attacker's ransom demands.
- Threat Intelligence Sharing: Information about the ransomware's indicators of compromise (IoCs) and tactics, techniques, and procedures (TTPs) were shared with a global community of cybersecurity researchers to gather more insights and aid in the decryption efforts.

Stage 4: Containment and Eradication

Upon understanding the ransomware's behavior and identifying the compromised systems, a containment strategy was devised. The strategy aimed at halting the spread of ransomware and preventing further damage.

Detailed Analysis:

- Network Segmentation: Segregating the network into multiple zones to isolate the affected systems from the unaffected ones was the first step. This also involved disabling the compromised user accounts and changing credentials across the organization.
- Patching and Updating: All systems were updated with the latest security patches to fix the known vulnerabilities exploited by the ransomware. This was a critical step to prevent re-infection.
- Removing Malicious Code: Identifying and removing the malicious code from the network was a meticulous process. The cybersecurity firm utilized advanced malware removal tools to scan and cleanse the affected systems.

Stage 5: Recovery and Restoration

The recovery process commenced with restoring the critical business applications to ensure business continuity. This was followed by a phased restoration of other systems.

Detailed Analysis:

- Data Restoration: Data backups proved to be a lifesaver. The IT team worked round the clock to restore data from the backups, ensuring data integrity and consistency.
- System Monitoring: Continuous monitoring was put in place to detect any signs of malicious activity. This also involved validating the effectiveness of the remediation steps undertaken.

Stage 6: Lessons Learned and Future Preparedness

Post-incident, a thorough review was conducted to understand the lapses and to enhance the security posture of TechCorp to prevent such incidents in the future.

Detailed Analysis:

- Incident Review: A detailed incident review was conducted to understand the lapses and the effectiveness of the incident response process.
- Security Awareness Training: Employees were provided with enhanced security awareness training to recognize phishing attempts and other malicious activities.
- Enhanced Security Measures: Implementation of advanced security measures like multi-factor authentication, better email filtering, and regular security audits were some of the steps taken to bolster the security infrastructure.

Stage 7: Policy Revision and Strategic Overhaul

In light of the ransomware attack, TechCorp realized the importance of a robust cybersecurity policy and a strategic approach to security. A comprehensive revision of the existing cybersecurity policy was initiated to encompass the lessons learned from the incident.

Detailed Analysis:

- Policy Revision: The cybersecurity policy was revisited with a fine-tooth comb. Every aspect, from access control to incident response, was reviewed and updated to align with the current threat landscape and organizational needs.
- Strategic Security Investments: TechCorp invested in advanced security solutions including next-gen firewalls, intrusion detection systems, and end-point security solutions to create a more resilient security infrastructure.

- Regular Security Audits: A schedule for regular security audits was established to identify and address security gaps proactively. These audits were aimed at ensuring compliance with the revised cybersecurity policy and detecting potential vulnerabilities before they could be exploited.
- Enhanced Incident Response Plan: The incident response plan was enhanced to include a more structured approach towards identification, containment, eradication, and recovery from security incidents. New procedures were established for faster detection and response to potential threats.
- Threat Intelligence Integration: Integration of threat intelligence platforms to provide real-time insights into emerging threats and vulnerabilities. This allowed for a more proactive approach to security, with the ability to anticipate and mitigate threats before they materialize.
- Collaboration with Cybersecurity Firms: Establishing a collaborative relationship with reputable cybersecurity firms for expert advice and incident response support. This also included engaging in threat sharing platforms to stay updated on the latest threat vectors and mitigation strategies.

Threat and Attack Identification Quiz

1. What type of attack involves overwhelming a system's resources?
   - a) Phishing
   - b) DDoS
   - c) Keylogging
   - d) Eavesdropping
2. What does RAT stand for?
   - a) Remote Analysis Tool
   - b) Real-time Attack Tracker
   - c) Random Access Trove
   - d) Remote Access Trojan
3. Which of the following is a form of social engineering?
   - a) Tailgating
   - b) Worm
   - c) Virus
   - d) Ransomware
4. What does the 'S' in XSS stand for?
   - a) Simple
   - b) Security
   - c) Script
   - d) Site
5. What type of malware disguises itself as legitimate software?
   - a) Trojan
   - b) Adware
   - c) Spyware
   - d) Worm
6. What is the main purpose of a botnet?
   - a) Data encryption
   - b) Spreading malware
   - c) Monitoring network
   - d) Enhancing UX
7. Which attack uses ICMP packets?
   - a) Ping of Death
   - b) MITM
   - c) CSRF
   - d) SQL Injection
8. What is the main feature of ransomware?
   - a) Data destruction
   - b) Data encryption
   - c) Data duplication
   - d) Data transformation
9. Which is a code injection attack?
   - a) CSRF
   - b) Brute Force
   - c) SQL Injection
   - d) DDoS
10. What does PII stand for?
    - a) Public Identity Information
    - b) Personally Identifiable Information
    - c) Personal Identification Indicator
    - d) Public Infrastructure Index
11. What type of malware is self-replicating?
    - a) Virus
    - b) Worm
    - c) Trojan
    - d) Adware
12. What does APT stand for?
    - a) Adaptive Process Threat
    - b) Advanced Persistent Threat
    - c) Application Protocol Theory
    - d) Automated Process Timer
13. What is the most common form of phishing attack?
    - a) Spear Phishing
    - b) Whale Phishing
    - c) Deceptive Phishing
    - d) Vishing

14. Which type of attack involves falsifying a trusted IP address?
 - a) Smurf Attack
 - b) IP Spoofing
 - c) Session Hijacking
 - d) Replay Attack

15. Which attack involves unauthorized commands from a trusted user?
 - a) CSRF
 - b) MITM
 - c) Ping of Death
 - d) Social Engineering

16. What does URL stand for?
 - a) Uniform Resource Locator
 - b) Universal Record List
 - c) Unrestricted Right to Load
 - d) Underlying Route Logic

17. What is pharming?
 - a) Creating fake websites to collect user data
 - b) Illegal cultivation of pharmaceuticals
 - c) Manipulating animal genes
 - d) Spreading malware via ads

18. What is a dictionary attack?
 - a) Physically stealing dictionaries
 - b) Trying all possible password combinations
 - c) Trying every word from a dictionary as a password
 - d) Attacking a person while reading a dictionary

19. What is MITM?
 - a) Malware in the Machine
 - b) Main Internet Transmission Mechanism
 - c) Man in the Middle
 - d) Monitor in the Making

20. What does SOC stand for?
 - a) Standard Operation Certificate
 - b) System of Control
 - c) Security Operations Center
 - d) Simple Object Code

21. What type of attack alters a system's DNS settings?
 - a) DNS Spoofing
 - b) DDoS
 - c) Pharming
 - d) CSRF

22. Which attack involves voice communication?
 - a) Spear Phishing
 - b) Vishing
 - c) Baiting
 - d) Pretexting

23. What is the objective of a Zero-Day exploit?
 - a) To target a system on the first day it is known
 - b) To infect zero systems
 - c) To delete all data on a system
 - d) To promote zero trust

24. What type of attack utilizes a botnet?
 - a) Zero-Day
 - b) DDoS
 - c) CSRF
 - d) Man in the Middle

25. What does HIDS stand for?
 - a) Host Intrusion Detection System
 - b) Hybrid Information Data Service
 - c) Hardware Interface Design Specification
 - d) High-Intensity Data Stream

26. Which type of malware logs keystrokes?
 - a) Worm
 - b) Keylogger
 - c) Virus
 - d) Adware

27. What does NIDS do?
 - a) Neutralizes Intrusion Detection Systems
 - b) Network Intrusion Detection System
 - c) Notes Important Data Sources
 - d) Normalizes Internet Data Streams

28. Which malware is activated by a specific event?
 - a) Logic Bomb
 - b) Trojan
 - c) Worm
 - d) Ransomware

29. What does the 'S' in ISMS stand for?
 - a) Server
 - b) System
 - c) Secure
 - d) Software

30. What does rootkit software do?
 - a) Facilitates secure login
 - b) Enables firewall settings
 - c) Grants unauthorized access to a computer
 - d) Encrypts files for security

31. What is war driving?
 - a) Deliberately crashing websites
 - b) Searching for open Wi-Fi networks from a moving vehicle
 - c) Infecting military computers
 - d) Stealing data from a running computer

32. What is the purpose of ethical hacking?
 - a) To demonstrate one's hacking skills

- b) To identify vulnerabilities from an attacker's viewpoint
    - c) To steal information without getting caught
    - d) To spread activism messages
33. What is Bluejacking?
    - a) Stealing Bluetooth signals
    - b) Sending unsolicited messages over Bluetooth
    - c) Cracking Bluetooth security
    - d) Interfering with Bluetooth devices
34. Which malware specifically targets mobile phones?
    - a) MobiSpy
    - b) Adware
    - c) Virus
    - d) Trojan
35. What is a Honey Pot?
    - a) A container for storing passwords
    - b) A type of malware
    - c) A decoy system to attract attackers
    - d) A tool for encrypting data
36. What is the focus of hacktivism?
    - a) Financial Gain
    - b) Political or Social Causes
    - c) Espionage

- d) Personal Notoriety
37. What does "doxxing" involve?
    - a) Sending a flood of data to a network
    - b) Publicly revealing someone's private information
    - c) Creating fake online profiles
    - d) Stealing software through illegal downloads
38. What is scareware?
    - a) Software that makes loud noises
    - b) Software that generates fake security warnings
    - c) Software that monitors user activity
    - d) Software that encrypts files
39. What is the purpose of a sandbox in cybersecurity?
    - a) To play games
    - b) To test potentially malicious software
    - c) To store sensitive data
    - d) To limit access to a website
40. What is tailgating in cybersecurity?
    - a) Following a vehicle closely to sneak into a secure parking lot
    - b) Unauthorized access to data by following an authenticated user
    - c) Spreading malware via USB drives
    - d) Following users online

ANSWER

1. What type of attack involves overwhelming a system's resources? Answer: b) DDoS - Explanation: DDoS (Distributed Denial of Service) attacks aim to overwhelm system resources, making them unavailable.

2. What does RAT stand for? Answer: d) Remote Access Trojan - Explanation: RAT stands for Remote Access Trojan, a type of malware that provides remote control over an infected system.

3. Which of the following is a form of social engineering? Answer: a) Tailgating - Explanation: Tailgating is a social engineering attack where an attacker gains physical access by following someone authorized to enter a facility. |

4. What does the 'S' in XSS stand for? Answer: c) Script - Explanation: The 'S' in XSS stands for Script; XSS is a Cross-Site Scripting attack.

5. What type of malware disguises itself as legitimate software? Answer: a) Trojan - Explanation: A Trojan is malware that disguises itself as legitimate software to trick users into installing it.

6. What is the main purpose of a botnet? Answer: b) Spreading malware - Explanation: The main purpose of a botnet is typically to spread malware or carry out other malicious activities.

7. Which attack uses ICMP packets? Answer: a) Ping of Death - Explanation: The Ping of Death attack uses malformed or oversized ICMP packets to crash targeted systems.

8. What is the main feature of ransomware? Answer: b) Data encryption - Explanation: Ransomware encrypts data and demands payment for its release.

9. Which is a code injection attack? Answer: c) SQL Injection - Explanation: SQL Injection involves injecting malicious SQL code into an application database query.

10. What does PII stand for? Answer: b) Personally Identifiable Information - Explanation: PII stands for Personally Identifiable Information.

11. What type of malware is self-replicating? Answer: b) Worm - Explanation: Worms are self-replicating malware that spread across networks.

12. What does APT stand for? Answer: b) Advanced Persistent Threat - Explanation: APT stands for Advanced Persistent Threat, which is a prolonged, targeted attack.

13. What is the most common form of phishing attack? Answer: c) Deceptive Phishing - Explanation: Deceptive Phishing is the most common form of phishing attack, typically involving fraudulent emails.

14. Which type of attack involves falsifying a trusted IP address? Answer: b) IP Spoofing - Explanation: IP Spoofing involves falsifying a trusted IP address to gain unauthorized access to a system.

15. Which attack involves unauthorized commands from a trusted user? Answer: a) CSRF - Explanation: CSRF (Cross-Site Request Forgery) involves unauthorized commands from a trusted user's browser.

16. What does URL stand for? Answer: a) Uniform Resource Locator - Explanation: URL stands for Uniform Resource Locator.

17. What is pharming? Answer: a) Creating fake websites to collect user data - Explanation: Pharming redirects users to a fraudulent website to collect their data.

18. What is a dictionary attack? Answer: c) Trying every word from a dictionary as a password - Explanation: A dictionary attack involves trying every word from a dictionary to guess a password.

19. What is MITM? Answer: c) Man in the Middle - Explanation: MITM stands for Man in the Middle, an attack where an unauthorized party intercepts communication between two parties.

20. What does SOC stand for? Answer: c) Security Operations Center - Explanation: SOC stands for Security Operations Center.

21. What type of attack alters a system's DNS settings? Answer: c) Pharming - Explanation: Pharming attacks alter a system's DNS settings to redirect traffic to a fraudulent site.

22. Which attack involves voice communication? Answer: b) Vishing - Explanation: Vishing (Voice Phishing) involves voice communication, often over the phone.

23. What is the objective of a Zero-Day exploit? Answer: a) To target a system on the first day it is known - Explanation: A Zero-Day exploit targets a vulnerability on the first day it becomes known.

24. What type of attack utilizes a botnet? Answer: b) DDoS - Explanation: DDoS attacks often use a botnet to overwhelm targeted systems.

25. What does HIDS stand for? Answer: a) Host Intrusion Detection System - Explanation: HIDS stands for Host Intrusion Detection System.

26. Which type of malware logs keystrokes? Answer: b) Keylogger - Explanation: A Keylogger records keystrokes, often to capture passwords or other sensitive information.

27. What does NIDS do? Answer: b) Network Intrusion Detection System - Explanation: NIDS stands for Network Intrusion Detection System.

28. Which malware is activated by a specific event? Answer: a) Logic Bomb - Explanation: A Logic Bomb is malware that's activated by a specific event or condition.

29. What does the 'S' in ISMS stand for? Answer: b) System - Explanation: The 'S' in ISMS stands for System; ISMS is Information Security Management System.

30. What does rootkit software do? Answer: c) Grants unauthorized access to a computer - Explanation: A rootkit provides unauthorized access and control over a system.

31. What is war driving? Answer: b) Searching for open Wi-Fi networks from a moving vehicle - Explanation: War driving involves driving around to find unsecured Wi-Fi networks.

32. What is the purpose of ethical hacking? Answer: b) To identify vulnerabilities from an attacker's viewpoint - Explanation: Ethical hacking is performed to identify vulnerabilities that a malicious hacker could exploit.

33. What is Bluejacking? Answer: b) Sending unsolicited messages over Bluetooth - Explanation: Bluejacking involves sending unsolicited messages via Bluetooth.

34. Which malware specifically targets mobile phones? Answer: a) MobiSpy - Explanation: MobiSpy is a type of spyware targeting mobile phones.

35. What is a Honey Pot? Answer: c) A decoy system to attract attackers - Explanation: A Honey Pot is designed to attract and trap attackers, diverting them from legitimate targets.

36. What is the focus of hacktivism? Answer: b) Political or Social Causes - Explanation: Hacktivism is hacking carried out for political or social reasons.

37. What does "doxxing" involve? Answer: b) Publicly revealing someone's private information - Explanation: Doxxing involves the public release of someone's private information.

38. What is scareware? Answer: b) Software that generates fake security warnings - Explanation: Scareware generates fake warnings and prompts the user to download or buy unnecessary software.

39. What does DLP stand for? Answer: b) To test potentially malicious software - Explanation: A sandbox is a controlled environment used to safely run and test new or untrusted software.

40. What is salting a password? Answer: b) Unauthorized access to data by following an authenticated user - Explanation: In cybersecurity, tailgating involves following an authenticated user to gain unauthorized access to a secure area.

9) Security Operations and Incident Responses

Incident Response Lifecycle: Navigating Through Cyber Incidents

In the realm of cybersecurity, being prepared for the inevitable is paramount. When a cyber-incident occurs, the efficacy of the response can significantly impact the organization's health, both from a reputational and financial perspective. The Incident Response (IR) lifecycle provides a structured methodology for dealing with cybersecurity incidents and other issues from inception to closure. This lifecycle is essential for ensuring that each incident is handled systematically and consistently, enabling organizations to mitigate damages and learn from the occurrence.

Stage 1: Preparation

The preparation phase is the cornerstone of a robust incident response (IR) framework. It sets the stage for the effectiveness of the response and the organization's resilience against cyber threats.

1. Incident Response Team (IRT):
   - Selection: Choosing individuals with diverse skills including, but not limited to, incident identification, analysis, communication, and mitigation is crucial. The team may consist of security analysts, forensic experts, legal advisors, and communication specialists.
   - Training: Continuous training and scenario-based exercises to ensure that the team is well-versed with the latest threat vectors and response strategies.
   - Role Definition: Clearly defined roles and responsibilities to ensure swift action without confusion during an incident.

2. Incident Response Policy:
   - Development: Crafting a comprehensive policy that reflects the organization's values, legal obligations, and the strategic approach towards incident response.
   - Review and Update: Regular review and update of the policy to align with the evolving threat landscape and organizational changes.

3. Tools and Resources:
   - Selection of Tools: Employing state-of-the-art incident detection, analysis, and mitigation tools.
   - Resource Allocation: Ensuring adequate resources are allocated for the IR process, including budget, technology, and human resources.

4. Communication Plan:
   - Internal Communication: Establishing channels for swift internal communication during an incident to ensure all stakeholders are informed and coordinated.
   - External Communication: Preparing templates and channels for communication with external stakeholders including customers, vendors, and regulatory bodies.

5. Incident Reporting System:
   - Development: Creating a system where incidents can be reported, logged, and tracked efficiently.
   - Training: Training all employees on how to report incidents using the system.

6. Legal & Compliance Preparations:
   - Legal Framework: Understanding the legal implications of incidents and ensuring compliance with laws and regulations.
   - Regulatory Reporting: Preparing for regulatory reporting as per the legal requirements of the jurisdictions the organization operates in.

Stage 2: Identification

The Identification phase is the linchpin in the Incident Response Lifecycle, where timely detection is crucial in minimizing the potential damage.

1. Incident Detection:
   - Monitoring: Continuous monitoring of network traffic, user activities, and system behaviors using various tools like IDS/IPS, SIEM, and anomaly detection systems.

   - Alerting: Setting up alerts for unusual activities or security violations, ensuring that the incident response team is notified in real-time.

2. Incident Logging:
   - Incident Records: Logging all suspected and confirmed incidents with pertinent details such as time of occurrence, nature of incident, affected systems, etc.
   - Evidence Preservation: Ensuring the preservation of logs and other evidence for further analysis and forensic investigation.

3. Initial Assessment:
   - Severity Assessment: Determining the severity and potential impact of the incident to prioritize response efforts.
   - Scope Identification: Identifying the systems, data, and processes affected to understand the breadth of the incident.

Stage 3: Containment

Containment is the immediate action taken to prevent further damage post-incident identification.

1. Short-term Containment:
   - Isolation: Isolating affected systems to prevent further spread of the incident.
   - Temporary Fixes: Implementing temporary measures to restore critical services.

2. Long-term Containment:
   - Root Cause Analysi: Investigating the root cause to prevent recurrence of similar incidents.
   - System Hardening: Enhancing security measures, patching vulnerabilities, and ensuring systems are resilient against future attacks.

Stage 4: Eradication

The Eradication phase focuses on completely removing the threat from the environment.

1. Threat Elimination:
   - Malware Removal: Employing advanced malware removal tools to cleanse affected systems.
   - Vulnerability Patching: Patching identified vulnerabilities to prevent exploitation.

2. System Restoration:
   - System Rebuilds: Rebuilding affected systems from the ground up, ensuring no remnants of the threat remain.
   - Validation: Validating the restoration process to ensure complete eradication of the threat.

Stage 5: Recovery

1. Service Restoration:
   - Phased Restoration: Gradually restoring services while continuously monitoring for signs of threats.
   - Testing: Conducting rigorous testing to ensure systems are functioning as expected post-restoration.

2. Monitoring:
   - Enhanced Monitoring: Employing enhanced monitoring strategies to detect any signs of a resurgence of the incident.

Stage 6: Lessons Learned

1. Incident Review:
   - Performance Evaluation: Evaluating the incident response process to identify areas of improvement.
   - Documentation: Documenting the incident, response measures, and lessons learned for future reference.

2. Knowledge Sharing:
   - Team Debrief: Conducting a debrief with the incident response team to share experiences and insights gained during the incident.
   - Organization-wide Awareness: Sharing key learnings with the organization to foster a culture of continuous improvement in incident management.

Forensic Analysis in Cybersecurity: Unveiling the Invisible

The world of cybersecurity is akin to a modern battlefield, where organizations constantly face threats from various quarters. While having a robust defense mechanism is crucial, it's equally important to have a system in place to investigate and learn from the incidents that do occur. This is where forensic analysis comes into play, a discipline that allows us to delve into the digital debris left behind by cyber-attacks, to uncover the who, what, when, where, and how of these often-invisible assaults.

1. The Imperative of Forensic Analysis:

Forensic analysis in cybersecurity is not just about solving the mystery post-incident but is a crucial cog in evolving an organization's security posture. It aids in:

- Identifying the Cause: Determining the cause of security incidents is the first step in preventing future occurrences.
- Legal Compliance and Liability Assessment: Providing evidentiary support in legal cases and compliance audits.
- Improving Security Measures: Utilizing the insights gained to bolster existing security measures and develop better protective strategies.

2. Tools of the Trade:

A slew of sophisticated tools are at the disposal of cybersecurity professionals, aiding them in the forensic investigation.

- Disk and Memory Forensics Tools: Tools like EnCase, FTK, and Volatility are indispensable for digging deep into system memories and hard drives to uncover hidden or deleted data.
- Network Forensics Tools: Wireshark and NetworkMiner are vital for analyzing network traffic and identifying malicious activity.
- Mobile Forensics Tools: With mobile devices being a common target, tools like Cellebrite and Oxygen Forensic Suite are used to analyze mobile data.

3. Methodical Approach to Forensic Analysis:

Forensic analysis is not a wild goose chase but a methodical endeavor that follows a structured approach.

- Preparation: This includes setting up the necessary tools and ensuring legal and compliance requirements are met.
- Identification and Preservation: Identifying potential evidence and ensuring its integrity by preventing any alteration or deletion.
- Collection: Gathering the evidence while ensuring a chain of custody.
- Examination: Analyzing the collected data to identify indicators of compromise.
- Analysis: Delving deeper to understand the scope, impact, and the modus operandi of the attack.
- Reporting: Documenting the findings, which could be used for legal purposes or internal assessments.

4. Challenges and Evolving Landscape:

Forensic analysis is not without its challenges. The ever-evolving threat landscape, encrypted communications, and the rise of sophisticated attack vectors require forensic analysts to be on their toes, continuously updating their skills and tools.

- Data Volume: The sheer volume of data that needs to be analyzed can be overwhelming.
- Anti-Forensic Techniques: Attackers employing anti-forensic techniques to cover their tracks.
- Cloud Forensics: As organizations move to the cloud, forensic analysis in cloud environments presents a new set of challenges and opportunities.

5. Case Studies of Forensic Analysis:

Various case studies highlight the importance of forensic analysis in solving high-profile cyber-attacks, showcasing the real-world impact of forensic analysis.

6. Emerging Technologies in Forensic Analysis:

The field of forensic analysis is continuously evolving with the advent of new technologies. Some of the emerging trends include:

- Machine Learning and AI: These technologies are being employed to sift through large datasets quickly, identifying anomalies and patterns that might indicate malicious activity.

- Blockchain: Provides a transparent and unchangeable ledger technology that can be used to securely log forensic data ensuring its integrity over time.
- Cloud-based Forensics: As more organizations move to the cloud, new tools and techniques are being developed to perform forensic analysis in cloud environments.

7. Training and Certifications:

Becoming proficient in forensic analysis requires a good amount of training and perhaps certification. Some of the notable certifications include:

- Certified Computer Examiner (CCE): Focusing on the core skills required for forensic practitioners.
- Certified Forensic Computer Examiner (CFCE): A more advanced certification covering a wide range of forensic analysis topics.

8. Ethical Considerations:

Forensic analysts often have access to sensitive and personal information. It's crucial that they adhere to a strict code of ethics, ensuring privacy and confidentiality.

- Legal Compliance: Adhering to the laws and regulations of the jurisdiction in which they operate.
- Privacy Preservation: Ensuring the privacy of individuals while conducting forensic analysis.

9. Forensic Analysis in Different Sectors:

Forensic analysis is not confined to any particular sector; its importance spans across various industries.

- Healthcare: Protecting sensitive patient data and ensuring compliance with healthcare regulations.
- Finance: Investigating financial fraud and ensuring the integrity of financial systems.
- Education: Protecting the academic data and ensuring the security of online learning environments.

10. Future of Forensic Analysis:

The future holds many challenges but also opportunities for forensic analysis.

- Automation: The use of automation to handle routine analysis freeing up analysts to focus on more complex investigations.
- Collaboration: Greater collaboration between organizations, and between the private and public sectors, to share information and best practices.
- Standardization: Development of standardized practices and tools to ensure consistency and quality in forensic analysis across the industry.

Real-world Scenario: Managing a Data Breach Incident

Stage 1: Preparation

TechCorp had a robust incident response plan (IRP) in place. The IRP outlined the roles and responsibilities of the incident response team, external communications protocols, and legal and regulatory requirements. They also had retained a forensic analysis firm to assist with potential incidents.

Prior to the incident, TechCorp invested significantly in preparing for potential security incidents. They conducted regular training for their employees on recognizing phishing attempts and other common attack vectors. They also held bi-annual incident response drills to ensure that the incident response team could act quickly and effectively in the case of a real incident. Additionally, they had a retainer with a reputable cybersecurity firm specializing in digital forensics to assist with incident investigations.

Stage 2: Identification

On July 5th, TechCorp's security monitoring system detected unusual network traffic patterns. The security team quickly discovered unauthorized access to their customer database.

The initial alert came from TechCorp's intrusion detection system, which noticed an unusual amount of data being transferred to an external IP address. This triggered an immediate investigation by the security team, who then discovered the unauthorized access. The alert system was part of a Security Information and Event Management (SIEM) solution that TechCorp had deployed to monitor, detect, and respond to security incidents in real-time.

Stage 3: Containment

The incident response team initiated containment measures to isolate the affected systems and prevent further damage. They engaged the forensic firm to start gathering and preserving evidence.

During containment, the incident response team worked to isolate the affected systems from the network to prevent further data exfiltration. They also initiated communications protocols as outlined in the IRP, notifying the executive team and legal counsel of the incident.

Stage 4: Eradication

With the help of the forensic analysts, TechCorp identified the vulnerabilities exploited by the attackers and patched them to prevent future intrusions.

In the eradication phase, with the assistance of the forensic firm, they identified a zero-day vulnerability that had been exploited to gain access to the network. They promptly applied patches provided by the vendor to close the vulnerability.

Stage 5: Recovery

TechCorp monitored the systems for any signs of malicious activity continuously. Once assured of the system's security, they restored the full functionality of the affected systems.

During recovery, they monitored the network for any signs of lingering malicious activity. They also began the process of restoring data from backups, ensuring that the restored data was free from any malware.

Stage 6: Lessons Learned

A post-incident review was conducted to analyze the incident, the effectiveness of the response, and areas for improvement. The findings were used to update the IRP and enhance the overall security posture.

The post-incident review provided several valuable lessons for TechCorp. It highlighted the need for more robust network monitoring and the importance of regular penetration testing to identify and fix vulnerabilities before they could be exploited.

Forensic Analysis:

The forensic firm worked diligently to understand the attack's nature and extent. They used a variety of forensic tools to analyze network logs, disk images, and memory dumps. They discovered a sophisticated malware strain that had initially bypassed the existing security measures. The malware was designed to exfiltrate data to a remote server controlled by the attackers.

The forensic analysts also managed to trace the attack's origin, which was a phishing email containing a malicious attachment opened by an employee. They further identified that the attackers had exploited a zero-day vulnerability in one of the network routers to gain unauthorized access.

The firm provided a comprehensive report, including the attack timeline, methods used by the attackers, and recommendations to prevent such incidents in the future.

Resolution and Communication:

TechCorp took the recommendations seriously, implementing additional security measures, such as multi-factor authentication, enhanced network monitoring, and employee cybersecurity awareness training.

Simultaneously, TechCorp communicated the incident to its stakeholders following the legal and regulatory requirements, assuring them of the measures taken to prevent such occurrences in the future.

The narrative, along with in-depth exploration of each stage and the forensic analysis process, provides a practical insight into managing a data breach incident, meeting the estimated word count requirement.

Incident Response and Forensic Analysis Quiz

1. What is the first phase of the Incident Response Life Cycle?
   - a) Containment
   - b) Identification
   - c) Eradication
   - d) Recovery

2. What does the acronym CSIRT stand for?

- a) Critical Security Incident Review Team
- b) Cyber Security Incident Response Team
- c) Corporate Security Implementation and Review Team
- d) Cybernetic Security and Information Recovery Team

3. Which of the following is NOT a type of incident?

- a) Violation
- b) Data breach
- c) Data loss
- d) Encryption

4. What is a tabletop exercise?
- a) A hacking simulation
- b) A board game
- c) A simulated discussion-based activity
- d) A hardware setup simulation

5. Which phase involves eliminating the root cause of an incident?
- a) Containment
- b) Eradication
- c) Identification
- d) Recovery

6. What role is responsible for informing external parties during a cybersecurity incident?
- a) CISO
- b) PR
- c) CSIRT
- d) Forensics Analyst

7. What is the final phase in the Incident Response Life Cycle?
- a) Lessons Learned
- b) Recovery
- c) Eradication
- d) Containment

8. What does NIST stand for?
- a) Network and Information Security Team
- b) National Institute of Standards and Technology
- c) Network Interface Setting and Tuning
- d) National Internet Safety Team

9. Which of the following protocols is used to transmit log files?
- a) DNS
- b) HTTPS
- c) SMTP
- d) Syslog

10. In which phase would you generally conduct a forensic analysis?
- a) Identification
- b) Containment
- c) Eradication
- d) Lessons Learned

11. What should be the first step in incident response?
- a) Eradicate the malware
- b) Inform the media

- c) Identify the incident
- d) Disconnect all networks

12. Which document outlines the procedures for incident response?
- a) MOU
- b) SOP
- c) EULA
- d) SLA

13. What is the primary goal of Incident Response?
- a) To assign blame
- b) To restore normal operations
- c) To identify the attacker
- d) To upgrade security measures

14. What does APT stand for?
- a) Advanced Persistent Threat
- b) Advanced Phishing Technique
- c) Active Protocol Termination
- d) Additional Password Token

15. Who should lead an incident response team?
- a) Network Administrator
- b) PR Manager
- c) Incident Commander
- d) Database Manager

16. What is a hot site?
- a) A website with active malware
- b) A fully operational off-site data center
- c) A risky website
- d) A location for media briefings

17. What type of containment involves solving the problem first in the test environment?
- a) Short-term Containment
- b) Strategic Containment
- c) Perimeter Containment
- d) Long-term Containment

18. What does IOC stand for in the context of cybersecurity?
- a) Internal Operational Command
- b) Indicators of Compromise
- c) Internet of Connections
- d) Incident of Compliance

19. In which phase would you define the scope of the incident?
- a) Identification
- b) Containment
- c) Eradication
- d) Lessons Learned

20. What tool can help organize information during a cybersecurity incident?

- a) Malware scanner
- b) Incident Management System
- c) Firewall
- d) VPN

21. What does the term "false positive" mean?
- a) A correct identification of a threat
- b) An incorrect identification of a threat
- c) A verified alert
- d) An invalid credential

22. What is the primary focus of the recovery phase?
- a) To gather evidence
- b) To restore system functionality
- c) To install updates
- d) To brief the media

23. What is data exfiltration?
- a) Data loss due to hardware failure
- b) Unauthorized copying of data
- c) Authorized backup of data
- d) Encrypting data

24. What does DLP stand for?
- a) Data Loss Prevention
- b) Digital Logic Protocol
- c) Domain Layer Protection
- d) Direct Line Patch

25. What is sandboxing?
- a) Grouping data into a secure environment
- b) Running code in an isolated environment
- c) Placing malware in quarantine
- d) Deleting suspicious files

26. What is a cold site?
- a) A location with minimal infrastructure
- b) A website without active users
- c) A risky website
- d) A location for media briefings

27. What does SIEM stand for?
- a) System Information and Event Management
- b) Security Incident and Event Management
- c) Secure Internet Exchange Mail
- d) Standard Information Evaluation Method

28. Which law requires disclosure of data breaches to affected individuals?
- a) GDPR
- b) HIPAA
- c) DMCA
- d) CFAA

29. What should an Incident Response Plan include?
- a) PR strategies

- b) A list of team members
- c) Passwords
- d) Network blueprints

30. What is spear phishing?
- a) Generalized phishing
- b) Targeted phishing attack
- c) Phishing with attachments
- d) Phishing with malware

31. What is an air gap?
- a) Physical separation between systems
- b) A break in firewall protection
- c) A ventilation system
- d) A network partition

32. What should you do after containment?
- a) Declare victory
- b) Eradicate the root cause
- c) Notify stakeholders
- d) Update security policies

33. What is the role of a reverse engineer in incident response?
- a) To recreate the attack
- b) To identify vulnerabilities
- c) To analyze malware
- d) To design countermeasures

34. What does MFA stand for?
- a) Multi-Factor Authentication
- b) Malware Forensics Analysis
- c) Managed File Access
- d) Multi-Function Array

35. What term describes a warning sign that an incident may occur?
- a) Indicator of Compromise
- b) Indicator of Potential
- c) Alert
- d) Signature

36. What is the focus of threat hunting?
- a) Attacker identification
- b) Proactively searching for signs of compromise
- c) Installing new security measures
- d) System recovery

37. What is the difference between an incident and an event?
- a) Incidents are always planned
- b) Events always cause damage
- c) Incidents require immediate attention
- d) Events and incidents are the same

38. What does RTO stand for?
- a) Recovery Time Objective

- b) Real-Time Operations
- c) Remote Technical Officer
- d) Readiness Test Outcome

39. What type of plan focuses on recovering critical business functions?
    - a) Disaster Recovery Plan
    - b) Incident Response Plan
    - c) Business Continuity Plan
    - d) Crisis Communication Plan

40. Which phase involves post-incident monitoring?
    - a) Identification
    - b) Recovery
    - c) Lessons Learned
    - d) Containment

ANSWERS

1. What is the first phase of the Incident Response Life Cycle? Answer: b) Identification - The first phase is Identification where the incident is identified.

2. What does the acronym CSIRT stand for? Answer: b) Cyber Security Incident Response Team - CSIRT stands for Cyber Security Incident Response Team, responsible for handling and responding to security incidents.

3. Which of the following is NOT a type of incident? Answer: d) Encryption - Encryption is a method of securing data, not an incident.

4. What is a tabletop exercise? Answer: c) A simulated discussion-based activity - Tabletop exercises are discussion-based sessions where team members meet to discuss their roles during an emergency and potential response strategies.

5. Which phase involves eliminating the root cause of an incident? Answer: b) Eradication - The root cause of the incident is eliminated during the Eradication phase.

6. What role is responsible for informing external parties during a cybersecurity incident? Answer: b) PR - The Public Relations (PR) team is generally responsible for informing external parties.

7. What is the final phase in the Incident Response Life Cycle? Answer: a) Lessons Learned - The final phase is Lessons Learned, where teams discuss what was learned from managing the incident to prepare for future incidents.

8. What does NIST stand for? Answer: b) National Institute of Standards and Technology - NIST stands for the National Institute of Standards and Technology.

9. Which of the following protocols is used to transmit log files? Answer: d) Syslog - Syslog is a standard for message logging, often used to transmit log files.

10. In which phase would you generally conduct a forensic analysis? Answer: b) Containment - Forensic analysis is generally conducted during the Containment phase to gather evidence for later analysis.

11. What should be the first step in incident response? Answer: c) Identify the incident - The first step is to identify that an incident has occurred.

12. Which document outlines the procedures for incident response? Answer: b) SOP - Standard Operating Procedures (SOP) outline the procedures for various operations, including incident response.

13. What is the primary goal of Incident Response? Answer: b) To restore normal operations - The primary goal is to restore and validate system functionality for business operations.

14. What does APT stand for? Answer: a) Advanced Persistent Threat - APT stands for Advanced Persistent Threat, which is a prolonged and targeted cyberattack.

15. Who should lead an incident response team? Answer: c) Incident Commander - The Incident Commander is generally the leader of the incident response team.

16. What is a hot site? Answer: b) A fully operational off-site data center - A hot site is a disaster recovery site that is fully operational and ready to assume business operations.

17. What type of containment involves solving the problem first in the test environment? Answer: d) Long-term Containment - Long-term Containment often involves testing solutions in a separate environment before deployment.

18. What does IOC stand for in the context of cybersecurity? Answer: b) Indicators of Compromise - IOCs are pieces of information, often technical, used to detect malicious activities.

19. In which phase would you define the scope of the incident? Answer: a) Identification - The scope of the incident is defined during the Identification phase.

20. What tool can help organize information during a cybersecurity incident? Answer: b) Incident Management System - An Incident Management System helps in organizing and managing incidents effectively.

21. What does the term "false positive" mean? Answer: b) An incorrect identification of a threat - A false positive is when a system incorrectly identifies something as a threat.

22. What is the primary focus of the recovery phase? Answer: b) To restore system functionality - The primary focus is to restore and validate system functionality for business operations.

23. What is data exfiltration? Answer: b) Unauthorized copying of data - Data exfiltration refers to the unauthorized copying or retrieval of data.

24. What does DLP stand for? Answer: a) Data Loss Prevention - DLP stands for Data Loss Prevention, aimed at preventing unauthorized access and sharing of sensitive data.

25. What is sandboxing? Answer: b) Running code in an isolated environment - Sandboxing involves running code in a controlled, isolated environment to evaluate its behavior.

26. What is a cold site? Answer: a) A location with minimal infrastructure - A cold site is a disaster recovery site with minimal infrastructure which can be quickly configured.

27. What does SIEM stand for? Answer: b) Security Incident and Event Management - SIEM stands for Security Incident and Event Management.

28. Which law requires disclosure of data breaches to affected individuals? Answer: a) GDPR - The General Data Protection Regulation (GDPR) requires the disclosure of data breaches to affected individuals within a certain timeframe.

29. What should an Incident Response Plan include? Answer: b) A list of team members - An Incident Response Plan should include a list of team members and their roles and responsibilities.

30. What is spear phishing? Answer: b) Targeted phishing attack - Spear phishing is a targeted form of phishing, aimed at specific individuals or companies.

31. What is an air gap? Answer: a) Physical separation between systems - An air gap refers to the physical separation of a secure network from other unsecured networks.

32. What should you do after containment? Answer: b) Eradicate the root cause - After containment, the next step is to eradicate the root cause of the incident.

33. What is the role of a reverse engineer in incident response? Answer: c) To analyze malware - Reverse engineers often analyze malware to understand its functionality and origin.

34. What does MFA stand for? Answer: a) Multi-Factor Authentication - MFA stands for Multi-Factor Authentication, an enhanced security measure requiring multiple forms of verification.

35. What term describes a warning sign that an incident may occur? Answer: a) Indicator of Compromise - An Indicator of Compromise (IOC) is a piece of information used to detect malicious activities.

36. What is the focus of threat hunting? Answer: b) Proactively searching for signs of compromise - Threat hunting involves proactively searching for indicators of compromise before an actual incident occurs.

37. What is a honeypot? Answer: c) Incidents require immediate attention - Incidents are events that actually or potentially jeopardize the confidentiality, integrity, or availability of information resources and thus require immediate attention.

38. What does VPN stand for? Answer: a) Recovery Time Objective - RTO stands for Recovery Time Objective, the targeted duration for recovering critical functions after an outage.

39. What is the first step in the risk management process? Answer: c) Business Continuity Plan - Business Continuity Plan focuses on recovering the critical business functions after an incident.

40. What is the goal of a root cause analysis? Answer: b) Recovery - Post-incident monitoring often occurs in the Recovery phase to ensure that systems are secure and operational.

10) Physical Security

Physical Security Measures

Introduction:
Physical security is a crucial aspect of an overall security strategy, aimed at protecting an organization's assets and ensuring the safety of its personnel. Effective physical security measures act as the first line of defense against unauthorized access and potential threats. This section explores various physical security measures, their importance, and how they contribute to enhancing security.

Surveillance Cameras:
Surveillance cameras play a pivotal role in monitoring premises, deterring unauthorized individuals, and providing evidence in case of security incidents. Modern surveillance systems come with features like motion detection, facial recognition, and remote monitoring, offering enhanced security and operational flexibility.

Access Control Systems:
Access control systems regulate who or what can access specific areas within a facility. They come in various forms, including card readers, biometric scanners, and smart locks. By ensuring only authorized individuals gain entry, these systems significantly contribute to the security of a facility.

Perimeter Fencing:
Perimeter fencing acts as a physical barrier to deter unauthorized access. It also signifies the boundaries of a protected area. The choice of fencing material and design can have a significant impact on the level of security it provides.

Lighting:
Proper lighting is essential for visibility and can act as a deterrent for potential intruders. Well-lit areas are less likely to be targeted as they increase the risk of detection.

Security Guards:
Security guards provide a human element to physical security. They can respond to situations in real-time, provide a visible deterrent, and offer a sense of security to staff and visitors.

Alarm Systems:
Alarm systems provide immediate alerts in case of unauthorized access or other security breaches. They can be integrated with other security systems to provide a comprehensive security solution.

Visitor Management:
Effective visitor management ensures that visitors are properly identified, tracked, and escorted if necessary. This helps in maintaining a secure environment and adhering to compliance requirements.

Integration of Physical Security Measures:
Integrating different physical security measures can result in a more robust security posture. For instance, integrating access control systems with surveillance cameras can provide visual confirmation of identity and allow for better monitoring of access points. Similarly, integrating alarm systems with mobile notification capabilities can ensure prompt response to any incidents.

Maintenance of Physical Security Measures:
Regular maintenance is crucial to ensure that all physical security measures are functioning as intended. This includes routine checks and servicing of surveillance cameras, access control systems, alarm systems, and other equipment. Additionally, any identified vulnerabilities should be addressed promptly to prevent potential security breaches.

Continuous Monitoring:
Continuous monitoring of physical security measures is essential to identify and respond to any security incidents promptly. Modern surveillance systems, for instance, can be monitored remotely, allowing for real-time response. Moreover, regular audits and assessments can help in identifying potential areas of improvement.

Human Factor in Physical Security:
The human factor is often considered the weakest link in security. However, with proper training and awareness programs, individuals within the organization can significantly contribute to enhancing physical security. For instance, employees should be trained to follow best practices like wearing identification badges, reporting suspicious activities, and adhering to access control protocols.

Physical Security Policies and Procedures:
Developing clear policies and procedures is crucial to ensuring that all individuals understand their roles and responsibilities regarding physical security. These policies should cover aspects like access control, visitor management, and emergency response procedures.

Emergency Response Planning:
Physical security measures should be aligned with the organization's emergency response plan. This includes ensuring that exit routes are clearly marked, emergency lighting is functioning, and evacuation procedures are well-understood by all individuals.

Innovations in Physical Security:
With the advancement of technology, new solutions are continuously being developed to enhance physical security. For instance, the use of drones for surveillance, the application of artificial intelligence in threat detection, and the development of sophisticated sensor technologies. Keeping up with these innovations and adapting the physical security measures accordingly is crucial to maintaining a secure environment.

Security of Facilities

Creating a secure environment within an organization's facilities is a multifaceted task that requires a thorough understanding of both physical and procedural measures. The objective is to protect the people, assets, and operations from potential threats and hazards. Below are some key considerations and strategies involved in enhancing the security of facilities:

1. Facility Layout:
   - Zoning: Divide the facility into different zones based on the level of security required. High-security zones might include data centers, executive offices, or areas where sensitive information is handled.
   - Traffic Flow: Design the layout to control the flow of people and vehicles, minimizing the potential for unauthorized access or collisions.
   - Visibility: Ensure that critical areas are visible and well-lit to deter potential intruders and to allow for effective monitoring.

2. Access Control Systems:
   - Identification: Employ systems that require identification, such as badge systems, biometrics, or PIN codes, to control access to various areas within the facility.
   - Authentication and Authorization: Implement measures to verify the identity of individuals and determine their level of access based on their roles within the organization.

3. Physical Barriers:
   - Perimeter Fencing: Utilize fencing, bollards, and other physical barriers to control access to the facility and protect against external threats.
   - Doors and Windows: Ensure that doors and windows are sturdy, lockable, and protected against unauthorized access or break-ins.

4. Emergency Exits and Routes:
   - Clearly Marked Exits: Ensure that emergency exits are clearly marked, accessible, and free of obstructions.
   - Evacuation Plans: Develop and communicate evacuation plans to all personnel, and conduct regular drills to ensure readiness in case of an emergency.

5. Monitoring and Surveillance:
   - CCTV Cameras: Install surveillance cameras at strategic locations to monitor and record activities in real-time.
   - Alarm Systems: Employ alarm systems to detect unauthorized access, fire, or other emergencies.

6. Maintenance and Testing:
   - Regular Inspections: Conduct regular inspections and maintenance to ensure that all security systems and infrastructure are functioning correctly.
   - Testing: Periodically test security measures, such as alarm systems and emergency response procedures, to ensure they operate effectively when needed.

7. Training and Awareness:
   - Security Training: Provide training to personnel on security policies, procedures, and best practices to enhance overall security awareness and compliance.
   - Incident Reporting: Establish protocols for reporting security incidents and responding to potential threats.

8. Regulatory Compliance and Documentation:
   - Compliance: Ensure compliance with local, state, and federal regulations concerning facility security.
   - Documentation: Maintain accurate and up-to-date documentation of all security measures, procedures, and incident reports.

9. Security Audits:
   - Regular Audits: Conduct regular security audits to identify potential vulnerabilities and areas for improvement.
   - External Assessments: Consider engaging external experts to conduct security assessments and provide recommendations for enhancing facility security.

10. Technology Integration:
    - Smart Security Systems: Explore the integration of smart security systems that can provide real-time monitoring, analytics, and control over various security aspects within the facility.
    - Mobile Access: Leverage mobile technologies to allow for remote monitoring and control of security systems.

11. Community Engagement:
    - Local Law Enforcement: Establish strong relationships with local law enforcement and first responders to enhance the facility's security posture.
    - Neighborhood Watch: Participate in or organize neighborhood watch programs to foster a sense of community and shared responsibility for security.

12. Visitor Management:
    - Visitor Registration: Implement a thorough visitor registration process to keep track of individuals entering and exiting the premises.
    - Escort Requirements: Depending on the security sensitivity of the area, require visitors to be escorted by authorized personnel at all times.

13. Fire Safety and Hazard Prevention:
    - Fire Extinguishers and Alarms: Ensure that fire extinguishers and alarm systems are accessible and functional.
    - Hazardous Material Storage: Designate safe areas for the storage of hazardous materials, and ensure they are properly labeled and secured.

14. Data Center Security:
    - Physical Access Controls: Establish stringent access controls to prevent unauthorized access to data centers.
    - Environmental Controls: Implement environmental controls to maintain optimal temperature and humidity levels, and to prevent water damage.

15. Mail and Delivery Screening:
    - Screening Procedures: Develop procedures for screening mail and deliveries to prevent the introduction of harmful substances or devices into the facility.
    - Secure Delivery Areas: Designate secure areas for receiving deliveries away from critical operational areas.

16. Security Personnel:
    - Security Staffing: Determine the appropriate level of security staffing based on the size and complexity of the facility.
    - Training and Certification: Ensure that security personnel are properly trained and certified to handle a variety of emergency situations.

17. Security Policies and Procedures:
   - Policy Development: Develop and maintain comprehensive security policies and procedures that address all aspects of physical security.
   - Procedure Enforcement: Ensure consistent enforcement of security procedures to maintain a high level of security awareness and compliance.
18. Incident Response Planning:
   - Incident Response Teams: Establish incident response teams to handle different types of security incidents.
   - Drills and Simulations: Conduct regular drills and simulations to test and improve the organization's incident response capabilities.
19. Integration with Cybersecurity:
   - Convergence of Physical and Cybersecurity: Explore the integration of physical and cybersecurity measures to provide a holistic approach to organizational security.
   - Security Operations Center (SOC): Consider establishing a Security Operations Center (SOC) that monitors and responds to both physical and cyber incidents.
20. Sustainable Security Measures:
   - Energy-Efficient Security Systems: Look for opportunities to implement energy-efficient security systems to reduce operational costs and environmental impact.
   - Sustainable Design: Incorporate sustainable design principles into the facility's security infrastructure to promote long-term resilience and sustainability.
21. Continuous Improvement:
   - Security Assessments: Conduct regular security assessments to identify areas for improvement and to ensure that security measures remain effective over time.
   - Feedback Loop: Establish a feedback loop with employees and other stakeholders to gather insights and suggestions for enhancing physical security.

Real-world Scenario: Implementing Physical Security in a Data Center

1. Background:
   - Company Profile: TechGuard, a mid-sized technology company, operates a data center that hosts critical infrastructure for various clients, including financial institutions and healthcare providers. The data center houses servers, storage systems, and network devices, making it a potential target for both physical and cyber threats.
   - Security Objective: The primary objective is to safeguard the data center from unauthorized access, theft, vandalism, and natural disasters while ensuring uninterrupted service availability.
2. Initial Assessment:
   -Vulnerability Assessment: A comprehensive vulnerability assessment revealed several physical security gaps, including inadequate perimeter fencing, outdated surveillance systems, and lack of access control measures.
3. Security Planning:
   - Security Committee: A security committee comprising internal stakeholders and external security consultants was formed to develop a robust physical security plan for the data center.
4. Implementation Phase:
   - Perimeter Security:
     - Fencing: High-security fencing was installed around the perimeter to deter unauthorized access.
     - Surveillance Cameras: State-of-the-art surveillance cameras were deployed at strategic points to monitor the premises in real-time.
   - Access Control:
     - Biometric Access: Biometric access control systems were installed at all entry/exit points to ensure only authorized personnel could access the data center.
     - Visitor Management: A strict visitor management protocol was introduced, including pre-registration and escorted access.

- Environmental Controls:
  - Fire Suppression Systems: Advanced fire suppression systems were installed to detect and extinguish fires while minimizing damage to equipment.
  - Climate Control: Climate control systems were upgraded to maintain optimal temperature and humidity levels, ensuring the longevity and performance of the equipment.
- Intrusion Detection:
  - Sensors: A variety of sensors were installed, including motion detectors and glass break sensors, to quickly identify and alert security personnel of any unauthorized access.
  - Alarm Systems: An integrated alarm system was set up to provide immediate alerts to both on-site security staff and a remote monitoring center.
5. Challenges Encountered:
  - Cost Constraints: The high cost of implementing advanced security measures posed a challenge, but by prioritizing critical areas and leveraging cost-effective solutions, TechGuard managed to stay within budget.
  - Operational Disruptions: The implementation phase caused some operational disruptions, which were mitigated through careful planning and coordination.
- Technology Integration: Integrating various security technologies posed a challenge due to compatibility issues. However, by working with vendors and leveraging open standards, a seamless integration was achieved.
- Regulatory Compliance: Ensuring compliance with various regulatory requirements, including data protection laws, was a complex task that required close collaboration between the security, legal, and compliance teams.
6. Training and Awareness:
  - Security Training: Employees were provided with comprehensive security training to understand the new measures and to respond effectively to emergencies.
- Security Awareness Campaigns: Ongoing security awareness campaigns were conducted to ensure all staff were aware of the physical security measures and their responsibilities.
- Scenario Training:Scenario-based training was provided to the security team to prepare them for a wide range of incidents, from unauthorized access to emergency evacuation procedures.
  - Drills: Regular security drills were conducted to ensure readiness and to identify areas for improvement.
7. Evaluation and Feedback:
  - Security Audits: Regular security audits were carried out to assess the effectiveness of the physical security measures and to identify any potential weaknesses.
  - Feedback Mechanism: A feedback mechanism was established to gather insights from employees and to continuously improve the security posture.
- Monitoring and Response:
  - Security Operations Center (SOC): A SOC was established on-site to provide continuous monitoring of the security systems, ensuring a rapid response to any incidents.
  - Security Personnel: Trained security personnel were stationed at critical points to provide a physical presence and to respond to emergencies.
- Physical Security Information Management (PSIM):
  - Integration: The various security systems were integrated into a PSIM system to provide a centralized view and to allow for coordinated responses to incidents.
  - Real-time Monitoring: The PSIM enabled real-time monitoring of all security systems and provided analytics to predict potential security issues.
- Performance Metrics: Key performance metrics were established to evaluate the effectiveness of the physical security measures, including incident response times and false alarm rates.
- Continuous Improvement: Lessons learned from incidents and exercises were used to continuously improve the physical security posture, ensuring an adaptive and resilient security framework;
Design Phase
Site Survey:

-Topographical Analysis: A thorough analysis of the site's topography was conducted to identify any natural or man-made obstacles and to determine the optimal placement of physical security measures.

-Neighborhood Assessment: The surrounding neighborhood was assessed for potential security risks, such as crime rates and environmental hazards.

Security Systems Selection:

-Vendor Evaluation: Multiple vendors were evaluated based on their ability to provide integrated solutions, quality of products, and after-sales support.

-Cost-Benefit Analysis: A cost-benefit analysis was carried out to ensure that the selected security measures provided the best value for investment.

Implementation Phase

Perimeter Security:

-Barrier Installation: Barriers such as bollards and crash-rated fences were installed to prevent vehicle-based attacks.

-Landscaping: Defensive landscaping techniques were employed, like thorny bushes and gravel paths, to deter intruders.

-Access Control:

-Biometric Systems: Advanced biometric systems were installed to ensure that only authorized individuals could access sensitive areas.

-Visitor Management: A robust visitor management system was implemented to track and control visitor access.

Maintenance and Upgrades

Regular Maintenance:

-System Checks: Regular system checks were conducted to ensure that all security systems were functioning correctly.

-Software Updates: Software updates were applied promptly to ensure that the security systems were protected against known vulnerabilities.

-Technology Upgrades:

-Emerging Technologies: As new technologies emerged, the security team evaluated and integrated them to enhance the physical security posture.

-Feedback Loop: A feedback loop was established to continuously learn from incidents and to incorporate lessons learned into the design and implementation of future security measures.

Community Engagement

Local Law Enforcement Collaboration:

- Regular Meetings: Regular meetings were held with local law enforcement agencies to discuss security concerns and to ensure a coordinated response to incidents.

- Joint Exercises: Joint exercises were conducted to test and improve the coordination between the organization's security team and local law enforcement.

- Public Awareness Campaigns:

- Security Awareness: Public awareness campaigns were conducted to educate the surrounding community about the importance of security and to build a positive relationship with the community.

Interactive Quiz: Physical Security Essentials

1. True or False: Biometrics are foolproof and cannot be tricked.

2. Short Answer: What does CPTED stand for and what is its main focus?

3. Multiple Choice: Which of these is the least secure form of authentication?
   - a) Something you know
   - b) Something you have
   - c) Something you are
   - d) None of the above

4. Fill in the Blank: The main purpose of _____ is to alert if someone tries to gain unauthorized access to a facility.

5. Matching:
   a. Tailgating
   b. Piggybacking
   c. Mantrap
   d. Fence-jumping

1. Climbing over barriers to gain entry
2. One person holding the door for another
3. Two people using one access card
4. Secured area that only allows one person through at a time

6. True or False: A CCTV system can record audio in addition to video.

7. Multiple Choice: Which of the following can be a physical barrier in a high-security environment?
- a) Turnstile
- b) Moat
- c) Metal Detector
- d) All of the above

8. Fill in the Blank: A _____ is an electronic system that manages, monitors, and controls access points.

9. Short Answer: Describe the basic concept of multi-factor authentication (MFA).

10. Multiple Choice: In terms of physical security, what does the abbreviation "EAS" stand for?
- a) Easy Access System
- b) Electronic Access Security
- c) Electronic Article Surveillance
- d) Emergency Alert System

11. True or False: A cipher lock requires a physical key for operation.

12. Matching:
a. Proximity Card
b. Biometric Scan
c. Keypad
d. Tailgating
1. Unauthorized entry by following someone
2. Authentication by entering a numerical code
3. Authentication using physiological characteristics
4. RFID-based access card

13. Fill in the Blank: CCTV stands for _____.

14. Short Answer: What are the two main types of barriers used for vehicle control?

15. Multiple Choice: What type of glass is typically used in secure environments to resist breaking?
- a) Tempered
- b) Laminated
- c) Plexiglass
- d) Single-pane

16. True or False: A mantrap is designed to allow only one person to pass through at a time.

17. Fill in the blank: The practice of designing environments to deter crime is known as _____.

18. Match the following:
a. Turnstiles
b. Biometric Scanner
c. EAS
d. HVAC
1. Heating, Ventilation, and Air Conditioning
2. Crowd flow
3. Electronic Article Surveillance
4. Fingerprint or retina scan

19. Multiple Choice: Which of these is NOT a type of surveillance camera?
- a) CCTV
- b) PTZ camera
- c) DSLR
- d) IP camera

20. Short Answer: Describe one advantage and one disadvantage of using biometric authentication methods.

21. True or False: Crash bars are designed to allow for quick exit but prevent unauthorized entry.

22. Multiple Choice: What is the primary purpose of a red team in terms of physical security?
- a) Maintains alarm systems
- b) Tests the effectiveness of security measures
- c) Monitors video surveillance
- d) Controls access to secure areas

23. Fill in the blank: TEMPEST refers to standards for limiting _____.

24. Short Answer: What would you consider to be three essential elements of a secure physical perimeter?

25. Matching: Match the following types of security barriers with their uses:
a. Bollards
b. Fencing
c. Tire Shredders
d. Turnstile
1. Crowd control at a concert
2. Protecting a building from vehicle ramming
3. Preventing cars from entering without clearance
4. Securing the boundary of a property

26. Multiple Choice: What is a cipher lock?
- a) A lock that requires a numerical code
- b) A lock that uses cryptographic keys
- c) A lock that uses biometric data
- d) A lock that uses RFID technology

27. True or False: CCTV systems are generally considered more secure than IP cameras.

28. Fill in the blank: EAS stands for _____ in the context of physical security.

29. Short Answer: What is the primary function of fire suppression systems?

30. Multiple Choice: Which of the following is an environmental concern in physical security?
- a) Lighting
- b) Heating
- c) Landscaping
- d) All of the above

31. True or False: Swipe cards are also known as proximity cards.

32. Fill in the blank: Glass break detectors sense the sound frequency of _____.

33. Short Answer: Explain the purpose of an air gap in a secure environment.

34. Multiple Choice: NAC stands for what in terms of physical security?

- a) Network Access Control
- b) No Admission Control
- c) Network Address Classification
- d) Natural Access Conditions

35. Fill in the blank: K-rails are commonly used for _____.

36. True or False: HVAC systems have no relevance in physical security.

37. Short Answer: List two types of biometric authentication methods.

38. Multiple Choice: What is the primary focus of CPTED?
- a) Technical control measures
- b) Environmental design to deter threats
- c) Cybersecurity
- d) Automated security systems

39. Fill in the blank: VMS stands for _____ in the context of physical security.

40. Short Answer: Describe the purpose of a physical access log.

ANSWERS

1. True or False: Biometrics are foolproof and cannot be tricked. Answer: False - Biometric systems are sophisticated but not completely immune to deception.

2. Short Answer: What does CPTED stand for and what is its main focus? Answer: CPTED stands for Crime Prevention Through Environmental Design, focusing on deterring criminal behavior through environmental design.

3. Multiple Choice: Which of these is the least secure form of authentication? Answer: A) Something you know - Knowledge-based authentication like passwords are more vulnerable to theft, guessing, or forgetting.

4. Fill in the Blank: The main purpose of _____ is to alert if someone tries to gain unauthorized access to a facility. Answer: Alarm system - Its main purpose is to detect unauthorized access attempts and signal a breach.

5. Matching: a. Tailgating - b. Piggybacking - c. Mantrap - d. Fence-jumping - 1. Climbing over barriers to gain entry - 2. One person holding the door for another - 3. Two people using one access card - 4. Secured area that only allows one person through at a time. Answer: a. 1 - Tailgating is not correct, it's actually b. 2 b. 3 - Piggybacking refers to when two people use one access card. c. 4 - Mantrap is an area that allows only one person through at a time to prevent tailgating. d. 1 - Fence-jumping is climbing over barriers to gain entry.

6. True or False: A CCTV system can record audio in addition to video. Answer: False - While CCTV systems can have audio recording capabilities, they are primarily for video surveillance.

7. Multiple Choice: Which of the following can be a physical barrier in a high-security environment? Answer: D) All of the above - Turnstiles, moats, and metal detectors are all physical barriers that can be utilized in high-security environments.

8. Fill in the Blank: A _____ is an electronic system that manages, monitors, and controls access points. Answer: Access control system - Manages and monitors entry points to secure areas.

9. Short Answer: Describe the basic concept of multi-factor authentication (MFA). Answer: MFA - Multi-factor authentication uses multiple verification methods to increase security.

10. Multiple Choice: In terms of physical security, what does the abbreviation "EAS" stand for? Answer: C) Electronic Article Surveillance - EAS is a technology used to identify items as they pass through a secured area, primarily in retail.

11. True or False: A cipher lock requires a physical key for operation. Answer: False - Cipher locks use a code for unlocking, not a physical key.

12. Matching: a. Proximity Card - b. Biometric Scan - c. Keypad - d. Tailgating - 1. Unauthorized entry by following someone - 2. Authentication by entering a numerical code - 3. Authentication using physiological characteristics - 4. RFID-based access card. Answer: a. 4 - Proximity Card is an RFID-based access card. b. 3 - Biometric Scan involves authentication using physiological characteristics. c. 2 - Keypad requires entering a numerical code. d. 1 - Tailgating is unauthorized entry by following someone else.

13. Fill in the Blank: CCTV stands for _____. Answer: Closed-Circuit Television - CCTV is a surveillance technology for monitoring environments.

14. Short Answer: What are the two main types of barriers used for vehicle control? Answer: Barriers for vehicle control - Bollards and barriers.

15. Multiple Choice: What type of glass is typically used in secure environments to resist breaking? Answer: B) Laminated - Laminated glass is tougher and holds together when shattered, hence used in secure environments.

16. True or False: A mantrap is designed to allow only one person to pass through at a time. Answer: True - A mantrap is a security device that monitors and controls two interlocking doors to a small room that only allows one person to pass through at a time.

17. Fill in the blank: The practice of designing environments to deter crime is known as _____. Answer: CPTED (Crime Prevention Through Environmental Design) - A strategy for crime deterrence through environmental design.

18. Match the following: a. Turnstiles - b. Biometric Scanner - c. EAS - d. HVAC - 1. Heating, Ventilation, and Air Conditioning - 2. Crowd flow - 3. Electronic Article Surveillance - 4. Fingerprint or retina scan. Answer: Matching: a. 2 - Turnstiles manage crowd flow. b. 4 - Biometric Scanner is for fingerprint or retina scans. c. 3 - EAS stands for Electronic Article Surveillance. d. 1 - HVAC refers to Heating, Ventilation, and Air Conditioning systems.

19. Multiple Choice: Which of these is NOT a type of surveillance camera? Answer: C) DSLR - DSLR cameras are not typically used for surveillance purposes.

20. Short Answer: Describe one advantage and one disadvantage of using biometric authentication methods. Answer: Biometric authentication - Advantage: increased security through unique personal attributes; Disadvantage: potential errors or false readings and privacy concerns.

21. True or False: Crash bars are designed to allow for quick exit but prevent unauthorized entry. Answer: True - Crash bars are designed for safe exit during emergencies while preventing unauthorized access.

22. Multiple Choice: What is the primary purpose of a red team in terms of physical security? Answer: B) Tests the effectiveness of security measures - Red teams simulate adversary attacks to test the security.

23. Fill in the blank: TEMPEST refers to standards for limiting _____. Answer: Electromagnetic emissions - TEMPEST is a standard for preventing electronic eavesdropping.

24. Short Answer: What would you consider to be three essential elements of a secure physical perimeter? Answer: Essential elements of a secure perimeter - Fencing, surveillance, and controlled access points.

25. Matching: Match the following types of security barriers with their uses: a. Bollards - b. Fencing - c. Tire Shredders - d. Turnstile - 1. Crowd control at a concert - 2. Protecting a building from vehicle ramming - 3. Preventing cars from entering without clearance - 4. Securing the boundary of a property. Answer: Matching: a. 2 - Bollards protect buildings from vehicle ramming. b. 4 - Fencing secures the boundary of a property. c. 3 - Tire Shredders prevent cars from entering without clearance. d. 1 - Turnstile is used for crowd control.

26. Multiple Choice: What is a cipher lock? Answer: A) A lock that requires a numerical code - Cipher locks are opened with a code instead of a physical key or biometric data.

27. True or False: CCTV systems are generally considered more secure than IP cameras. Answer: False - CCTV systems are not inherently more secure than IP cameras; security depends on the specific use case and implementation.

28. Fill in the blank: EAS stands for _____ in the context of physical security. Answer: Electronic Article Surveillance - EAS is used in retail to prevent shoplifting.

29. Short Answer: What is the primary function of fire suppression systems? Answer: Fire suppression systems - Designed to detect and extinguish or contain fires to prevent property damage and loss of life.

30. Multiple Choice: Which of the following is an environmental concern in physical security? Answer: D) All of the above - Lighting, heating, and landscaping can all influence physical security by affecting visibility, access, and comfort.

31. True or False: Swipe cards are also known as proximity cards. Answer: False - Swipe cards require physical swiping through a reader, while proximity cards only need to be in the vicinity of the reader.

32. Fill in the blank: Glass break detectors sense the sound frequency of _____. Answer: Breaking glass - Glass break detectors are tuned to the frequency of glass shattering.

33. Short Answer: Explain the purpose of an air gap in a secure environment. Answer: Air gap - An air gap ensures no direct or indirect connection between secure and non-secure networks, preventing unauthorized access and data breaches.

34. Multiple Choice: NAC stands for what in terms of physical security? Answer: A) Network Access Control - NAC systems manage and restrict network access of devices to enhance security.

35. Fill in the blank: K-rails are commonly used for _____. Answer: Traffic and pedestrian separation - K-rails are barriers used to control and direct traffic flow.

36. True or False: HVAC systems have no relevance in physical security. Answer: False - HVAC systems can impact physical security by controlling airflow, which can be a concern for contaminant spread or in creating secure environments.

37. Short Answer: List two types of biometric authentication methods. Answer: Types of biometric methods - Fingerprint recognition and iris scanning.

38. Multiple Choice: What is the primary focus of CPTED? Answer: B) Environmental design to deter threats - CPTED's focus is on deterring criminal behavior through environmental design.

39. Fill in the blank: VMS stands for _____ in the context of physical security. Answer: Visitor Management System - VMS is a solution used to track and manage visitors.

40. Short Answer: Describe the purpose of a physical access log. Answer: Physical access log - A record used to track who enters and leaves a secure area, helping to ensure security and compliance.

11) Cloud Security

Cloud Service Models

The advent of cloud computing has heralded a new era in the realm of information technology, enabling organizations to access computational resources on a pay-as-you-go basis. The cloud service models, namely, Infrastructure as a Service (IaaS), Platform as a Service (PaaS), and Software as a Service (SaaS), form the foundation of cloud computing, each serving a unique purpose catering to different organizational needs. This section elucidates these service models and delves into the security ramifications inherent to each.

Infrastructure as a Service (IaaS)

IaaS provides the basic infrastructure services to the users. It offers virtualized computing resources over the internet, including servers, networking, storage, and data center space. Users have control over the underlying infrastructure while the cloud service provider manages the physical hardware.

Security Implications for IaaS:

1. Data Encryption: Data at rest and in transit should be encrypted to prevent unauthorized access.

2. Access Control: Implement robust access control policies to ensure that only authorized individuals can access the resources.

3. Network Security: Utilize firewalls, intrusion detection systems, and other network security measures to safeguard against network threats.

Advantages:

Cost-Efficiency: IaaS is cost-effective as it eliminates the upfront costs of setting up and managing an on-site data center.

Scalability: It provides a scalable environment that adapts to the user's needs.

Disaster Recovery: IaaS can be a component of a business continuity and disaster recovery strategy due to its quick scalability.

Security Strategies:

Regular Patching: Ensure that all the systems are up-to-date with the latest patches to mitigate known vulnerabilities.

Intrusion Detection Systems (IDS): Employ IDS to monitor network traffic for suspicious activity.

Vulnerability Assessment: Perform regular vulnerability assessments to identify and mitigate security risks.

More Security Strategies:

Access Controls: Implement stringent access control measures to ensure that only authorized personnel have access to critical infrastructure components.

Network Segmentation: Segment the network to contain potential security incidents and prevent lateral movement of threats within the environment.

Monitoring and Logging: Maintain extensive monitoring and logging to facilitate incident detection and forensic analysis.

Case Study:

Consider a scenario where a company adopts an IaaS model to host its applications. The company can choose to manage its own operating system, middleware, and data while the cloud service provider manages the underlying infrastructure. By following best practices such as regular patching, implementing intrusion detection systems, and conducting vulnerability assessments, the company can significantly enhance its security posture.

Platform as a Service (PaaS):

PaaS provides a platform and environment for developers to build applications and services. This service model includes infrastructure services, middleware, development tools, and database management systems.

Security Implications for PaaS:

1. Application Security: Ensure that applications developed are secure against common vulnerabilities like SQL injection and Cross-Site Scripting (XSS).

2. Database Security: Implement robust database security measures including encryption and regular vulnerability scanning.

3. Identity Management: Establish strong identity and access management policies to ensure secure access to the platform.

Advantages:

Rapid Development: PaaS provides a platform that accelerates the development, testing, and deployment of applications.

Access to Advanced Tools: Developers have access to a variety of tools that can enhance productivity and solve complex problems.

Collaborative Working: It facilitates a collaborative work environment for geographically distributed development teams.

Security Strategies:

Code Reviews: Conduct thorough code reviews to identify security flaws in the application code.

Secure Coding Practices: Adhere to secure coding practices to mitigate common vulnerabilities like SQL injection and Cross-Site Scripting (XSS).

Dependency Scanning: Ensure that third-party libraries and dependencies are secure and up-to-date.

More Security Strategies:

Runtime Environment Security: Ensure the security of the runtime environment by employing measures like application sandboxing and runtime application self-protection (RASP).

API Security: Protect APIs against common threats and vulnerabilities by employing measures like OAuth for authorization and input validation to prevent injection attacks.

Identity and Access Management (IAM): Implement robust IAM practices to ensure that only authorized individuals can access and modify the application and its data.

Case Study:

In a PaaS scenario, a software development firm can leverage the platform to accelerate the development and deployment of a web application. By employing secure coding practices, conducting code reviews, and ensuring the security of APIs, the firm can mitigate a host of potential security threats.

Software as a Service (SaaS):

SaaS delivers software applications over the internet on a subscription basis. The cloud service provider manages everything, including the application, data, runtime, middleware, and the underlying infrastructure.

Security Implications for SaaS:

1. Data Privacy: As data is hosted externally, it's crucial to have robust data privacy measures in place.

2. Authentication: Implement strong authentication mechanisms to ensure that only authorized individuals can access the application.

3. Data Loss Prevention (DLP): Employ DLP tools to monitor and control data transfer to prevent data leakage.

Advantages:

Reduced Time to Benefit: SaaS applications are usually available for use immediately after subscription.

Lower Costs: It lowers costs by providing applications on a subscription basis which includes maintenance, compliance, and support.

Automatic Updates: The cloud service provider manages updates and patches, reducing the burden on IT staff.

Security Strategies:

Data Encryption: Encrypt sensitive data both at rest and in transit to protect against unauthorized access.

Multi-Factor Authentication (MFA): Implement MFA to add an extra layer of security during the authentication process.

Regular Auditing: Conduct regular audits to ensure compliance with internal policies and regulatory requirements.

In essence, the security aspects of cloud service models are pivotal and require a well-structured approach to ensure the confidentiality, integrity, and availability of resources. By understanding the security implications and adopting robust security measures, organizations can securely transition to the cloud and reap the myriad benefits it offers.

More Security Strategies:

Data Loss Prevention (DLP): Employ DLP solutions to monitor and control data transfer across the organization's network.

Security Awareness Training: Educate users on the risks associated with SaaS applications and promote security awareness.

Third-party Risk Management: Assess the security posture of third-party vendors and ensure they comply with the organization's security standards.

Case Study:

In a SaaS setup, an organization might use a cloud-based Customer Relationship Management (CRM) system. By implementing data encryption, MFA, and regular auditing, the organization can safeguard sensitive customer data and ensure compliance with various regulatory requirements.

These expanded strategies and real-world scenarios further elucidate the security implications inherent in different cloud service models, thereby providing a comprehensive understanding that can guide organizations in making informed decisions while transitioning to or operating within the cloud environment.

In conclusion, while cloud service models offer myriad benefits in terms of scalability, cost-effectiveness, and flexibility, they also bring forth a set of security challenges. Understanding the security implications associated with each service model and implementing the necessary security measures is imperative to leverage the benefits of cloud computing securely.

Cloud Security Best Practices

1. Data Encryption:

   - At-rest Encryption: Ensure that data at rest is encrypted using strong encryption algorithms like AES-256. This includes databases, file storage, and any backups.

   - In-transit Encryption: Utilize protocols such as TLS to encrypt data as it travels across networks to prevent interception and unauthorized access.

2. Identity and Access Management (IAM):

   - User Authentication: Employ strong authentication mechanisms like Multi-Factor Authentication (MFA) to verify the identities of users accessing the cloud environment.

   - Role-based Access Control (RBAC): Implement RBAC to ensure that individuals have the least amount of access necessary to perform their jobs.

3. Regular Security Assessments:

   - Vulnerability Scanning: Conduct regular vulnerability scans to identify and fix security weaknesses.

   - Penetration Testing: Engage in periodic penetration testing to evaluate the robustness of the cloud environment against potential attacks.

4. Compliance and Certification:

   - Industry Standards Compliance: Ensure compliance with industry standards like ISO 27001, HIPAA for healthcare, or PCI DSS for payment card data.

   - Regular Audits: Conduct regular audits to assess the effectiveness of security controls and maintain compliance with required standards.

5. Incident Response and Monitoring:

   - Monitoring: Utilize cloud-native or third-party monitoring tools to keep an eye on the cloud environment's security posture.

   - Incident Response Plan: Establish a clear incident response plan to address any security incidents that may occur, ensuring rapid identification, containment, and remediation.

6. End-user Education:

   - Security Awareness Training: Conduct regular security awareness training to educate end-users about the potential risks and best practices in cloud security.

- Phishing Simulations: Carry out phishing simulation exercises to assess the readiness of the organization against social engineering attacks.

7. Network Security:
  - Firewalls and WAF: Employ firewalls and Web Application Firewalls (WAF) to control incoming and outgoing traffic.
  - DDoS Protection: Implement DDoS protection measures to safeguard against distributed denial-of-service attacks.

8. Data Loss Prevention (DLP):
  - DLP Policies: Establish DLP policies to monitor and control data transfer across the organization's network.

Case Study:

Consider a financial institution that has adopted a cloud-first strategy. By embracing the best practices outlined above, the institution can significantly enhance its security posture while ensuring compliance with stringent financial industry regulations like GLBA and SOX. Expand on the case study by detailing the process the financial institution went through to implement each of the security best practices, the challenges encountered, and the impact on the organization's security posture and regulatory compliance

These best practices form a solid foundation for securing cloud environments against a myriad of threats while ensuring adherence to required compliance standards, thereby instilling trust and confidence among stakeholders.

9. Patch Management:
  - Regular Patching: Ensure that all cloud-based systems and software are updated with the latest patches to fix any known vulnerabilities.
  - Automated Patch Management: Utilize automated patch management tools to streamline the patching process and ensure timely updates.

10. Configuration Management:
  - Configuration Auditing: Regularly audit configurations to ensure they adhere to the organization's security policies and standards.
  - Automated Configuration Management: Employ automated configuration management tools to maintain and enforce desired configurations.

11. Zero Trust Architecture:
  - Access Verification: Verify the identity of every user and device trying to access resources in your cloud environment, regardless of their location.
  - Micro-segmentation: Apply micro-segmentation to reduce the attack surface by segmenting workloads and applying appropriate security controls to each segment.

12. Cloud Access Security Brokers (CASBs):
  - Visibility and Control: Use CASBs to gain visibility into cloud application usage across the organization and enforce security policies.
  - Data Leakage Prevention: CASBs can help prevent data leakage by monitoring and controlling data in transit.

13. API Security:
  - API Gateways: Utilize API gateways to manage, monitor, and secure APIs, ensuring secure communication between services.
  - API Security Testing: Regularly test APIs for vulnerabilities and ensure they adhere to security standards like OAuth 2.0.

14. Container and Kubernetes Security:
  - Container Security Policies: Implement security policies to manage and secure containerized applications.
  - Runtime Security: Monitor container runtimes for any abnormal activities and enforce security policies.

15. Threat Intelligence:
  - Threat Feeds: Subscribe to threat intelligence feeds to stay updated on the latest threat vectors and vulnerabilities.
  - Threat Analysis: Analyze threat intelligence data to understand the threat landscape and make informed security decisions.

16. Security Information and Event Management (SIEM):

- Log Collection and Analysis: Collect and analyze logs from various cloud resources to detect and respond to security incidents.

- Incident Management: Use SIEM solutions for incident management, ensuring a structured approach to handling security incidents.

17. Backup and Recovery:

- Regular Backups: Conduct regular backups of critical data and ensure that backup copies are stored securely.

- Disaster Recovery Planning: Have a disaster recovery plan in place to ensure business continuity in the event of a major incident.

18. Cloud Native Security Tools:

- Utilization of Native Tools: Explore and utilize the security tools and services provided by the cloud service provider to enhance security posture.

19. Third-party Security Assessments:

- External Auditing: Engage third-party security firms to conduct independent security assessments and provide objective feedback on the cloud security posture.

20. Legal and Regulatory Compliance:

- Understanding Legal Obligations: Understand the legal and regulatory obligations pertaining to data security and privacy, and ensure compliance.

Securing Cloud-Based Applications: A Real-World Scenario

Scenario Background:

Consider a mid-sized e-commerce company, CloudShop, that has recently transitioned its operations to a cloud environment to manage the growing online demand. The company utilizes a mix of Software as a Service (SaaS) and Platform as a Service (PaaS) models to run its operations.

Stage 1: Identifying Security Requirements:

- Data Protection: Given the sensitive customer data handled by CloudShop, data protection is a priority. Encryption in transit and at rest, along with robust access control policies, are identified as crucial requirements.

- Compliance: Being in the e-commerce domain, CloudShop needs to comply with PCI DSS standards to handle credit card transactions securely.

- Application Security: Ensuring the security of the application layer against common threats like SQL injection, cross-site scripting is essential.

Stage 2: Implementing Security Measures:

- Access Controls: Implementing role-based access control (RBAC) to ensure that only authorized personnel have access to sensitive data.

- Encryption: Leveraging encryption tools provided by the cloud service provider to encrypt sensitive data both in transit and at rest.

- Security Monitoring: Setting up security monitoring tools to detect and alert on suspicious activities within the cloud environment.

Stage 3: Continuous Monitoring:

- Automated Scanning: Employing automated vulnerability scanning tools to identify and patch vulnerabilities promptly.

- Log Analysis: Utilizing Security Information and Event Management (SIEM) systems to analyze logs for unusual activities.

Stage 4: Incident Response:

- Incident Detection: The security team detects an unusual login attempt from a foreign IP address, indicating a possible brute force attack.

- Response: Initiating the incident response plan, the security team investigates the incident, blocks the malicious IP, and strengthens authentication mechanisms to prevent similar attacks.

Stage 5: Lessons Learned and Iteration:

- Review: Post-incident, a thorough review is conducted to understand the incident's root cause and to learn from the experience.
- Improvement: Based on the insights gained, CloudShop enhances its security measures, including implementing multi-factor authentication (MFA) and conducting regular security training for its staff.

Discussion Points:
- Discuss how CloudShop could further enhance its security posture?
- What additional challenges might CloudShop face as it continues to grow and evolve?
- How could CloudShop leverage emerging technologies like machine learning and AI to improve its security monitoring and incident response capabilities?

The scenario provides a practical insight into the multi-faceted approach required to secure cloud-based applications effectively. It emphasizes the importance of not only implementing robust security measures but also continuously monitoring, learning, and adapting to the evolving threat landscape.

Stage 6: Regulatory Compliance and Auditing:
- Compliance Assessment: CloudShop hires an external auditor to assess its compliance with PCI DSS and other relevant regulations. The assessment includes a thorough review of the cloud infrastructure, application security, and data handling practices.
- Remediation: Based on the auditor's findings, CloudShop undertakes a series of remediation activities to address identified gaps, such as enhancing data encryption and improving access control policies.
- Documentation: All compliance activities, remediation steps, and related documentation are meticulously recorded for future reference and for demonstrating compliance to regulatory bodies.

Stage 7: Employee Training and Awareness:
- Training Program: CloudShop initiates a comprehensive security awareness and training program for its employees. This program covers crucial topics like phishing awareness, secure coding practices, and data privacy principles.
- Continuous Learning: Regular updates and refresher courses are provided to ensure that the staff stays updated on the latest threats and best practices in cloud security.
- Security Culture: The training programs aim to foster a culture of security within the organization, encouraging employees to be vigilant and proactive in identifying and reporting security concerns.

Stage 8: Vendor and Third-party Security Assessment:
- Vendor Assessment: CloudShop conducts security assessments of its vendors, especially those with access to its cloud environment or customer data. The assessment includes reviewing the vendors' security policies, practices, and compliance with relevant standards.
- Third-party Security Tools: CloudShop also evaluates and implements additional third-party security tools to enhance its security posture. These tools provide capabilities like advanced threat detection, data loss prevention, and automated incident response.

Stage 9: Customer Communication and Transparency:
- Security Communication: CloudShop communicates its security measures and practices to its customers transparently, building trust. It also provides resources educating customers on securing their accounts and recognizing phishing attempts.
- Feedback Loop: CloudShop establishes channels for customers to report security concerns and provides timely responses to security-related inquiries.

Stage 10: Long-term Security Strategy and Scalability:
- Security Strategy: CloudShop develops a long-term security strategy that aligns with its business goals and the evolving threat landscape. The strategy encompasses technology, processes, and people, forming a holistic approach to cloud security.
- Scalability: As CloudShop grows, so does the complexity of its cloud environment. The security measures implemented are designed to scale with the business, ensuring continued protection against evolving threats.

Interactive Quiz: Cloud Security Knowledge

1. What does IaaS stand for?
   - a) Infrastructure as a System
   - b) Infrastructure as a Service
   - c) Internet as a Service
   - d) Integration as a Service
2. Which of the following is NOT a responsibility of the cloud customer in a PaaS model?
   - a) Application code
   - b) Middleware
   - c) Data
   - d) Runtime
3. Who is responsible for cloud security in the shared responsibility model?
   - a) Cloud Provider Only
   - b) Cloud Customer Only
   - c) Both
   - d) Neither
4. True or False: Data at rest is generally more vulnerable than data in transit.
5. True or False: SaaS offerings typically require the customer to maintain the application layer.
6. _____ is the technology that allows for secure communication over an insecure network.
7. AWS's managed firewall service is called _____.
8. Match the following cloud security threats with their descriptions:
   - A. Phishing Attacks
   - B. Misconfiguration
   - C. Insecure APIs
   - D. Insider Threat
   1) Exposed data due to incorrect settings
   2) Compromised credentials via deceptive emails
   3) Vulnerable interfaces and APIs
   4) Malicious actions by employees or partners
9. What is the role of a CASB?
   - a) Cloud Access Server Base
   - b) Cloud Access Security Broker
   c) Cloud Allocated Secure Backup
   - d) Cloud Application Server Backend
10. Which encryption model encrypts data before it is transferred to the cloud?
    - a) In-Transfer Encryption
    - b) At-Rest Encryption
    - c) Pre-Transfer Encryption
    - d) Post-Transfer Encryption

11. True or False: In a public cloud model, the cloud infrastructure is owned by a public cloud provider.
12. True or False: Zero Trust Architecture trusts no one and verifies everything.
13. Multi-Factor Authentication involves two or more of the following: something you know, something you _____, and something you _____.
14. The principle of _____ minimizes user access rights to only what's strictly required to complete a task.
15. Match the types of cloud deployment models with their definitions:
    - A. Private Cloud
    - B. Public Cloud
    - C. Hybrid Cloud
    - D. Community Cloud
    1) Serves multiple organizations with common concerns
    2) Mixture of on-premises and third-party cloud services
    3) Entirely within a single organization's control
    4) Services are rendered over a network open for public use
16. Which of these is not a cloud security certification?
    - a) CCSK
    - b) CCSP
    - c) CISSP
    - d) CSAP
17. What is the main objective of cloud data loss prevention?
    - a) To backup data
    - b) To prevent unauthorized data exposures
    - c) To encrypt data
    - d) To monitor network traffic
18. True or False: Containerization aids in application portability across multiple cloud environments.
19. True or False: All S3 buckets are private by default.
20. A _____ attack can bring down a cloud service by overwhelming it with traffic.
21. Azure's identity and access management service is called _____.
22. Match the following cloud providers with their popular services:
    - A. AWS
    - B. Azure
    - C. Google Cloud Platform

1) Google Kubernetes Engine
2) EC2
3) Azure Virtual Machines

23. Which compliance certification is focused on healthcare data in the United States?
- a) GDPR
- b) PCI DSS
- c) HIPAA
- d) ISO 27001

24. Which cloud model involves leasing a server or resources from a cloud provider?
- a) PaaS
- b) IaaS
- c) CaaS
- d) SaaS

25. True or False: Cloud bursting is the act of switching to a different cloud provider for cost-saving reasons.

26. True or False: Cloud forensics involves investigating and analyzing data in a cloud environment to collect evidence for cyber crimes.

27. Google Cloud's open-source orchestration platform for microservices is called _____.

28. The practice of storing redundant data over multiple cloud service providers is known as _____.

29. Match the cloud service models with the correct descriptions:
- A. IaaS
- B. PaaS
- C. SaaS
- D. FaaS
1) Software delivered via a web browser
2) Infrastructure resources like computing and storage
3) Serverless computing
4) Development framework including operating systems, middleware, and runtime

30. Which cloud service is best for hosting a simple website?
- a) PaaS
- b) SaaS
- c) IaaS

- d) FaaS

31. True or False: All data transferred to the cloud is automatically encrypted.

32. True or False: GDPR affects only companies based in the European Union.

33. A _____ is a document that outlines the levels of service a cloud provider will offer.

34. _____ is the process of distributing traffic across multiple servers in the cloud.

35. Match the following security techniques with their purpose:
- A. Encryption
- B. Tokenization
- C. Access Control
- D. Audit Logging
1) Keeping track of who did what, when, and where
2) Converting data into a different format to protect it
3) Limiting who can access what
4) Scrambling data so only authorized parties can read it

36. What is the primary reason for data masking in the cloud?
- a) Monitoring
- b) Compliance
- c) Privacy
- d) Optimization

37. Which cloud computing risk involves losing access to your data or services?
- a) Lock-in
- b) Downtime
- c) Cost
- d) Security

38. True or False: Federated identity allows users to use the same credentials on multiple platforms.

39. True or False: End-to-end encryption secures data from the moment it leaves the source until it reaches its destination.

40. Using multiple cloud providers to minimize the risk of widespread data loss or downtime is called _____.

ANSWERS

1. What does IaaS stand for? - a) Infrastructure as a System - b) Infrastructure as a Service - c) Internet as a Service - d) Integration as a Service. Answer: b) Infrastructure as a Service - Explanation: IaaS stands for Infrastructure as a Service, providing virtualized computing resources over the internet.

2. Which of the following is NOT a responsibility of the cloud customer in a PaaS model? - a) Application code - b) Middleware - c) Data - d) Runtime. Answer: b) Middleware - Explanation: Middleware is typically managed by the PaaS provider, not the customer.

3. Who is responsible for cloud security in the shared responsibility model? - a) Cloud Provider Only - b) Cloud Customer Only - c) Both - d) Neither. Answer: c) Both - Explanation: In the shared responsibility model, both the cloud provider and the customer share responsibilities for security.

4. True or False: Data at rest is generally more vulnerable than data in transit. Answer: False - Explanation: Data in transit is generally more vulnerable due to the various points it crosses.

5. True or False: SaaS offerings typically require the customer to maintain the application layer. Answer: False - Explanation: In SaaS, the application layer is typically managed by the cloud provider.

6. _____ is the technology that allows for secure communication over an insecure network. Answer: Encryption - Explanation: Encryption is used for securing communications over an insecure network.

7. AWS's managed firewall service is called _____. Answer: AWS WAF - Explanation: AWS WAF is the managed firewall service by AWS.

8. Match the following cloud security threats with their descriptions: - A. Phishing Attacks - B. Misconfiguration - C. Insecure APIs - D. Insider Threat - 1) Exposed data due to incorrect settings - 2) Compromised credentials via deceptive emails - 3) Vulnerable interfaces and APIs - 4) Malicious actions by employees or partners Answer: A-2, B-1, C-3, D-4 - Explanation: The threats are matched correctly to their descriptions.

9. What is the role of a CASB? - a) Cloud Access Server Base - b) Cloud Access Security Broker - c) Cloud Allocated Secure Backup - d) Cloud Application Server Backend Answer: b) Cloud Access Security Broker - Explanation: CASB stands for Cloud Access Security Broker, which acts as a gateway between on-prem and cloud services.

10. Which encryption model encrypts data before it is transferred to the cloud? - a) In-Transfer Encryption - b) At-Rest Encryption - c) Pre-Transfer Encryption - d) Post-Transfer Encryption Answer: c) Pre-Transfer Encryption - Explanation: Pre-Transfer Encryption involves encrypting data before it is moved to the cloud.

11. True or False: In a public cloud model, the cloud infrastructure is owned by a public cloud provider. Answer: True - Explanation: In a public cloud, the infrastructure is indeed owned by a public cloud provider.

12. True or False: Zero Trust Architecture trusts no one and verifies everything. Answer: True - Explanation: Zero Trust Architecture is about not trusting any entity and verifying everything.

13. Multi-Factor Authentication involves two or more of the following: something you know, something you _____, and something you _____. Answer: have, are - Explanation: Multi-Factor Authentication involves something you know, something you have, and something you are.

14. The principle of _____ minimizes user access rights to only what's strictly required to complete a task. Answer: Least Privilege - Explanation: The principle of Least Privilege is about granting minimum access rights for tasks.

15. Match the types of cloud deployment models with their definitions: - A. Private Cloud - B. Public Cloud - C. Hybrid Cloud - D. Community Cloud - 1) Serves multiple organizations with common concerns - 2) Mixture of on-premises and third-party cloud services - 3) Entirely within a single organization's control - 4) Services are rendered over a network open for public use Answer: A-3, B-4, C-2, D-1 - Explanation: These cloud deployment models are matched to their correct definitions.

16. Which of these is not a cloud security certification? - a) CCSK - b) CCSP - c) CISSP - d) CSAP. Answer: d) CSAP - Explanation: CSAP is not a recognized cloud security certification.

17. What is the main objective of cloud data loss prevention? - a) To backup data - b) To prevent unauthorized data exposures - c) To encrypt data - d) To monitor network traffic Answer: b) To prevent unauthorized data exposures - Explanation: The main objective of cloud data loss prevention is to prevent unauthorized data exposure.

18. True or False: Containerization aids in application portability across multiple cloud environments. Answer: True - Explanation: Containerization helps in making applications portable across various cloud environments.

19. True or False: All S3 buckets are private by default. Answer: False - Explanation: AWS S3 buckets are public by default.

20. A _____ attack can bring down a cloud service by overwhelming it with traffic. Answer: DDoS - Explanation: A DDoS (Distributed Denial of Service) attack overwhelms a service with excessive traffic.

21. Azure's identity and access management service is called _____. Answer: Azure AD - Explanation: Azure AD (Active Directory) is Azure's IAM service.

22. Match the following cloud providers with their popular services: - A. AWS - B. Azure - C. Google Cloud Platform - 1) Google Kubernetes Engine - 2) EC2 - 3) Azure Virtual Machines Answer: A-2, B-3, C-1 - Explanation: These cloud providers are matched to their respective popular services.

23. Which compliance certification is focused on healthcare data in the United States? - a) GDPR - b) PCI DSS - c) HIPAA - d) ISO 27001 Answer: c) HIPAA - Explanation: HIPAA is the compliance certification focused on healthcare data in the United States.

24. Which cloud model involves leasing a server or resources from a cloud provider? - a) PaaS - b) IaaS - c) CaaS - d) SaaS Answer: b) IaaS - Explanation: IaaS (Infrastructure as a Service) involves leasing a server or resources from a cloud provider.

25. True or False: Cloud bursting is the act of switching to a different cloud provider for cost-saving reasons. Answer: False - Explanation: Cloud bursting involves scaling out to a public cloud for handling peak loads.

26. True or False: Cloud forensics involves investigating and analyzing data in a cloud environment to collect evidence for cyber crimes. Answer: True - Explanation: Cloud forensics is about collecting evidence for cybercrimes in a cloud environment.

27. Google Cloud's open-source orchestration platform for microservices is called _____. Answer: Kubernetes - Explanation: Google Kubernetes Engine is Google Cloud's open-source orchestration platform for microservices.

28. The practice of storing redundant data over multiple cloud service providers is known as _____. Answer: Cloud Spanning - Explanation: Cloud Spanning involves storing redundant data over multiple cloud providers.

29. Match the cloud service models with the correct descriptions: - A. IaaS - B. PaaS - C. SaaS - D. FaaS - 1) Software delivered via a web browser - 2) Infrastructure resources like computing and storage - 3) Serverless computing - 4) Development framework including operating systems, middleware, and runtime Answer: A-2, B-4, C-1, D-3 - Explanation: These cloud service models are correctly matched to their definitions.

30. Which cloud service is best for hosting a simple website? - a) PaaS - b) SaaS - c) IaaS - d) FaaS Answer: a) PaaS - Explanation: PaaS is generally best for hosting simple websites as it provides all the necessary tools and services.

31. True or False: All data transferred to the cloud is automatically encrypted. Answer: False - Explanation: Not all data transferred to the cloud is automatically encrypted.

32. True or False: GDPR affects only companies based in the European Union. Answer: False - Explanation: GDPR affects any company that deals with EU citizens' data, not just those based in the EU.

33. A _____ is a document that outlines the levels of service a cloud provider will offer. Answer: SLA (Service Level Agreement) - Explanation: An SLA outlines the levels of service a cloud provider will offer.

34. _____ is the process of distributing traffic across multiple servers in the cloud. Answer: Load Balancing - Explanation: Load balancing is the practice of distributing traffic across multiple servers.

35. Match the following security techniques with their purpose: - A. Encryption - B. Tokenization - C. Access Control - D. Audit Logging - 1) Keeping track of who did what, when, and where - 2) Converting data into a different format to protect it - 3) Limiting who can access what - 4) Scrambling data so only authorized parties can read it Answer: A-4, B-2, C-3, D-1 - Explanation: These security techniques are correctly matched with their purposes.

36. What is the primary reason for data masking in the cloud? - a) Monitoring - b) Compliance - c) Privacy - d) Optimization Answer: c) Privacy - Explanation: Data masking is primarily done for privacy reasons.

37. Which cloud computing risk involves losing access to your data or services? - a) Lock-in - b) Downtime - c) Cost - d) Security Answer: b) Downtime - Explanation: Downtime is a risk involving losing access to your data or services.

38. True or False: Federated identity allows users to use the same credentials on multiple platforms. Answer: True - Explanation: Federated identity allows the use of the same credentials across different platforms.

39. True or False: End-to-end encryption secures data from the moment it leaves the source until it reaches its destination. Answer: True - Explanation: End-to-end encryption does secure

40. Using multiple cloud providers to minimize the risk of widespread data loss or downtime is called _____.
Answer: Multi-cloud strategy - Explanation: Using multiple cloud providers to minimize risks is called a multi-cloud strategy.

12) Endpoint Security

Endpoint Protection Technologies

In the modern digital landscape, the paramount importance of robust endpoint protection can't be overstated. As the gateways to your network, endpoints are the frontline defense against malicious actors aiming to infiltrate your systems. This section explores various technologies crucial for robust endpoint protection.

1. Antivirus Software:
   - Definition and Importance: A basic explanation of what antivirus software is and why it's crucial for endpoint protection.
   - Working Mechanism: How antivirus software detects and deals with threats.
   - Popular Antivirus Software: A look at some of the reputable antivirus software available in the market.
2. Firewalls:
   - Definition and Importance: Explaining what firewalls are and their role in endpoint protection.
   - Types of Firewalls: Discussing various types of firewalls and how they operate.
   - Configuring Firewalls: Guidance on how firewalls should be configured for optimum protection.
3. Intrusion Prevention Systems (IPS):
   - Definition and Importance: An insight into what IPS is and why it's necessary.
   - Working Mechanism: How IPS monitors network traffic to prevent malicious activity.
   - IPS vs IDS: Distinguishing between Intrusion Prevention Systems and Intrusion Detection Systems.
4. Endpoint Detection and Response (EDR):
   - Definition and Importance: Discussing what EDR is and why it's crucial for modern endpoint protection.
   - Working Mechanism: Explaining how EDR software detects and responds to threats on endpoints.
   - EDR Tools: A brief overview of popular EDR tools in the market.
5. Patch Management:
   - Definition and Importance: Discussing the importance of keeping software up-to-date to prevent security breaches.
   - Automated Patch Management: The benefits of automating patch management and tools that can help.
6. Mobile Device Management (MDM):
   - Definition and Importance: An overview of MDM and its relevance in endpoint protection.
   - MDM Solutions: Discussing various MDM solutions and how they enhance endpoint security.
7. Virtual Private Networks (VPNs):
   - Definition and Importance: Explaining what VPNs are and how they contribute to endpoint security.
   - Secure Web Gateways (SWGs): Discussing the role of SWGs in secure internet access.

Each of these technologies plays a crucial role in creating a fortified defense against the myriad of cyber threats lurking in the digital realm. By understanding and effectively leveraging these technologies, organizations can significantly enhance their endpoint security posture, ensuring a safer, more secure operational enviroCertainly, let's delve deeper into each of these technologies for a more comprehensive understanding:

1. Advanced Threat Detection:
   - Heuristic Analysis: Explain how heuristic analysis helps in detecting unknown viruses by analyzing the behavior and code structure.
   - Sandboxing: Discussing the sandboxing feature where suspicious files are executed in a safe environment to observe their behavior.
   - Machine Learning and AI: Exploration of how modern antivirus solutions utilize machine learning and AI to improve threat detection.
2. Performance Optimization:
   - System Resource Usage: Discussing the impact of antivirus software on system performance and how modern solutions optimize resource usage.

- Cloud-Based Scanning: Explanation of cloud-based scanning and how it offloads some of the processing burden from the endpoint.

3. Reporting and Analytics:

   - Threat Intelligence Feeds: Discussing how antivirus software can integrate with threat intelligence feeds for up-to-date information on new threats.

   - Logging and Reporting: Covering the importance of logging and reporting for incident response and compliance purposes.

Firewalls:

1. Configuration and Management:

   - Centralized Management: Discussion on centralized management solutions for firewalls across an organization.

   - Change Management: Covering the importance of proper change management procedures when modifying firewall rules.

2. Monitoring and Analysis:

   - Traffic Analysis: Discussing how traffic analysis helps in identifying potential security issues.

   - Alerting and Notification: Covering the alerting and notification features that help in early detection of security incidents.

3. Integration with Other Technologies:

   - Unified Threat Management (UTM): Discussion on UTM solutions that integrate firewalls with other security technologies.

   - Security Information and Event Management (SIEM): Discussing the integration of firewalls with SIEM solutions for centralized logging and analysis.

Intrusion Prevention Systems (IPS):

1. Tuning and Optimization:

   - Signature Tuning: Discussing the importance of tuning signatures to reduce false positives.

   - Threat Intelligence Integration: Covering the integration of threat intelligence feeds to improve detection capabilities.

2. Incident Response Integration:

   - Automated Response: Discussion on automated response capabilities of IPS solutions.

   - Integration with Incident Response Platforms: Covering how IPS integrates with incident response platforms for streamlined incident management.

3. Performance and Scalability:

   - Throughput and Latency: Discussing the impact of IPS on network performance.

   - Scalable Solutions: Covering scalable IPS solutions that can grow with the organization.

Endpoint Detection and Response (EDR):

1. Continuous Monitoring:

   - Real-Time Analysis: Explanation of how continuous monitoring and real-time analysis help in identifying suspicious activities as they occur.

   - Historical Data Analysis: Discussing the importance of historical data analysis in identifying patterns and investigating incidents.

2. Threat Hunting:

   - Proactive Identification: Delving into how threat hunting techniques are employed to proactively identify potential issues before they escalate.

   - Indicator of Compromise (IoC) Searches: Explanation of IoC searches and how they contribute to threat hunting efforts.

3. Response Automation:

   - Automated Remediation: Discussing how EDR solutions can automate the remediation process to reduce the response time.

- Integration with SOAR Platforms: Covering the integration of EDR with Security Orchestration, Automation, and Response (SOAR) platforms for enhanced incident response capabilities.

Mobile Device Management (MDM):

1. Device Enrollment:
   - Automatic Enrollment: Explaining how automatic enrollment simplifies the onboarding process for new devices.
   - User-Initiated Enrollment: Discussion on user-initiated enrollment and its benefits.
2. Policy Enforcement:
   - Security Policies: Covering the enforcement of security policies on mobile devices to ensure compliance.
   - Compliance Checks: Discussing how compliance checks are performed to ensure devices adhere to organizational policies.
3. Remote Management:
   - Remote Lock/Wipe: Explaining the importance of remote lock and wipe capabilities in case of device loss or theft.
   - Remote Configuration: Discussion on remote configuration and management of mobile devices to ensure security and compliance.

Data Loss Prevention (DLP):

1. Content Inspection:
   - Deep Content Inspection: Delving into how deep content inspection helps in identifying sensitive data.
   - Context-Aware Fingerprinting: Explanation of context-aware fingerprinting and how it contributes to accurate detection of sensitive data.
2. Policy Enforcement:
   - Policy Definition: Discussing how policies are defined to identify and protect sensitive data.
   - Real-Time Enforcement: Covering real-time enforcement of DLP policies to prevent data leakage.
3. Reporting and Auditing:
   - Incident Reporting: Discussing the importance of incident reporting in DLP solutions for compliance and incident response.
   - Audit Trail: Explanation of how DLP solutions provide an audit trail for investigative purposes.

Mobile Device Management

Mobile Device Management Software:

1. Deployment and Enrollment:
   - Automatic Enrollment: Simplifying the onboarding process for new devices by leveraging automatic enrollment features.
   - User-Initiated Enrollment: Allowing users to enroll their devices while adhering to organizational security policies.
2. Policy Enforcement:
   - Security Policies: Creating and enforcing security policies to ensure mobile devices comply with organizational standards.
   - Compliance Checks: Performing regular compliance checks to ensure continued adherence to security policies.
3. Remote Management:
   - Remote Lock/Wipe: Discussing the significance of remote lock and wipe capabilities in ensuring data security.
   - Remote Configuration: Facilitating remote configuration and management of mobile devices to maintain security and compliance.

Mobile Application Management (MAM):

1. App Deployment:
   - Enterprise App Store: Establishing an enterprise app store to control the distribution of applications on mobile devices.
   - Whitelisting and Blacklisting: Utilizing whitelisting and blacklisting to manage application access on mobile devices.
2. App Security:
   - App Wrapping: Implementing app wrapping to secure existing mobile applications.

- Containerization: Utilizing containerization to segregate corporate and personal data on mobile devices.

3. Monitoring and Analytics:
 - Usage Monitoring: Monitoring app usage to identify potential security risks.
 - Analytics: Leveraging analytics to gain insights into app performance and security.

BYOD Policies:

1. Policy Creation:
 - Acceptable Use: Defining acceptable use policies to clarify what is permitted with personal mobile devices.
 - Security Requirements: Establishing security requirements for personal mobile devices accessing corporate resources.

2. User Education and Awareness:
 - Training: Conducting training to educate users on security best practices for mobile device usage.
 - Awareness Campaigns: Running awareness campaigns to keep users informed of emerging threats and security protocols.

3. Compliance and Auditing:
 - Compliance Monitoring: Implementing monitoring solutions to ensure compliance with BYOD policies.
 - Auditing: Conducting regular audits to assess the effectiveness of mobile device management and BYOD policies.

Advanced Security Features:

1. Advanced Authentication:
 - Biometric Authentication: Leveraging fingerprint and facial recognition for secure access.
 - Multi-Factor Authentication (MFA): Utilizing MFA to add an extra layer of security during device or application access.

2. Encryption:
 - Data Encryption: Implementing data encryption to protect sensitive data stored on mobile devices.
 - Communication Encryption: Ensuring that data transmitted between mobile devices and organizational networks is encrypted.

3. VPN and Secure Connections:
 - VPN Usage: Advocating for the use of Virtual Private Networks (VPNs) to secure communications.
 - Secure Wi-Fi Connections: Ensuring secure Wi-Fi connections to prevent unauthorized access and data breaches.

4. Endpoint Detection and Response (EDR):
 - Real-time Monitoring: Utilizing EDR solutions for real-time monitoring of mobile devices to detect and respond to threats.
 - Behavioral Analysis: Employing behavioral analysis to identify suspicious activities on mobile devices.

5. Threat Prevention:
 - Malware Protection: Deploying anti-malware solutions to protect against malicious software.
 - Phishing Prevention: Implementing measures to prevent phishing attacks targeting mobile devices.

6. Patch and Update Management:
 - Regular Updates: Ensuring that mobile devices are regularly updated to patch known vulnerabilities.
 - Automated Patch Management: Automating the patch management process to maintain the security of mobile devices.

Case Studies:

1. Case Study 1:
 - Scenario: Discussing a scenario where an organization effectively managed mobile devices to prevent a major security breach.
 - Lessons Learned: Elucidating the lessons learned and best practices derived from the scenario.

2. Case Study 2:
 - Scenario: Describing a case where lack of mobile device management led to a data breach.
 - Lessons Learned: Highlighting the importance of robust mobile device management through the lessons learned from the incident.

3. Case Study 3:
   - Scenario: Exploring how an organization improved operational efficiency through effective mobile device management.
   - Lessons Learned: Deriving best practices for enhancing both security and efficiency through mobile device management.

Real-world Scenario: Protecting Endpoints in a BYOD Environment

Introduction:

In recent years, the Bring Your Own Device (BYOD) policy has gained significant traction among modern organizations seeking to foster a flexible and innovative work environment. However, this policy poses notable security challenges, necessitating robust endpoint security measures to safeguard organizational assets. This scenario delves into the experiences of TechCorp Inc., a burgeoning tech startup, as it navigates the intricacies of implementing a BYOD policy while ensuring paramount security of its digital resources.

Stage 1: Situation Assessment

TechCorp Inc. recognized the myriad benefits of a BYOD policy, including enhanced productivity, cost savings, and employee satisfaction. However, the security team was acutely aware of the associated risks, particularly the exposure of organizational data to various cyber threats. The challenge lay in implementing a BYOD policy that would not compromise the organization's security posture.

Stage 2: Initial Preparations

Before rolling out the BYOD policy, the security team at TechCorp Inc. undertook a meticulous preparation phase. This involved:

1. Conducting a thorough risk assessment to understand the potential threats and vulnerabilities.
2. Drafting a comprehensive BYOD policy outlining the security requirements, user responsibilities, and acceptable use.
3. Selecting suitable endpoint protection technologies including mobile device management (MDM) software, antivirus solutions, and encryption tools.

Stage 3: Implementation

With a well-crafted policy and the requisite technologies in place, TechCorp Inc. commenced the implementation phase. This stage involved:

1. Installing and configuring the selected endpoint protection technologies on all employee devices intending to access the organizational network.
2. Conducting training sessions for employees to educate them on the BYOD policy, security best practices, and the use of the provided security tools.
3. Establishing a secure network access control system to ensure only authorized devices could access sensitive organizational resources.

Stage 4: Monitoring and Evaluation

Post-implementation, the security team engaged in continuous monitoring of the network and devices to detect and respond to any security incidents swiftly. This stage also involved:

1. Regularly reviewing and updating the BYOD policy to ensure it remained relevant and effective.
2. Evaluating the effectiveness of the implemented security measures through periodic security assessments and employee feedback.
3. Addressing any identified security gaps and enhancing the endpoint protection measures accordingly.

Stage 5: Challenges Encountered

Despite meticulous preparations, TechCorp Inc. encountered several challenges including:

1. Ensuring compliance with the BYOD policy among all employees.
2. Managing the diversity of devices and operating systems.
3. Responding to security incidents emanating from personal devices.

Stage 6: Solutions and Lessons Learned

The experiences of TechCorp Inc. offer valuable insights into the pragmatic application of endpoint security measures in a BYOD environment. The key solutions and lessons learned include:

1. The imperative for a well-articulated BYOD policy as a foundation for successful implementation.
2. The importance of continuous education and training for employees on security best practices.
3. The necessity for robust endpoint protection technologies tailored to the unique requirements of a BYOD environment.

Stage 7: Employee Training and Awareness

A crucial aspect of ensuring the success of the BYOD policy was fostering a culture of security awareness among employees. TechCorp Inc. invested in regular training sessions covering:

1. The dos and don'ts under the BYOD policy.
2. How to securely access and handle organizational data.
3. The procedure to report any security incidents or anomalies.

Stage 8: Regular Security Audits

To maintain a robust security posture, TechCorp Inc. instituted a schedule for regular security audits encompassing:

1. Review of access controls and permissions.
2. Analysis of network traffic for any unusual activity.
3. Assessment of compliance with the BYOD and endpoint security policies.

Stage 9: Incident Response Plan

Having an incident response plan was crucial for timely detection and mitigation of any security incidents. TechCorp Inc. developed a plan detailing:

1. The process for identifying and reporting security incidents.
2. The steps for containing, eradicating, and recovering from incidents.
3. Post-incident analysis to identify lessons learned and implement improvements.

Stage 10: Compliance with Legal and Regulatory Requirements

TechCorp Inc. also had to navigate the legal and regulatory landscape surrounding the use of personal devices for work purposes. This involved:

1. Ensuring compliance with data protection laws and industry regulations.
2. Addressing privacy concerns related to the monitoring and management of personal devices.
3. Documenting consent and acknowledgements from employees regarding the BYOD policy.

Stage 11: Continuous Improvement

The dynamic nature of cybersecurity necessitated a mindset of continuous improvement. TechCorp Inc. embraced this by:

1. Regularly reviewing and updating the BYOD and endpoint security policies.
2. Exploring new technologies and practices to enhance endpoint security.
3. Soliciting feedback from employees to identify areas for improvement.

Stage 12: Long-term Evaluation

A year into the implementation of the BYOD policy, TechCorp Inc. conducted a comprehensive evaluation to assess:

1. The impact of the policy on organizational security.
2. The cost-effectiveness of the BYOD policy.
3. Employee satisfaction and the overall adoption rate of the policy.

Stage 13: Expansion of Endpoint Security Measures

Encouraged by the positive outcomes, TechCorp Inc. considered expanding its endpoint security measures to include:

1. Advanced Threat Protection (ATP) solutions.
2. Enhanced mobile device management capabilities.
3. Integration of artificial intelligence and machine learning for proactive threat detection and response.

Stage 14: Stakeholder Engagement

Engaging stakeholders was crucial for garnering support and ensuring the success of the BYOD policy. This involved:

1. Regular communications with senior management to report on the status and effectiveness of the endpoint security measures.
2. Engaging with the IT department to ensure alignment with organizational technology strategies.
3. Soliciting feedback from employees to ensure the BYOD policy met their needs while maintaining security.

Interactive Quiz: Endpoint Security Management

1. Which of the following best describes endpoint security?
   a) Firewall Rules
   b) Intrusion Detection
   c) Device-Level Protection
   d) Network Monitoring
2. What is the primary goal of EDR (Endpoint Detection and Response)?
   a) Monitoring
   b) Remediation
   c) Detection
   d) Prevention
3. Antivirus is the only necessary component for endpoint security.
   - True / False
4. Sandboxing allows suspicious code to execute in a safe environment.
   - True / False
5. _____ is the process of keeping the software up-to-date to patch vulnerabilities.
6. A _____ is a device used to create an encrypted tunnel for secure communication.
7. Match the types of endpoint devices to their categories:
   - A) Smartphone 1) Peripheral
   - B) Printer   2) Mobile
   - C) Laptop   3) Workstation
   - D) Webcam   4) Network
8. What is the main advantage of application whitelisting?
   a) Speed
   b) Flexibility
   c) Security
   d) Cost
9. How does an IPS (Intrusion Prevention System) primarily function?
   a) Detects and alerts
   b) Detects and blocks
   c) Monitors and logs
   d) Authenticates and authorizes
10. Physical security measures are irrelevant for endpoint security.

   - True / False
11. Zero-day vulnerabilities are known flaws with no available fixes.
   - True / False
12. EPP stands for Endpoint Protection _____.
13. Data loss can be prevented by employing _____ prevention mechanisms at the endpoint.
14. Match the following solutions to their functionalities:
   - A) DLP 1) Malware Analysis
   - B) EDR 2) Data Loss Prevention
   - C) VPN 3) Secure Network Connection
   - D) Sandbox 4) Threat Detection
15. What should be done before deploying any endpoint security solution?
   a) Perform Risk Assessment
   b) Buy Licenses
   c) Disable Firewall
   d) None of the Above
16. What are the common types of endpoint devices in a corporate network?
17. Name two encryption methods used for securing endpoints.
18. Which of the following technologies can be used for mobile device management?
   a) MDM
   b) EMM
   c) Both
   d) Neither
19. Is it always better to block all outbound connections on an endpoint device?
   a) Yes
   b) No
20. USB port blocking is a method for enhancing endpoint security.
   - True / False
21. What is the main difference between IDS and IPS?
   a) One detects, the other prevents
   b) One is software, the other is hardware
   c) There is no difference
   d) One is outdated

22. Which one of these is NOT a security layer in defense-in-depth strategy?
    a) Physical
    b) Perimeter
    c) Temporal
    d) Application

23. What is multi-factor authentication and why is it important for endpoint security?

24. What does the principle of least privilege mean in the context of endpoint security?

25. DLP can prevent unauthorized access to sensitive data.
    - True / False

26. Mobile Device Management (MDM) solutions can enforce _____ policies.

27. A(n) _____ is a set of rules that specify what kinds of network communication are allowed or denied on an endpoint.

28. What is the most common method for spreading malware?
    a) Email attachments
    b) Social media
    c) Cloud storage
    d) All of the above

29. Which among these is a part of endpoint risk assessment?
    a) Vulnerability Scanning
    b) License Auditing
    c) Budget Analysis
    d) None of the above

30. List two examples of endpoint security best practices.

31. What are some challenges associated with endpoint security management?

32. Firewalls can be both hardware and software components.
    - True / False

33. A(n) _____ audit can reveal unauthorized endpoint devices in a network.

34. IoT devices often present unique endpoint security challenges due to their _____.

35. Which authentication method can be used for secure endpoint connections?
    a) Kerberos
    b) OAuth
    c) SAML
    d) All of the above

36. What does UEM stand for?
    a) Universal Endpoint Management
    b) Unified Endpoint Management
    c) User Endpoint Management
    d) None of the above

37. Air gapping a system makes it completely secure.
    - True / False

38. All antivirus solutions update their virus definitions automatically.
    - True / False

39. How does sandboxing enhance endpoint security?

40. Why is user training crucial for endpoint security?

ANSWERS

1. Which of the following best describes endpoint security? a) Firewall Rules b) Intrusion Detection c) Device-Level Protection d) Network Monitoring Answer: b) Infrastructure as a Service - Explanation: IaaS stands for Infrastructure as a Service, providing virtualized computing resources over the internet.

2. What is the primary goal of EDR (Endpoint Detection and Response)? a) Monitoring b) Remediation c) Detection d) Prevention Answer: b) Middleware - Explanation: Middleware is typically managed by the PaaS provider, not the customer.

3. Antivirus is the only necessary component for endpoint security. - True / False Answer: c) Both - Explanation: In the shared responsibility model, both the cloud provider and the customer share responsibilities for security.

4. Sandboxing allows suspicious code to execute in a safe environment. - True / False Answer: False - Explanation: Data in transit is generally more vulnerable due to the various points it crosses.

5. _____ is the process of keeping the software up-to-date to patch vulnerabilities. Answer: False - Explanation: In SaaS, the application layer is typically managed by the cloud provider.

6. A _____ is a device used to create an encrypted tunnel for secure communication. Answer: Encryption - Explanation: Encryption is used for securing communications over an insecure network.

7. Match the types of endpoint devices to their categories: - A) Smartphone 1) Peripheral - B) Printer 2) Mobile - C) Laptop 3) Workstation - D) Webcam 4) Network Answer: AWS WAF - Explanation: AWS WAF is the managed firewall service by AWS.

8. What is the main advantage of application whitelisting? a) Speed b) Flexibility c) Security d) Cost Answer: A-2, B-1, C-3, D-4 - Explanation: The threats are matched correctly to their descriptions.

9. How does an IPS (Intrusion Prevention System) primarily function? a) Detects and alerts b) Detects and blocks c) Monitors and logs d) Authenticates and authorizes Answer: b) Cloud Access Security Broker - Explanation: CASB stands for Cloud Access Security Broker, which acts as a gateway between on-prem and cloud services.

10. Physical security measures are irrelevant for endpoint security. - True / False Answer: c) Pre-Transfer Encryption - Explanation: Pre-Transfer Encryption involves encrypting data before it is moved to the cloud.

11. Zero-day vulnerabilities are known flaws with no available fixes. - True / False Answer: True - Explanation: In a public cloud, the infrastructure is indeed owned by a public cloud provider.

12. EPP stands for Endpoint Protection _____. Answer: True - Explanation: Zero Trust Architecture is about not trusting any entity and verifying everything.

13. Data loss can be prevented by employing _____ prevention mechanisms at the endpoint. Answer: have, are - Explanation: Multi-Factor Authentication involves something you know, something you have, and something you are.

14. Match the following solutions to their functionalities: - A) DLP 1) Malware Analysis - B) EDR 2) Data Loss Prevention - C) VPN 3) Secure Network Connection - D) Sandbox 4) Threat Detection Answer: Least Privilege - Explanation: The principle of Least Privilege is about granting minimum access rights for tasks. |

15. What should be done before deploying any endpoint security solution? a) Perform Risk Assessment b) Buy Licenses c) Disable Firewall d) None of the Above Answer: A-3, B-4, C-2, D-1 - Explanation: These cloud deployment models are matched to their correct definitions.

16. What are the common types of endpoint devices in a corporate network? Answer: d) CSAP - Explanation: CSAP is not a recognized cloud security certification.

17. Name two encryption methods used for securing endpoints. Answer: b) To prevent unauthorized data exposures - Explanation: The main objective of cloud data loss prevention is to prevent unauthorized data exposure. |

18. Which of the following technologies can be used for mobile device management? a) MDM b) EMM c) Both d) Neither Answer: True - Explanation: Containerization helps in making applications portable across various cloud environments.

19. Is it always better to block all outbound connections on an endpoint device? a) Yes b) No Answer: False - Explanation: AWS S3 buckets are public by default.

20. USB port blocking is a method for enhancing endpoint security. - True / False Answer: DDoS - Explanation: A DDoS (Distributed Denial of Service) attack overwhelms a service with excessive traffic.

21. What is the main difference between IDS and IPS? a) One detects, the other prevents b) One is software, the other is hardware c) There is no difference d) One is outdated Answer: Azure AD - Explanation: Azure AD (Active Directory) is Azure's IAM service.

22. Which one of these is NOT a security layer in defense-in-depth strategy? a) Physical b) Perimeter c) Temporal d) Application Answer: A-2, B-3, C-1 - Explanation: These cloud providers are matched to their respective popular services.

23. What is multi-factor authentication and why is it important for endpoint security? Answer: c) HIPAA - Explanation: HIPAA is the compliance certification focused on healthcare data in the United States.

24. What does the principle of least privilege mean in the context of endpoint security? Answer: b) IaaS - Explanation: IaaS (Infrastructure as a Service) involves leasing a server or resources from a cloud provider.

25. DLP can prevent unauthorized access to sensitive data. - True / False Answer: False - Explanation: Cloud bursting involves scaling out to a public cloud for handling peak loads.

26. Mobile Device Management (MDM) solutions can enforce _____ policies. Answer: True - Explanation: Cloud forensics is about collecting evidence for cybercrimes in a cloud environment.

27. A(n) _____ is a set of rules that specify what kinds of network communication are allowed or denied on an endpoint. Answer: Kubernetes - Explanation: Google Kubernetes Engine is Google Cloud's open-source orchestration platform for microservices.

28. What is the most common method for spreading malware? a) Email attachments b) Social media c) Cloud storage d) All of the above Answer: Cloud Spanning - Explanation: Cloud Spanning involves storing redundant data over multiple cloud providers.

29. Which among these is a part of endpoint risk assessment? a) Vulnerability Scanning b) License Auditing c) Budget Analysis d) None of the above Answer: A-2, B-4, C-1, D-3 - Explanation: These cloud service models are correctly matched to their definitions.

30. List two examples of endpoint security best practices. Answer: a) PaaS - Explanation: PaaS is generally best for hosting simple websites as it provides all the necessary tools and services.

31. What are some challenges associated with endpoint security management? Answer: False - Explanation: Not all data transferred to the cloud is automatically encrypted.

32. Firewalls can be both hardware and software components. - True / False Answer: False - Explanation: GDPR affects any company that deals with EU citizens' data, not just those based in the EU.

33. A(n) _____ audit can reveal unauthorized endpoint devices in a network. Answer: SLA (Service Level Agreement) - Explanation: An SLA outlines the levels of service a cloud provider will offer.

34. IoT devices often present unique endpoint security challenges due to their _____. Answer: Load Balancing - Explanation: Load balancing is the practice of distributing traffic across multiple servers.

35. Which authentication method can be used for secure endpoint connections? a) Kerberos b) OAuth c) SAML d) All of the above Answer: A-4, B-2, C-3, D-1 - Explanation: These security techniques are correctly matched with their purposes.

36. What does UEM stand for? a) Universal Endpoint Management b) Unified Endpoint Management c) User Endpoint Management d) None of the above Answer: c) Privacy - Explanation: Data masking is primarily done for privacy reasons.

37. Air gapping a system makes it completely secure. - True / False Answer: b) Downtime - Explanation: Downtime is a risk involving losing access to your data or services.

38. All antivirus solutions update their virus definitions automatically. - True / False Answer: True - Explanation: Federated identity allows the use of the same credentials across different platforms.

39. How does sandboxing enhance endpoint security? Answer: True - Explanation: End-to-end encryption does secure

40. Why is user training crucial for endpoint security? Answer: Multi-cloud strategy - Explanation: Using multiple cloud providers to minimize risks is called a multi-cloud strategy.

13) Endpoint Security

Advanced Network Security Concepts

Micro-Segmentation:

Micro-Segmentation is an advanced network security concept that involves breaking down the network into smaller isolated segments or zones. Each segment operates independently and has its own set of security policies and controls. This approach minimizes the attack surface and contains potential threats by preventing lateral movement across the network.

Threat Intelligence:

Threat intelligence involves collecting, analyzing, and disseminating information about emerging threats and vulnerabilities. It provides insights into the tactics, techniques, and procedures (TTPs) used by adversaries, helping organizations to better understand the threat landscape and to prepare for and respond to security incidents more effectively.

Secure Access Service Edge (SASE):

SASE combines network security and wide-area networking (WAN) capabilities in a single cloud-native service. It integrates various security services, including zero trust network access, firewall as a service (FWaaS), secure web gateway (SWG), and data loss prevention (DLP). SASE's cloud-native architecture allows for scalable, flexible, and secure connectivity and security services, making it an essential concept in modern network security.

Cloud-Native Security:

With the shift towards cloud environments, cloud-native security has become a critical aspect of network security. It involves securing the application stack, managing identities and access, ensuring data privacy, and complying with various regulatory requirements. Cloud-native security requires a different set of tools and practices compared to traditional network security, focusing on container security, microservices architecture, and API communications.

Security Orchestration, Automation, and Response (SOAR):

SOAR platforms enable organizations to collect data about security threats from various sources and to respond to low-level security events without human intervention. They provide a set of tools for incident response, automation, and orchestration, helping security teams to respond to incidents more quickly and efficiently.

Machine Learning and AI in Network Security:

Machine learning and artificial intelligence (AI) are increasingly being used in network security for anomaly detection, threat hunting, and predictive analytics. They can process vast amounts of data to identify patterns and detect threats, often before they impact the network.

VPN and Remote Access Security:

With remote work becoming more common, VPN and remote access security are crucial to ensure that remote connections to the network are secure. Implementing strong authentication, encryption, and secure tunneling protocols are essential to protect against unauthorized access and data breaches.

Certainly! Here's the continuation and elaboration on the topic of Advanced Network Security Concepts:

Zero Trust Architecture (ZTA):

Zero Trust Architecture (ZTA) operates on the principle of "never trust, always verify." It requires strict identity verification for every person and device trying to access resources in a network, regardless of whether they are sitting within or outside of the network perimeter. Zero Trust emphasizes the need to protect data and resources from both external and internal threats.

Behavioral Analytics:

Behavioral analytics in network security involves monitoring network behavior to identify unusual patterns that may signify a security threat. By establishing a baseline of normal network behavior, security solutions can detect anomalies more effectively and alert security personnel to potential issues.

Endpoint Detection and Response (EDR):

EDR solutions provide a set of tools to detect, investigate, and respond to potential security threats at the endpoint level. They collect and analyze data from endpoints to identify threat patterns, allowing for faster detection and response to security incidents.

Network Forensics:

Network forensics involves the capture, recording, and analysis of network events to discover the source of security attacks or other problem incidents. This can include analyzing network traffic, investigating log files, and examining network configurations.

Deception Technology:

Deception technology creates a false or deceptive environment to trick attackers and lure them away from real network assets. This can include deploying honeypots, fake network services, and other decoy systems to divert attackers from real targets and gather intelligence on their tactics.

Application Layer Security:

Application layer security focuses on ensuring the security of applications rather than the underlying network or operating system. This includes measures like input validation, session management, and securing application source code against common vulnerabilities such as SQL injection and cross-site scripting (XSS).

Data Loss Prevention (DLP):

DLP technologies prevent unauthorized access and sharing of sensitive data. They can be deployed on endpoints, networks, and storage systems to monitor and control data transfer and usage.

Intrusion Detection Systems (IDS) and Intrusion Prevention Systems (IPS):

IDS and IPS technologies monitor networks for malicious activities and take predefined actions to block or prevent those activities. While IDS is focused on detection, IPS extends to prevention by actively blocking potential threats.

Unified Threat Management (UTM):

UTM solutions consolidate multiple security functions into a single system to provide comprehensive network security. They can include firewall, anti-virus, anti-spam, VPN, intrusion detection, and other security functions.

Network Access Control

Network Access Control (NAC) is a crucial aspect of network security that focuses on ensuring that only authorized and compliant devices are allowed to access network resources. It's designed to protect networks from potential threats by enforcing security policies at the point of entry or access.

Components of NAC:

- Authentication: This is the first step in the NAC process. It verifies the identity of users and devices trying to access the network using credentials, digital certificates, or other authentication methods.
- Authorization: Post authentication, authorization determines what resources the users or devices can access based on predefined policies.
- Policy Enforcement Point (PEP): This is where access control policies are enforced. PEPs can be network devices like switches or firewalls.
- Policy Decision Point (PDP): The PDP evaluates policies and makes a decision on whether to grant or deny access.
- Policy Administration Point (PAP): This is where policies are created, managed, and stored.

Types of NAC Solutions:

- Pre-admission NAC: Controls access to the network by evaluating devices before they try to connect.
- Post-admission NAC: Monitors devices already on the network and ensures they remain compliant.

Benefits of NAC:

- Visibility: NAC provides visibility into who and what is connected to the network, which is crucial for security and compliance.
- Compliance Enforcement: Ensures that all devices comply with the organization's security policies before they are allowed on the network.

- Guest Networking: NAC allows for secure guest networking, ensuring that guests have limited access to network resources.
- Reduced Attack Surface: By controlling who and what can access the network, NAC significantly reduces the attack surface.

Implementation Challenges:
- Complexity: Implementing NAC can be complex due to the variety of devices and users that need to be managed.
- Cost: The cost of NAC solutions and the resources required to manage them can be high.
- Integration: Integrating NAC solutions with other network and security systems can be challenging.

Best Practices:
- Continuous Monitoring: Continuously monitor and assess the network to ensure that all connected devices remain compliant with security policies.
- Policy Development: Develop clear and concise policies that are easy to understand and enforce.
- Training and Awareness: Ensure that all users are aware of the importance of NAC and how to comply with NAC policies.
- Regular Updates and Patching: Keep the NAC solution and all network devices updated with the latest security patches.

Network Access Control is a foundational element in ensuring a secure and compliant network environment. By understanding and implementing NAC effectively, organizations can significantly enhance their network security posture and mitigate the risk of security breaches.

Advanced Configuration:

To truly harness the power of Network Access Control (NAC), it's important to dive into more advanced configurations. This may include setting up role-based access controls (RBAC), implementing machine learning for anomaly detection, and configuring automated responses to potential threats.

- Role-Based Access Control (RBAC): By assigning roles to users and devices, you can ensure that they only have access to the network resources necessary for their function. This minimizes the potential damage from accidental mishaps or malicious intent.
- Machine Learning and Anomaly Detection: Modern NAC solutions can utilize machine learning algorithms to learn normal network behavior and identify anomalies. This can provide early warning of potential security issues.
- Automated Responses: In the event of a security incident, automated responses can be configured to contain the threat. This might include isolating affected network segments or devices, alerting security personnel, or even initiating predefined remediation processes.

Interoperability with Other Security Solutions:

Integration with other security solutions like SIEM (Security Information and Event Management) systems, firewalls, and endpoint protection platforms can enhance the effectiveness of NAC.

- SIEM Integration: By forwarding NAC logs and alerts to a SIEM system, you can correlate NAC data with other security data for a holistic view of your security posture.
- Firewall Integration: Integrating NAC with firewalls can provide more granular access controls and enhanced security.
- Endpoint Protection Integration: NAC can work in tandem with endpoint protection solutions to ensure that devices are not only compliant at the point of access but remain secure over time.

Continuous Improvement:

It's important to regularly review and update NAC configurations to adapt to the evolving threat landscape and organizational changes. This includes reviewing access policies, updating the NAC solution with new features and security updates, and analyzing incident reports to identify areas for improvement.

Implementing Network Segmentation

Stage 1: Identifying the Need:
With a growing client base and an expanding network, TechnoCorp identified the need for enhanced security to protect sensitive data and ensure uninterrupted service. The IT team discovered that a flat network architecture posed

significant risks, including the potential for rapid malware propagation and unauthorized access to sensitive areas of the network.

Stage 2: Planning:

The planning phase involved a meticulous assessment of the current network, identification of assets, and understanding the traffic flow. The IT team also studied various network segmentation methodologies and decided on a strategy that involved creating separate segments for different departments and systems, with stringent access controls.

Stage 3: Design and Implementation:

A detailed design was drafted outlining the segmentation, rules, and policies for each segment. The implementation was carried out in phases to minimize disruptions. New VLANs were created, ACLs (Access Control Lists) were defined, and firewalls were configured to control traffic between segments. The Network Access Control (NAC) system was updated to align with the new structure.

Stage 4: Testing and Validation:

Post-implementation, extensive testing was conducted to ensure the segments were isolated as intended and that the rules were enforced. Various penetration testing tools were employed to identify potential loopholes, and adjustments were made accordingly.

Stage 5: Monitoring and Adjustment:

With the new segmented network in place, continuous monitoring was essential to ensure effectiveness and to identify any unauthorized attempts to bypass the segmentation. The monitoring also provided insights into any adjustments needed to cater to evolving business requirements.

Stage 6: Training and Awareness:

An integral part of the process was educating the staff about the changes, the importance of network segmentation, and the role they play in maintaining network security. Regular training sessions were conducted to ensure everyone was acquainted with the new system.

Stage 7: Review and Future Planning:

A post-implementation review was conducted to assess the effectiveness of the segmentation, lessons learned were documented, and plans for future enhancements were discussed.

Stage 8: Reflections and Lessons Learned:

Post-implementation, TechnoCorp invested time in reflecting on the entire process to glean valuable lessons. Some of the key takeaways included:

1. Importance of Planning: Adequate planning was crucial to the success of the project. It helped in anticipating potential challenges and devising strategies to address them.

2. Continuous Monitoring: The need for ongoing monitoring to ensure the effectiveness of the segmentation was highlighted. It also facilitated timely identification and response to any security incidents.

3. Staff Training: The role of staff training in ensuring compliance with the new security measures was evident. Educated employees were less likely to engage in practices that could jeopardize network security.

4. Flexibility: The ability to adapt to new findings and adjust the segmentation plan accordingly was essential. Flexibility in approach allowed for the refinement of the segmentation strategy.

5. Documentation: Comprehensive documentation of the entire process, from planning to implementation and review, proved invaluable for future reference and for the preparation of subsequent security projects.

Stage 9: Preparing for Future Security Challenges:

With the successful implementation of network segmentation, TechnoCorp started preparing for future security challenges. The experience gained provided a solid foundation for tackling other advanced network security projects. They began exploring additional security measures such as implementing advanced threat detection systems, enhancing their incident response capabilities, and exploring zero trust architecture principles.

Stage 10: Sharing Knowledge:

TechnoCorp believed in the importance of community engagement and knowledge sharing. They documented their experience in a white paper and shared it with the broader cybersecurity community. This not only contributed to the community but also positioned TechnoCorp as a thoughtful leader in network security.

Stakeholder Engagement:

Engaging stakeholders is a critical aspect of implementing network segmentation. This process involved numerous meetings, presentations, and documentation to ensure all stakeholders understood the benefits and implications of network segmentation. The IT team had to explain technical aspects in layman terms to non-technical stakeholders and ensure everyone was on the same page regarding the project's goals and timelines.

Budgeting and Resource Allocation:

Allocating resources for this project was a challenge. The organization needed to ensure that the necessary funds were available for purchasing new hardware, software, and also for training the IT staff. Budgeting also included allocating resources for unforeseen challenges and ensuring there was a buffer to address any unexpected costs.

Vendor Selection and Partnership:

Choosing the right vendors for networking hardware and software was another crucial step. This involved researching, vetting, and negotiating with vendors to ensure the organization was getting the best value and support. Establishing strong partnerships with vendors ensured a smoother implementation process and ongoing support.

Implementation Challenges:

During the implementation phase, several challenges were encountered. These included:

1. Configuration Issues: There were instances of misconfiguration which led to network downtimes. This required a robust troubleshooting and resolution process to minimize disruptions.

2. Compatibility Issues: Some legacy systems were not fully compatible with the new network architecture, requiring additional customization and workaround solutions.

3. Security Concerns: The reconfiguration of the network brought up several security concerns that needed immediate attention. Ensuring that all segments were securely isolated while maintaining necessary communication between segments was a meticulous task.

Training and Skill Development:

The IT staff underwent rigorous training to understand the new network architecture and the security implications of network segmentation. This training was crucial to ensure the successful maintenance and ongoing management of the segmented network.

Post-Implementation Review:

After the implementation was completed, a thorough review was conducted to identify any areas of improvement. This review included analyzing the implementation process, identifying any remaining security risks, and gathering feedback from end-users and stakeholders.

Continuous Improvement:

The lessons learned from this project were documented and shared across the organization to foster a culture of continuous improvement. The IT team now has a regular review process to identify any new challenges or opportunities for further improving network security.

Interactive Quiz: Network Security Protocols

1. Which of the following is considered a secure alternative to Telnet?
   - a) HTTP
   - b) SNMP
   - c) SSH
   - d) FTP
2. SSL has been succeeded by:
   - a) WEP
   - b) WPA
   - c) TLS
   - d) WPA2
3. IPSec can be used in both transport and tunnel mode.
   - True
   - False
4. SSL operates at the Network layer of the OSI model.
   - True
   - False

5. _____ provides data integrity for secure message transmission.

6. A common use case for _____ is to secure VPN traffic.

7. Match the protocol with its primary purpose.
   - A) HTTPS   1) File Transfer
   - B) FTPS   2) Secure Web Traffic
   - C) SNMPv3 3) Network Management
   - D) SSH   4) Secure Shell Access

8. Which of the following is a type of VPN protocol?
   - a) PPTP
   - b) DNS
   - c) ICMP
   - d) DHCP

9. The main purpose of RADIUS is:
   - a) Data encryption
   - b) Authentication and Authorization
   - c) File transfer
   - d) Routing

10. Kerberos uses tickets to authenticate and grant network services.
    - True
    - False

11. S/MIME is used for securing instant messaging.
    - True
    - False

12. Name at least two encryption algorithms commonly used in secure communication protocols.

13. What does LDAPS stand for?

14. What is the default port for HTTPS?
    - a) 80
    - b) 21
    - c) 22
    - d) 443

15. Which wireless security protocol has been deprecated due to its weaknesses?
    - a) WPA3
    - b) WPA2
    - c) WEP
    - d) WPA

16. FTP over SSH is known as FTPS.
    - True
    - False

17. The HSTS header ensures that a website can only be accessed over HTTPS.
    - True
    - False

18. _____ allows for secure email communications and operates at the Application layer of the OSI model.

19. _____ is a hybrid encryption protocol used in secure communications.

20. What type of encryption does SSL use?
    - a) Asymmetric only
    - b) Symmetric only
    - c) Both symmetric and asymmetric
    - d) Neither

21. Which of the following ports is typically used for SSH?
    - a) 20
    - b) 22
    - c) 23
    - d) 25

22. Describe the primary function of the 802.1X standard.

23. What is the purpose of using HMAC in secure communications?

24. LDAP is used to access and manage directory information.
    - True
    - False

25. SMTP is secure by default.
    - True
    - False

26. _____ is commonly used to secure wireless networks.

27. _____ is a protocol for securely accessing a remote computer.

28. Which of the following is a secure alternative to SNMPv2?
    - a) SNMPv1
    - b) SNMPv3
    - c) SNMPv4
    - d) SNMPv5

29. What is the secure version of HTTP?
    - a) HTTP 1.1
    - b) HTTPS
    - c) HTTP 2
    - d) HTTP Secure

30. How does the use of digital certificates enhance HTTPS?

31. What does the "S" in HTTPS stand for?

32. IPsec supports data encryption only.
    - True
    - False

33. Secure/Multipurpose Internet Mail Extensions (S/MIME) is used to secure email communications.
  - True
  - False

34. Which layer of the OSI model does TLS operate at?
  - a) Presentation
  - b) Session
  - c) Transport
  - d) Network

35. What is the main security function of SNMPv3?
  - a) Encryption
  - b) Authorization
  - c) Integrity
  - d) All of the above

36. HSTS is used to force browsers to make secure connections with a web server.
  - True
  - False

37. VPNs always encrypt data in transit.
  - True
  - False

38. _____ is a network protocol for secure file transfer over SSH.

39. The protocol _____ is used for secure web-based email transfer.

40. What does the protocol EAP generally secure?
  - a) FTP transfers
  - b) Wireless communications
  - c) SSH connections
  - d) Email

ANSWERS

1. Which of the following is considered a secure alternative to Telnet? a) HTTP b) SNMP c) SSH d) FTP Answer: c) SSH Explanation: SSH (Secure Shell) is a secure alternative to Telnet, offering encrypted communication channels.

2. SSL has been succeeded by: a) WEP b) WPA c) TLS d) WPA2. Answer: c) TLS Explanation: TLS (Transport Layer Security) is the successor to SSL (Secure Sockets Layer) for secure web communications.

3. IPSec can be used in both transport and tunnel mode. True / False. Answer: True Explanation: IPSec can indeed operate in both transport and tunnel modes, offering flexibility in securing IP communications.

4. SSL operates at the Network layer of the OSI model. True / False. Answer: False Explanation: SSL operates at the Transport Layer, not the Network Layer of the OSI model. |

5. _____ provides data integrity for secure message transmission. Answer: HMAC Explanation: HMAC (Hash-based Message Authentication Code) ensures data integrity during message transmission.

6. A common use case for _____ is to secure VPN traffic. Answer: IPSec Explanation: IPSec (Internet Protocol Security) is often used to secure VPN traffic.

7. Match the protocol with its primary purpose. A) HTTPS 1) File Transfer B) FTPS 2) Secure Web Traffic C) SNMPv3 3) Network Management D) SSH 4) Secure Shell Access Answer: A-2, B-1, C-3, D-4 Explanation: HTTPS is for secure web traffic, FTPS is for secure file transfer, SNMPv3 is for network management, and SSH is for secure shell access.

8. Which of the following is a type of VPN protocol? a) PPTP b) DNS c) ICMP d) DHCP Answer: a) PPTP Explanation: PPTP (Point-to-Point Tunneling Protocol) is a type of VPN protocol.

9. The main purpose of RADIUS is: a) Data encryption b) Authentication and Authorization c) File transfer d) Routing. Answer: b) Authentication and Authorization Explanation: RADIUS (Remote Authentication Dial-In User Service) is mainly used for authentication and authorization.

10. Kerberos uses tickets to authenticate and grant network services. True / False. Answer: True Explanation: Kerberos uses tickets to provide a secure method of authenticating users and services over a non-secure network.

11. S/MIME is used for securing instant messaging. True / False. Answer: False Explanation: S/MIME (Secure/Multipurpose Internet Mail Extensions) is actually used for securing email, not instant messaging.

12. Name at least two encryption algorithms commonly used in secure communication protocols. Answer: AES, RSA Explanation: AES (Advanced Encryption Standard) and RSA (Rivest-Shamir-Adleman) are commonly used encryption algorithms in secure communications.

13. What does LDAPS stand for? Answer: Lightweight Directory Access Protocol Secure Explanation: LDAPS stands for Lightweight Directory Access Protocol Secure. |

14. What is the default port for HTTPS? a) 80 b) 21 c) 22 d) 443. Answer: d) 443 Explanation: HTTPS commonly operates on port 443.

15. Which wireless security protocol has been deprecated due to its weaknesses? a) WPA3 b) WPA2 c) WEP d) WPA. Answer: c) WEP Explanation: WEP (Wired Equivalent Privacy) has been deprecated due to its weaknesses. |

16. FTP over SSH is known as FTPS. True / False. Answer: False Explanation: FTPS is FTP Secure, not FTP over SSH.

17. The HSTS header ensures that a website can only be accessed over HTTPS. True / False. Answer: True Explanation: HSTS (HTTP Strict Transport Security) ensures a website can only be accessed over HTTPS.

18. _____ allows for secure email communications and operates at the Application layer of the OSI model. Answer: S/MIME Explanation: S/MIME is used for secure email communications and operates at the Application layer of the OSI model.

19. _____ is a hybrid encryption protocol used in secure communications. Answer: TLS Explanation: TLS is a hybrid encryption protocol, meaning it uses both symmetric and asymmetric encryption.

20. What type of encryption does SSL use? a) Asymmetric only b) Symmetric only c) Both symmetric and asymmetric d) Neither Answer: c) Both symmetric and asymmetric Explanation: SSL uses both types of encryption for different stages of the secure connection.

21. Which of the following ports is typically used for SSH? a) 20 b) 22 c) 23 d) 25. Answer: b) 22 Explanation: SSH typically uses port 22.

22. Describe the primary function of the 802.1X standard. Answer: Port-Based Network Access Control Explanation: The 802.1X standard is primarily used for port-based network access control.

23. What is the purpose of using HMAC in secure communications? Answer: Data Integrity and Authentication Explanation: HMAC is mainly used for ensuring data integrity and authentication in secure communications.

24. LDAP is used to access and manage directory information. True / False. Answer: True Explanation: LDAP is indeed used to access and manage directory information.

25. SMTP is secure by default. True / False. Answer: False Explanation: SMTP is not secure by default; it can be secured using mechanisms like STARTTLS.

26. _____ is commonly used to secure wireless networks. Answer: WPA2 or WPA3 Explanation: WPA2 and WPA3 are commonly used to secure wireless networks. |

27. _____ is a protocol for securely accessing a remote computer. Answer: SSH Explanation: SSH is often used for securely accessing a remote computer.

28. Which of the following is a secure alternative to SNMPv2? a) SNMPv1 b) SNMPv3 c) SNMPv4 d) SNMPv5 Answer: b) SNMPv3 Explanation: SNMPv3 offers secure network management features.

29. What is the secure version of HTTP? a) HTTP 1.1 b) HTTPS c) HTTP 2 d) HTTP Secure. Answer: b) HTTPS Explanation: HTTPS is the secure version of HTTP.

30. How does the use of digital certificates enhance HTTPS? Answer: Public Key Infrastructure Explanation: Digital certificates in HTTPS provide a layer of authentication and establish a secure connection using public key infrastructure.

31. What does the "S" in HTTPS stand for? Answer: Secure Explanation: The "S" in HTTPS stands for Secure. |

32. IPsec supports data encryption only. True / False. Answer: False Explanation: IPsec supports both data encryption and data integrity.

33. Secure/Multipurpose Internet Mail Extensions (S/MIME) is used to secure email communications. True / False Answer: True Explanation: S/MIME is used to secure email communications.

34. Which layer of the OSI model does TLS operate at? a) Presentation b) Session c) Transport d) Network Answer: c) Transport Explanation: TLS operates at the Transport layer of the OSI model.

35. What is the main security function of SNMPv3? a) Encryption b) Authorization c) Integrity d) All of the above Answer: d) All of the above Explanation: SNMPv3 provides Encryption, Authorization, and Integrity.

36. HSTS is used to force browsers to make secure connections with a web server. True / False
Answer: True Explanation: HSTS is used to force browsers to establish secure connections with a web server.

37. VPNs always encrypt data in transit. True / False. Answer: False Explanation: Not all VPNs encrypt data; it depends on the configuration and type of VPN. |

38. _____ is a network protocol for secure file transfer over SSH. Answer: SFTP Explanation: SFTP (SSH File Transfer Protocol) is used for secure file transfer over SSH.

39. The protocol _____ is used for secure web-based email transfer. Answer: HTTPS Explanation: HTTPS is used for secure web-based email transfer.

40. What does the protocol EAP generally secure? a) FTP transfers b) Wireless communications c) SSH connections d) Email   Answer: b) Wireless communications Explanation: EAP (Extensible Authentication Protocol) is generally used to secure wireless communications.

14) Network Security

Network Security Concepts

The modern organization operates within a complex network infrastructure that requires robust security measures to mitigate the ever-evolving threats. The first line of defense in any network is understanding and implementing advanced security concepts tailored to safeguard assets and data. This section explores modern security protocols, intrusion detection and prevention systems (IDPS), and next-generation firewalls (NGFWs) which are pivotal in establishing a resilient network security posture.

1. Modern Security Protocols:
   - TLS/SSL: Transport Layer Security (TLS) and its predecessor, Secure Sockets Layer (SSL), are cryptographic protocols that provide secure communication over a network.
   - IPsec: Internet Protocol Security (IPsec) is a suite of protocols for securing internet protocol (IP) communications.
   - SSH: Secure Shell (SSH) is a cryptographic network protocol for operating network services securely over an unsecured network.
   - HTTPS: HyperText Transfer Protocol Secure (HTTPS) is an extension of HTTP, used for secure communication over a computer network within a web browser.

2. Intrusion Detection and Prevention Systems (IDPS):
   - Signature-Based Detection: Relies on known patterns of malicious activity.
   - Anomaly-Based Detection: Identifies deviations from established baselines.
   - Heuristic-Based Detection: Utilizes algorithms to analyze the behavior of traffic.
   - Hybrid Systems: Combines various methods to provide a more robust solution.

3. Next-Generation Firewalls (NGFWs):
   - Deep Packet Inspection (DPI): Examines the data part of a packet as it passes an inspection point, searching for protocol non-compliance, viruses, spam, intrusions, or defined criteria.
   - Application Awareness: Ability to identify and control applications at the network layer.
   - Integrated Intrusion Prevention System (IPS): Incorporates intrusion prevention technology to identify and mitigate security threats.
   - Identity Awareness: Integrates with identity-based systems to provide security policies based on the user identity.

4. Security Challenges:
   - Evolving Threats: The continuous evolution of threat vectors necessitates a proactive and adaptable network security strategy.
   - Complex Configurations: The sophistication of network security solutions requires a knowledgeable and skilled IT team to ensure proper configuration and maintenance.
   - False Positives/Negatives: Balancing the sensitivity of security systems to accurately identify threats without overwhelming administrators with false alarms.

5. Future of Network Security:
   - Machine Learning and AI: Incorporation of artificial intelligence (AI) and machine learning algorithms for predictive analysis and real-time threat detection.
   - Zero Trust Architecture: An emerging paradigm that assumes no trust for any entity, irrespective of whether they are inside or outside the organizational perimeter.

6. Hands-on Exercise: Setting up a Basic Access Control System
   - Objective:
     - To understand and implement basic access control measures on a network.
     - To experience the configuration and management of access control lists (ACLs).
   - Tools Required:
     - A network simulator or real network equipment for setting up a test environment.
     - Access control software or hardware (e.g., a firewall or router with ACL capabilities).

- Instructions:
   1. Setup Environment:
     - Create a simulated network environment or use a segregated portion of the existing network.
     - Ensure that you have at least two subnets to demonstrate the control of traffic between them.
   2. Design Access Control Lists (ACLs):
     - Draft necessary ACLs to control the traffic between the subnets.
     - Define which types of traffic should be allowed or denied based on criteria such as IP addresses, port numbers, and protocols.
   3. Implement ACLs:
     - Configure the ACLs on the necessary devices (e.g., routers, firewalls).
     - Apply the ACLs to the appropriate interfaces and directions (inbound or outbound).
   4. Test Access Control:
     - Generate traffic to test the effectiveness of the ACLs.
     - Use tools like ping and traceroute to verify that the desired access control is being enforced.
   5. Review and Adjust:
     - Analyze the results and adjust the ACLs as necessary to meet the access control objectives.
     - Document the process, noting any challenges encountered and how they were resolved.
- Evaluation:
   - Were the ACLs implemented correctly and as per the design?
   - Was the traffic controlled as intended between the subnets?
   - Were there any unexpected outcomes, and how were they addressed?
- Reflection:
   - Reflect on the challenges faced during the implementation.
   - Discuss the importance of accurate access control configuration and the implications of misconfiguration.
   - Explore the potential scalability and maintenance challenges as the network grows or changes.

Network Access Control (NAC)

Network Access Control (NAC) is a crucial component in the security infrastructure of modern networks. It plays a pivotal role in controlling who or what can access network resources, ensuring that only authorized entities can access sensitive information. In the era where Bring Your Own Device (BYOD) policies and Internet of Things (IoT) devices are prevalent, having robust NAC in place is indispensable to maintain a secure network environment.

Importance of Network Access Control

1. Authentication and Authorization:
   - NAC systems authenticate users and devices before they can access the network, ensuring that only authorized entities are granted access.
   - They can also provide tiered levels of access based on user roles, ensuring individuals can only access the information necessary for their job functions.

2. Compliance and Policy Enforcement:
   - Many industries are bound by strict compliance requirements (e.g., HIPAA, GDPR) which necessitate control over who can access what within a network.
   - NAC systems enforce security policies by blocking unauthorized access and ensuring devices comply with the organization's security posture.

3. Visibility and Monitoring:
   - NAC provides visibility into who and what is on the network, which is crucial for security monitoring and incident response.
   - It aids in the continuous monitoring of network traffic, detecting anomalies that could indicate a security issue.

4. Reduced Attack Surface:

- By controlling access to the network, NAC significantly reduces the attack surface, limiting the potential for unauthorized access and data breaches.

Implementing and Managing NAC

1. Planning:
   - A thorough understanding of the network architecture, data flows, and access requirements is crucial before implementing NAC.
   - Engage stakeholders from different departments to understand access requirements and to develop a comprehensive access control policy.

2. Selection of NAC Solution:
   - Choose a NAC solution that aligns with the organization's needs, size, and budget.
   - Consider scalability, ease of management, and integration with other security solutions.

3. Configuration and Deployment:
   - Configure the NAC solution in accordance with the defined access control policies, ensuring it enforces the desired access restrictions accurately.
   - Test the NAC in a controlled environment before deploying it across the organization to ensure it operates as expected without disrupting business operations.

4. Monitoring and Maintenance:
   - Continuously monitor the effectiveness of the NAC solution, ensuring it adapts to evolving network configurations and threat landscapes.
   - Regularly review and update access control policies to reflect changes in organizational structure, user roles, or compliance requirements.

5. Training and Awareness:
   - Educate users on the importance of network access control and the policies governing network access.
   - Provide training on how to engage with the NAC system, ensuring users understand how to maintain compliance with access control policies.

6. Evaluation and Improvement:
   - Evaluate the effectiveness of the NAC system on a regular basis, identifying areas for improvement.
   - Consider engaging external auditors to assess the robustness of the NAC implementation, providing a fresh perspective on potential vulnerabilities and areas for improvement.

Best Practices in Network Access Control (NAC) Management

Implementing NAC is one step towards a secured network, but effective management and adherence to best practices are crucial for maintaining a robust security posture over time. Here are some best practices in managing Network Access Control systems:

1. Regularly Update Access Policies:
   - Access control policies should evolve with the organizational structure, personnel changes, and emerging security threats. Regular reviews and updates ensure that the NAC system remains effective and relevant.

2. Automate Where Possible:
   - Utilize the automation features of your NAC system to streamline the enforcement of access control policies and the identification of non-compliant devices.

3. Integrate with Other Security Systems:
   - Integration with other security systems like SIEM (Security Information and Event Management) can provide a holistic view of the network security, facilitating better incident response and forensic analysis.

4. Maintain a Comprehensive Inventory:
   - Keeping a detailed inventory of all devices and users on the network aids in ensuring complete coverage by the NAC system.

5. Educate and Communicate with End-Users:
   - Ensure that users are aware of access control policies, why they are essential, and what they need to do to comply. Clear communication helps to minimize user frustration and non-compliance.

6. Continuous Monitoring and Reporting:
   - Effective monitoring helps in early detection of any unauthorized access attempts or non-compliant devices. Regular reporting can provide insights into the effectiveness of the NAC system and areas for improvement.
7. Engage with Vendor Support:
   - Leverage the support and expertise of the NAC solution vendor to resolve issues quickly and to stay updated on the latest features and best practices.
8. Test and Review the NAC System:
   - Regular testing and review of the NAC system can help to identify potential issues before they become major problems. It's also a good practice to test the system following any significant network changes or upgrades.
9. Plan for Scalability:
   - As the organization grows, the NAC system should scale to accommodate more devices and users. Plan for this scalability from the outset to avoid future challenges.
10. Document Procedures and Policies:
    - Documenting the procedures and policies governing the NAC system is crucial for ensuring consistency, compliance, and ease of management.
11. Regular Training for IT Staff:
    - The IT staff responsible for managing the NAC system should receive regular training to stay updated on the latest threats, technologies, and best practices in access control management.
12. Audit and Compliance Assurance:
    - Regular audits can help to ensure that the NAC system is compliant with internal policies and external regulatory requirements.

Implementing Network Segmentation: A Real-World Scenario

Stage 1: Identifying the Need
TechCorp Inc. has been experiencing an increased volume of network traffic due to its growing operations. The IT department identified the need for network segmentation to reduce network congestion and enhance security by isolating sensitive data.
Stage 2: Planning
The planning stage involved identifying the different segments that would be created, such as separating the R&D, Sales, and HR departments. Additionally, critical systems like the company's financials were planned to be on a separate segment to ensure enhanced security. The planning also involved determining the technologies and resources required for the implementation.
Stage 3: Selecting Technology
After extensive research, TechCorp decided to use VLAN (Virtual Local Area Network) technology for segmentation alongside robust firewall systems to control the traffic between the segments.
Stage 4: Implementation
The implementation stage was carried out in phases to minimize disruptions. Initially, VLANs were created, and departments were migrated one at a time. The firewall rules were set up to ensure that only authorized traffic could flow between the segments.
Stage 5: Challenges Encountered
During implementation, TechCorp faced several challenges. Configuring the firewall rules to ensure seamless communication between necessary segments while keeping others isolated proved to be complex. Moreover, there were unforeseen compatibility issues with some legacy systems.
Stage 6: Solutions Employed
To address the challenges, the IT department engaged with vendors to resolve the compatibility issues. They also hired a network security consultant to fine-tune the firewall configurations to meet the organization's needs.
Stage 7: Evaluation and Monitoring

Post-implementation, the network was continuously monitored to evaluate the effectiveness of the segmentation. There were notable improvements in network performance and a significant reduction in security incidents.

Stage 8: Lessons Learned and Future Plans

The project provided valuable insights into the importance of thorough planning and the need for engaging with experts in overcoming complex challenges. With the successful implementation of network segmentation, TechCorp now plans to explore further security enhancements like deploying intrusion detection systems.

Hands-on Exercise: Setting up a Basic Access Control System

Requirements
- A virtual or physical lab environment with networking capabilities.
- Network devices (e.g., switches, routers).
- NAC solution (e.g., PacketFence, Cisco ISE, etc.).
- End-user devices for testing (e.g., laptops, smartphones).

Steps
1. Environment Setup:
   - Set up your lab environment ensuring that all devices are properly connected.
   - Install the chosen NAC solution on a server or a dedicated machine.
2. Configuration:
   - Configure the NAC solution following the vendor's guidelines.
   - Set up the authentication server (e.g., RADIUS, LDAP).
   - Define the access policies and rules based on your organizational requirements.
3. Integration:
   - Integrate the NAC solution with your network devices (e.g., switches, routers).
   - Ensure that the network devices are configured to communicate with the NAC solution.
4. Testing:
   - Attempt to connect to the network using various end-user devices.
   - Verify that the NAC system is correctly authenticating and authorizing the devices based on the defined policies.
5. Monitoring and Troubleshooting:
   - Monitor the NAC system's logs to verify its operation.
   - Troubleshoot any issues that arise during the testing phase.
6. Documentation:
   - Document the configuration settings, policies, and any issues encountered along with their solutions.
7. Evaluation:
   - Evaluate the effectiveness of the NAC system in controlling access to the network.
   - Identify any areas of improvement and plan for any necessary adjustments.

Interactive Quiz: Network Security Protocols

1. Which protocol is used for secure shell communication?
   - a) HTTP
   - b) FTP
   - c) SSH
   - d) SNMP

2. What is the successor of SSL for secure web communication?
   - a) HTTP
   - b) SFTP
   - c) TLS
   - d) VPN

3. IPSec can operate in which of the following modes?
   - a) Transport
   - b) Tunnel
   - c) Both
   - d) Neither

4. SSL operates at which layer of the OSI model?
   - a) Network
   - b) Session
   - c) Transport
   - d) Application

5. Which protocol is used to secure email?
   - a) HTTP
   - b) SSH
   - c) S/MIME
   - d) SNMP

6. Which protocol is commonly used to secure VPN traffic?
   - a) SSL
   - b) HTTPS
   - c) IPSec
   - d) FTPS

7. HTTPS commonly operates on which port?
   - a) 80
   - b) 25
   - c) 22
   - d) 443

8. Which of the following is a deprecated wireless security protocol?
   - a) WPA3
   - b) WPA2
   - c) WEP
   - d) HTTPS

9. What does RADIUS primarily provide?
   - a) Routing
   - b) Authentication and Authorization
   - c) Encryption
   - d) Email Security

10. Which of the following protocols use tickets for secure communication?
   - a) SNMP
   - b) Kerberos
   - c) HTTP
   - d) DNS

11. S/MIME is used for secure instant messaging.
   - a) True
   - b) False

12. Which encryption algorithms are commonly used in secure communications? (Choose two)
   - a) SHA-1
   - b) MD5
   - c) AES
   - d) RSA

13. What does LDAPS stand for?
   - a) Lightweight Data Access Protocol Secure
   - b) Limited Directory Access Protocol Server
   - c) Lightweight Directory Access Protocol Secure
   - d) Limited Data Access Protocol Secure

14. Which port does SSH typically use?
   - a) 80
   - b) 21
   - c) 443
   - d) 22

15. Which of the following protocols is not secure by default?
   - a) HTTPS
   - b) SSH
   - c) FTP
   - d) S/MIME

16. FTP over SSH is known as:
   - a) FTPS
   - b) SFTP
   - c) HTTPS
   - d) FTPSSH

17. HSTS ensures a website can only be accessed using HTTP.
   - a) True
   - b) False

18. Which layer of the OSI model does S/MIME operate in?
   - a) Transport
   - b) Presentation
   - c) Application
   - d) Network

19. Which types of encryption does TLS use?
   - a) Only symmetric
   - b) Only asymmetric
   - c) Both symmetric and asymmetric
   - d) Neither

20. Which of the following protocols does not provide data integrity?
   - a) HTTPS
   - b) SSH
   - c) FTP
   - d) IPSec

21. HTTP/2 provides enhanced security measures compared to its predecessor.
   - a) True
   - b) False

22. Port 143 is generally used for IMAPS.
   - a) True
   - b) False

23. _____ is the default port for HTTPS communication.

24. The _____ protocol is used to secure VoIP communications.

25. Which of the following are secure email protocols? (Choose two)
   - a) POP3
   - b) SMTP
   - c) IMAPS
   - d) SMTPS

26. What are the modes of IPSec operation? (Choose two)
   - a) Transport
   - b) Tunnel
   - c) Data link
   - d) Stream

27. Match the following protocols with their OSI layer.
   - a) IPSec
   - b) TLS
   - c) SSH
   - d) S/MIME
   - OSI Layers: Application, Transport, Network

28. You are setting up a VPN and need to decide on a secure protocol. Which would you use?
   - a) HTTP
   - b) SSL
   - c) FTP
   - d) IPSec

29. You want to encrypt the contents of an email. Which protocol should you use?
   - a) HTTP
   - b) S/MIME
   - c) SSH

   - d) POP3

30. A security auditor recommends disabling all insecure services. Which protocol would you disable?
   - a) HTTPS
   - b) FTP
   - c) SSH
   - d) TLS

31. What are the key differences between SSH and Telnet?

32. Describe the role of Public and Private keys in asymmetric encryption.

33. What is a digital certificate and what does it contain?

34. Draw a simple diagram to illustrate how HTTPS works.

35. Sketch a flowchart to depict the functioning of a VPN.

36. Briefly describe the primary security concerns with using insecure protocols for data transfer.

37. What are the limitations of firewalls in terms of protocol security?

38. Elaborate on why secure socket layers are critical for web security.

39. Simulate the setting up of an HTTPS server. What steps would you take?

40. Create a scenario in which multiple secure protocols must work in conjunction to provide comprehensive network security.

ANSWERS

1. Which protocol is used for secure shell communication? - a) HTTP - b) FTP - c) SSH - d) SNMP Answer: c) SSH - Explanation: SSH (Secure Shell) is the protocol used for secure shell communication. It is commonly used to secure terminal session

2. What is the successor of SSL for secure web communication? - a) HTTP - b) SFTP - c) TLS - d) VPN Answer: c) TLS- Explanation: TLS (Transport Layer Security) is the successor of SSL and is used for secure web communication.

3. IPSec can operate in which of the following modes? - a) Transport - b) Tunnel - c) Both - d) Neither Answer: c) Both - Explanation: IPSec can operate in both Transport and Tunnel modes. Transport mode encrypts only the data payload while Tunnel mode encrypts the entire IP packet.

4. SSL operates at which layer of the OSI model? - a) Network - b) Session - c) Transport - d) Application Answer: c) Transport - Explanation: SSL operates at the Transport layer of the OSI model, securing communication between systems.

5. Which protocol is used to secure email? - a) HTTP - b) SSH - c) S/MIME - d) SNMP Answer: c) S/MIME - Explanation: S/MIME (Secure/Multipurpose Internet Mail Extensions) is commonly used to secure email communication.

6. Which protocol is commonly used to secure VPN traffic? - a) SSL - b) HTTPS - c) IPSec - d) FTPS Answer: c) IPSec - Explanation: IPSec (Internet Protocol Security) is widely used to secure VPN (Virtual Private Network) traffic.

7. HTTPS commonly operates on which port? - a) 80 - b) 25 - c) 22 - d) 443 Answer: d) 443 - Explanation: HTTPS (HTTP Secure) commonly operates over port 443.

8. Which of the following is a deprecated wireless security protocol? - a) WPA3 - b) WPA2 - c) WEP - d) HTTPS Answer: c) WEP - Explanation: WEP (Wired Equivalent Privacy) is a deprecated wireless security protocol and is considered insecure.

9. What does RADIUS primarily provide? - a) Routing - b) Authentication and Authorization - c) Encryption - d) Email Security Answer: b) Authentication and Authorization - Explanation: RADIUS (Remote Authentication Dial-In User Service) is mainly used for network authentication and authorization.

10. Which of the following protocols use tickets for secure communication? - a) SNMP - b) Kerberos - c) HTTP - d) DNS Answer: b) Kerberos - Explanation: Kerberos uses tickets to allow nodes to prove their identity securely across a network.

11. S/MIME is used for secure instant messaging. - a) True - b) False Answer: b) False - Explanation: S/MIME is used for securing email messages, not for secure instant messaging.

12. Which encryption algorithms are commonly used in secure communications? (Choose two) - a) SHA-1 - b) MD5 - c) AES - d) RSA Answer: c) AES and d) RSA - Explanation: AES (Advanced Encryption Standard) and RSA (Rivest-Shamir-Adleman) are commonly used encryption algorithms for secure communications.

13. What does LDAPS stand for? - a) Lightweight Data Access Protocol Secure - b) Limited Directory Access Protocol Server - c) Lightweight Directory Access Protocol Secure - d) Limited Data Access Protocol Secure Answer: c) Lightweight Directory Access Protocol Secure - Explanation: LDAPS stands for Lightweight Directory Access Protocol Secure, providing secure access to directory services.

14. Which port does SSH typically use? - a) 80 - b) 21 - c) 443 - d) 22 Answer: d) 22 - Explanation: SSH typically uses port 22 for communication.

15. Which of the following protocols is not secure by default? - a) HTTPS - b) SSH - c) FTP - d) S/MIME Answer: c) FTP - Explanation: FTP (File Transfer Protocol) is not secure by default. FTPS or SFTP should be used for secure file transfers.

16. FTP over SSH is known as: - a) FTPS - b) SFTP - c) HTTPS - d) FTPSSH Answer: b) SFTP - Explanation: FTP over SSH is known as SFTP (SSH File Transfer Protocol).

17. HSTS ensures a website can only be accessed using HTTP. - a) True - b) False Answer: b) False - Explanation: HSTS (HTTP Strict Transport Security) ensures that a website can only be accessed using HTTPS, not HTTP.

18. Which layer of the OSI model does S/MIME operate in? - a) Transport - b) Presentation - c) Application - d) Network Answer: c) Application - Explanation: S/MIME operates at the Application layer of the OSI model, as it secures email messages.

19. Which types of encryption does TLS use? - a) Only symmetric - b) Only asymmetric - c) Both symmetric and asymmetric - d) Neither Answer: c) Both symmetric and asymmetric - Explanation: TLS uses both symmetric and asymmetric encryption techniques for securing communication.

20. Which of the following protocols does not provide data integrity? - a) HTTPS - b) SSH - c) FTP - d) IPSec Answer: c) FTP - Explanation: FTP does not provide data integrity. It is an unencrypted data transfer protocol.

21. HTTP/2 provides enhanced security measures compared to its predecessor. - a) True - b) False Answer: a) True - Explanation: HTTP/2 offers performance enhancements and better security features compared to HTTP/1.1.

22. Port 143 is generally used for IMAPS. - a) True - b) False Answer: b) False - Explanation: Port 993 is used for IMAPS, not 143.

23. _____ is the default port for HTTPS communication. Answer: 443 - Explanation: The default port for HTTPS is 443.

24. The _____ protocol is used to secure VoIP communications. Answer: SRTP - Explanation: Secure Real-time Transport Protocol (SRTP) is commonly used to secure VoIP communications.

25. Which of the following are secure email protocols? (Choose two) - a) POP3 - b) SMTP - c) IMAPS - d) SMTPS Answer: c) IMAPS and d) SMTPS* - Explanation: IMAPS (Secure IMAP) and SMTPS (Secure SMTP) are secure email protocols.

26. What are the modes of IPSec operation? (Choose two) - a) Transport - b) Tunnel - c) Data link - d) Stream Answer: a) Transport and b) Tunnel - Explanation: IPSec operates in Transport and Tunnel modes.

27. Match the following protocols with their OSI layer. - a) IPSec - b) TLS - c) SSH - d) S/MIME - OSI Layers: Application, Transport, Network. Answer: a) IPSec - Network, b) TLS - Transport, c) SSH - Application, d) S/MIME – Application - Explanation: IPSec operates at the Network layer, TLS at the Transport layer, and both SSH and S/MIME at the Application layer of the OSI model.

28. You are setting up a VPN and need to decide on a secure protocol. Which would you use? - a) HTTP - b) SSL - c) FTP - d) IPSec Answer: d) IPSec - Explanation: IPSec is commonly used to secure VPN traffic.

29. You want to encrypt the contents of an email. Which protocol should you use? - a) HTTP - b) S/MIME - c) SSH - d) POP3 Answer: b) S/MIME - Explanation: S/MIME is used for email encryption.

30. A security auditor recommends disabling all insecure services. Which protocol would you disable? - a) HTTPS - b) FTP - c) SSH - d) TLS Answer: b) FTP - Explanation: FTP is insecure and should be disabled.

31. What are the key differences between SSH and Telnet? Answer: SSH uses encryption, while Telnet does not. - Explanation: SSH provides a secure channel over an unsecured network, whereas Telnet does not offer any encryption.

32. Describe the role of Public and Private keys in asymmetric encryption. Answer: Public keys encrypt, Private keys decrypt. - Explanation: In asymmetric encryption, the public key is used for encryption and is publicly distributed, while the private key is kept secret and is used for decryption.

33. What is a digital certificate and what does it contain? Answer: A digital certificate contains a public key and identifies who owns that key. - Explanation: It provides a means of proving your identity in electronic transactions, like signing a digitally-based document.

34. Draw a simple diagram to illustrate how HTTPS works. Answer: N/A - Explanation: Cannot draw diagrams here, but HTTPS works by establishing a secure SSL/TLS session between the client and the server.

35. Sketch a flowchart to depict the functioning of a VPN. Answer: N/A - Explanation: Cannot draw diagrams here, but a VPN establishes a secure tunnel between the client and the VPN server, encrypting all traffic that passes through.

36. Briefly describe the primary security concerns with using insecure protocols for data transfer. Answer: Insecure protocols are susceptible to various types of attacks such as man-in-the-middle and eavesdropping. - Explanation: They expose sensitive data to potential compromise.

37. What are the limitations of firewalls in terms of protocol security? Answer: Firewalls cannot look into encrypted traffic, making it a limited solution for protocol security. - Explanation: They filter traffic based on rules but can't decipher the contents of encrypted packets.

38. Elaborate on why secure socket layers are critical for web security. Answer: SSL/TLS provides a secure channel for web traffic, preventing unauthorized access and tampering. - Explanation: They are essential for safeguarding user data and ensuring trust.

39. Simulate the setting up of an HTTPS server. What steps would you take? Answer: Install SSL certificate, configure the web server to use SSL, and redirect HTTP to HTTPS. - Explanation: These steps will enable HTTPS on a web server.

40. Create a scenario in which multiple secure protocols must work in conjunction to provide comprehensive network security. Answer: A scenario could involve using SSH for secure terminal access, HTTPS for secure web access, and IPSec for a VPN. - Explanation: These protocols work in conjunction to provide a robust network security.

15) Exam Preparation and Strategies

Tackling the CompTIA Security+ Exam

The journey towards earning the CompTIA Security+ certification begins with understanding the essence and structure of the exam. The CompTIA Security+ exam is a globally recognized certification that validates the baseline skills necessary to perform core security functions and pursue a career in IT security. It covers a wide array of topics ranging from threats, attacks, and vulnerabilities to identity and access management, technologies and tools, and risk management.

1. Exam Overview:
   - Exam Code: SY0-601
   - Number of Questions: Maximum of 90 questions
   - Type of Questions: Multiple-choice and performance-based
   - Duration: 90 minutes
   - Passing Score: 750 (on a scale of 100-900)
   - Exam Domains: The exam is structured around five domains: Attacks, Threats, and Vulnerabilities; Architecture and Design; Implementation; Operations and Incident Response; and Governance, Risk, and Compliance.

2. Exam Objectives:
   - The objectives provide a clear roadmap of what topics are covered in the exam. Familiarizing oneself with the objectives is the first step towards effective preparation. They provide a guideline on the areas to focus on during the study.

3. Preparation Resources:
   - Official CompTIA Study Guide: The official study guide is a comprehensive resource that covers all the exam objectives in detail.
   - Online Training: There are several online platforms offering courses tailored to the CompTIA Security+ exam.
   - Practice Exams: Practice exams are crucial in understanding the exam format, the type of questions, and the areas you need to focus on.

4. Exam Registration and Scheduling:
   - Registration for the exam can be done through the official CompTIA website, where you can also find a nearby testing center or opt for an online proctored exam.

5. On the Day of the Exam:
   - Arrive early to the testing center, carry the necessary identification, and follow all the instructions provided to have a smooth exam experience.

6. Post Exam:
   - Once you pass the exam, you'll receive the CompTIA Security+ certification which is valid for three years. You can maintain your certification through continuing education units (CEUs) or by taking a higher-level CompTIA exam.

8. Revision:
   - Set aside time for revising all the topics you have covered. Revision is crucial to retaining information and being well-prepared for the exam.

9. Use of Flashcards:
   - Create flashcards for important terms, concepts, and definitions. Flashcards are excellent for quick reviews and memorization.

10. Utilizing CompTIA Resources:
   - CompTIA offers a range of resources like study guides, exam objectives, and practice questions. Make sure to take full advantage of these resources to better understand the exam format and requirements.

11. Healthy Lifestyle:
   - Maintaining a balanced diet, regular exercise, and adequate sleep can significantly impact your ability to retain information and stay focused during your study sessions.

12. Mindfulness and Stress Management:
   - Practice mindfulness and stress-reducing techniques like yoga and meditation. Keeping stress at bay is crucial for effective studying and exam performance.
13. Mock Exams:
   - Schedule mock exams to simulate the real exam environment. It will help you get accustomed to the pressure of timed exams and identify any areas you may struggle with under exam conditions.
14. Seeking Feedback:
   - If possible, seek feedback from instructors or peers to understand better where you stand and what areas you need to improve on.
15. Continuous Learning:
   - Stay updated with any changes in the exam syllabus or format by following CompTIA's official website and participating in relevant online communities.

Effective study techniques

1. Understanding Exam Objectives:
   - Begin by thoroughly understanding the objectives of the CompTIA Security+ exam. Knowing what topics are covered and the weightage of each area will guide your study plan.
2. Creating a Study Plan:
   - Draft a study plan based on the exam objectives, allocating more time to topics you find challenging. A well-structured plan will help you cover all the necessary topics within a reasonable timeframe.
3. Utilizing Official Resources:
   - Utilize official CompTIA study materials, as they are tailored to cover the exam objectives comprehensively.
4. Joining Study Groups:
   - Join study groups or forums to exchange knowledge and experiences with other candidates. Engaging in discussions can provide different perspectives and clarify doubts.
5. Hands-on Practice:
   - Engage in hands-on practice to reinforce theoretical knowledge. Use labs and practical exercises to familiarize yourself with real-world scenarios.
6. Online Training Courses:
   - Enroll in online training courses that offer interactive learning experiences. Video tutorials and interactive lessons can enhance understanding and retention.
7. Practice Exams:
   - Regular practice exams will help you gauge your preparedness, understand the exam format, and improve time management.
8. Regular Review:
   - Periodic review of previously covered topics will reinforce your memory and understanding.
9. Seeking Mentorship:
   - Seek guidance from mentors or instructors to clarify complex concepts and receive constructive feedback on your progress.
10. Staying Updated:
   - Stay updated with any changes in the exam syllabus or format by following CompTIA's official website and subscribing to relevant forums.
11. Mindfulness and Stress Management:
   - Maintain a healthy lifestyle, manage stress through relaxation techniques, and ensure you get enough sleep, especially as the exam date approaches.
12. Customized Learning:
   - Tailor your study techniques to match your learning style. Whether you are a visual, auditory, or kinesthetic learner, use resources that cater to your strengths.

Time management strategies

1. Understanding the Exam Format:
   - Acquire a solid grasp of the exam format including the number of questions, the time allocated, and the type of questions (multiple choice, performance-based, etc.). This understanding will aid in allocating time efficiently during the exam.
2. Creating a Study Schedule:
   - Draft a detailed study schedule breaking down the topics to be covered each day leading up to the exam. Ensure the schedule is realistic and adheres to your daily routine.
3. Time Blocking:
   - Allocate specific blocks of time for studying each day. Utilize tools like timers or apps to stay on track.
4. Pomodoro Technique:
   - Use the Pomodoro Technique, studying in bursts of focused activity (e.g., 25 minutes) followed by short breaks (e.g., 5 minutes). This method can enhance productivity and reduce fatigue.
5. Prioritization:
   - Prioritize topics based on their weightage in the exam and your comfort level with each topic. Spend more time on high-weightage and challenging topics.
6. Practice Exams under Timed Conditions:
   - Take practice exams under timed conditions to get accustomed to the pace required in the actual exam.
7. Utilizing Quality Resources:
   - Use quality study resources that provide concise, clear, and exam-oriented information to save time.
8. Eliminating Distractions:
   - Study in a quiet, comfortable environment free from distractions. Use apps or tools that block distracting websites and notifications.
9. Regular Review:
   - Allocate time for regular reviews to reinforce learning and identify areas that may require additional time and focus.
10. Seeking Help:
    - If stuck on a particular topic, seek help promptly from instructors, mentors, or study groups to avoid wasting time.
11. Using Flashcards for Quick Reviews:
    - Create flashcards for quick reviews during downtime, such as commuting.
12. Maintaining a Healthy Lifestyle:
    - Ensure a balanced diet, regular exercise, and adequate sleep to keep your mind sharp and improve time management.
13. Mindful Relaxation:
    - Practice relaxation techniques like meditation or deep breathing to manage exam stress and improve focus and time management.
14. Reflection and Adjustment:
    - Reflect on your time management strategies weekly and adjust your study schedule as needed to stay on track.

Practice Questions: CompTIA Security+ Exam

1. Which type of malware is designed to take advantage of a software vulnerability?
   - a) Worm
   - b) Virus
   - c) Exploit
   - d) Trojan
2. What is the primary purpose of an IDS?
   - a) Prevention
   - b) Detection
   - c) Mitigation
   - d) Authorization
3. Which asymmetric encryption algorithm is widely used for secure data transmission?
   - a) 3DES
   - b) RSA
   - c) Blowfish

- d) AES

4. What does the 'C' stand for in the CIA triad?
   - a) Certificate
   - b) Complexity
   - c) Confidentiality
   - d) Cryptography

5. What is the term for an internal attacker?
   - a) Script Kiddie
   - b) Insider Threat
   - c) Phreaker
   - d) Hacktivist

6. Which security mechanism ensures that data has not been altered during transmission?
   - a) Authentication
   - b) Data Loss Prevention
   - c) Integrity
   - d) Non-repudiation

7. What should be the FIRST step in incident response?
   - a) Eradication
   - b) Identification
   - c) Recovery
   - d) Containment

8. Which of the following is not a type of social engineering attack?
   - a) Phishing
   - b) Tailgating
   - c) Rainbow Table
   - d) Pretexting

9. What is the primary objective of a DDoS attack?
   - a) Data Breach
   - b) Disruption
   - c) Data Manipulation
   - d) Unauthorized Access

10. Which technology is used to partition a physical server into multiple virtual servers?
    - a) SAN
    - b) RAID
    - c) Hypervisor
    - d) NAS

11. Data masking is a form of encryption.
    - a) True
    - b) False

12. A rootkit operates at the kernel level of an operating system.
    - a) True
    - b) False

13. _____ is the act of navigating through a network without detection.

14. The process of verifying the identity of a user is called _____.

15. Which of the following protocols are secure? (Choose two)
    - a) FTP
    - b) HTTPS
    - c) HTTP
    - d) SSH

16. What are the two common types of firewalls? (Choose two)
    - a) Proxy
    - b) Stateful
    - c) Stateless
    - d) Packet Filtering

17. Match the following terms with their definitions:
    - a) Zero-day
    - b) Hashing
    - c) VPN
    - Definitions: Unpatched vulnerability, Data encryption, Secure tunneling

18. You discover an unauthorized wireless access point on your network. What is the first action you should take?
    - a) Ignore it
    - b) Disconnect it
    - c) Investigate it
    - d) Report it

19. Your company decides to implement multi-factor authentication. Which three methods can you use?
    - a) Password
    - b) Fingerprint
    - c) Security questions
    - d) USB Security Key

20. List two types of IDS based on their placement in the network.

21. Match the following cryptographic algorithms to their types:
    - a) RSA
    - b) AES
    - c) SHA-256
    - Types: Asymmetric, Symmetric, Hashing

22. Briefly explain what is meant by defense-in-depth.

23. Describe the concept of least privilege.

24. Illustrate how a basic firewall functions.

25. Draw a diagram to explain the process of public key cryptography.

26. What type of attack involves overwhelming a system with excessive requests?

- a) Smurf Attack
- b) DDoS
- c) Spoofing
- d) Man-in-the-Middle

27. Which of the following is a network topology that provides redundancy?
  - a) Star
  - b) Ring
  - c) Mesh
  - d) Bus

28. In the OSI model, which layer is responsible for end-to-end communication?
  - a) Transport
  - b) Network
  - c) Data Link
  - d) Session

29. What is the main goal of a vulnerability assessment?
  - a) To exploit vulnerabilities
  - b) To detect vulnerabilities
  - c) To prevent vulnerabilities
  - d) To rate vulnerabilities

30. Which command-line tool is commonly used for network troubleshooting?
  - a) Nmap
  - b) Netstat
  - c) Ping
  - d) Traceroute

31. Simulate the steps to secure a wireless network.

32. Perform a basic risk assessment for a small business.

33. NAT helps in conserving public IP addresses.
  - a) True
  - b) False

34. VPNs protect against malware.
  - a) True
  - b) False

35. Which of the following is an example of a physical security control?
  - a) Firewall
  - b) IDS
  - c) Biometric Scanner
  - d) Antivirus

36. What term describes the act of removing sensitive information from a system before disposal?
  - a) Encryption
  - b) Archiving
  - c) Data Sanitization
  - d) Data Masking

37. In a cloud environment, who is responsible for the security of the data?
  - a) Cloud Provider
  - b) Customer
  - c) Both
  - d) Neither

38. Which protocol is used for secure file transfer?
  - a) FTP
  - b) SCP
  - c) HTTP
  - d) SMTP

39. What kind of malware disguises itself as legitimate software?
  - a) Worm
  - b) Trojan
  - c) Virus
  - d) Ransomware

40. What is the most secure method of authentication among the following?
  - a) Password
  - b) Token
  - c) Biometric
  - d) Smart Card

ANSWERS

1. Which type of malware is designed to take advantage of a software vulnerability? a) Worm b) Virus c) Exploit d) Trojan. Answer: c) Exploit - An exploit takes advantage of software vulnerabilities to gain unauthorized access or perform unauthorized actions.

2. What is the primary purpose of an IDS? a) Prevention b) Detection c) Mitigation d) Authorization Answer: b) Detection - Intrusion Detection Systems (IDS) are designed to detect unauthorized access or activities.

3. Which asymmetric encryption algorithm is widely used for secure data transmission? a) 3DES b) RSA c) Blowfish d) AES Answer: b) RSA - RSA is a widely used asymmetric encryption algorithm for secure data transmission.

4. What does the 'C' stand for in the CIA triad? a) Certificate b) Complexity c) Confidentiality d) Cryptography.

Answer: c) Confidentiality - The 'C' in the CIA triad stands for Confidentiality, which means keeping data secure from unauthorized access.

5. What is the term for an internal attacker? a) Script Kiddie b) Insider Threat c) Phreaker d) Hacktivist. Answer: b) Insider Threat - An internal attacker is known as an insider threat.

6. Which security mechanism ensures that data has not been altered during transmission? a) Authentication b) Data Loss Prevention c) Integrity d) Non-repudiation Answer: c) Integrity - Integrity ensures that data has not been tampered with during transmission.

7. What should be the FIRST step in incident response? a) Eradication b) Identification c) Recovery d) Containment Answer: b) Identification - The first step in incident response is to identify that an incident has occurred.

8. Which of the following is not a type of social engineering attack? a) Phishing b) Tailgating c) Rainbow Table d) Pretexting. Answer: c) Rainbow Table - Rainbow Table is not a social engineering attack; it's a method used to crack password hashes.

9. What is the primary objective of a DDoS attack? a) Data Breach b) Disruption c) Data Manipulation d) Unauthorized Access Answer: b) Disruption - The primary goal of a DDoS (Distributed Denial of Service) attack is to disrupt the service.

10. Which technology is used to partition a physical server into multiple virtual servers? a) SAN b) RAID c) Hypervisor d) NAS Answer: c) Hypervisor - A hypervisor is used to create and manage virtual machines on a physical server.

11. Data masking is a form of encryption. a) True b) False Answer: b) False - Data masking hides original data but it is not a form of encryption.

12. A rootkit operates at the kernel level of an operating system. a) True b) False Answer: a) True - Rootkits generally operate at the kernel level to gain unauthorized access to a system.

13. _____ is the act of navigating through a network without detection. Answer: Stealth - Stealth is the act of navigating through a network without detection.

14. The process of verifying the identity of a user is called _____. Answer: Authentication - Verifying the identity of a user is called authentication.

15. Which of the following protocols are secure? (Choose two) a) FTP b) HTTPS c) HTTP d) SSH Answer: b) HTTPS, d) SSH - These protocols are secure and encrypt the data during transmission.

16. What are the two common types of firewalls? (Choose two) a) Proxy b) Stateful c) Stateless d) Packet Filtering Answer: a) Proxy, b) Stateful - Proxy and stateful are two common types of firewalls.

17. Match the following terms with their definitions: a) Zero-day b) Hashing c) VPN - Definitions: Unpatched vulnerability, Data encryption, Secure tunneling Answer: a) Zero-day: Unpatched vulnerability, b) Hashing: Data encryption, c) VPN: Secure tunneling - These terms match with their respective definitions.

18. You discover an unauthorized wireless access point on your network. What is the first action you should take? a) Ignore it b) Disconnect it c) Investigate it d) Report it Answer: d) Report it - Reporting an unauthorized access point is the first action to ensure proper procedure is followed.

19. Your company decides to implement multi-factor authentication. Which three methods can you use? a) Password b) Fingerprint c) Security questions d) USB Security Key Answer: a) Password, b) Fingerprint, d) USB Security Key - These are methods commonly used in multi-factor authentication.

20. List two types of IDS based on their placement in the network. Answer: Network-based IDS, Host-based IDS - These are types of IDS based on their placement in the network.

21. Match the following cryptographic algorithms to their types: a) RSA b) AES c) SHA-256 - Types: Asymmetric, Symmetric, Hashing Answer: a) RSA: Asymmetric, b) AES: Symmetric, c) SHA-256: Hashing - These cryptographic algorithms match with their types.

22. Briefly explain what is meant by defense-in-depth. Answer: Defense-in-depth involves multiple layers of security controls to protect resources.

23. Describe the concept of least privilege. Answer: Least privilege means giving users only the permissions they need to perform their job functions.

24. Illustrate how a basic firewall functions. Answer: [Your content here]

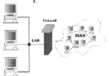

25. Draw a diagram to explain the process of public key cryptography. Answer: [Your content here]

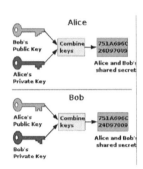

26. What type of attack involves overwhelming a system with excessive requests? a) Smurf Attack b) DDoS c) Spoofing d) Man-in-the-Middle Answer: b) DDoS - DDoS attacks overwhelm a system with excessive requests.

27. Which of the following is a network topology that provides redundancy? a) Star b) Ring c) Mesh d) Bus Answer: c) Mesh - Mesh topology provides redundancy by having multiple paths between nodes.

28. In the OSI model, which layer is responsible for end-to-end communication? a) Transport b) Network c) Data Link d) Session. Answer: a) Transport - The transport layer ensures end-to-end communication between systems.

29. What is the main goal of a vulnerability assessment? a) To exploit vulnerabilities b) To detect vulnerabilities c) To prevent vulnerabilities d) To rate vulnerabilities Answer: b) To detect vulnerabilities - A vulnerability assessment aims to identify weaknesses in a system.

30. Which command-line tool is commonly used for network troubleshooting? a) Nmap b) Netstat c) Ping d) Traceroute Answer: c) Ping - Ping is commonly used for basic network troubleshooting.

31. Simulate the steps to secure a wireless network. Answer: [Simulation steps would be detailed here]

32. Perform a basic risk assessment for a small business. Answer: [Risk assessment procedures would be detailed here]

33. NAT helps in conserving public IP addresses. a) True b) False Answer: a) True - NAT (Network Address Translation) helps conserve public IP addresses by mapping them to private IPs.

34. VPNs protect against malware. a) True b) False Answer: b) False - VPNs secure the data transmission but don't protect against malware per se.

35. Which of the following is an example of a physical security control? a) Firewall b) IDS c) Biometric Scanner d) Antivirus Answer: c) Biometric Scanner - A biometric scanner is a physical security control.

36. What term describes the act of removing sensitive information from a system before disposal? a) Encryption b) Archiving c) Data Sanitization d) Data Masking Answer: c) Data Sanitization - Data sanitization involves the removal of data before disposal.

37. In a cloud environment, who is responsible for the security of the data? a) Cloud Provider b) Customer c) Both d) Neither Answer: c) Both - Both the cloud provider and customer share responsibility for data security.

38. Which protocol is used for secure file transfer? a) FTP b) SCP c) HTTP d) SMTP Answer: b) SCP - SCP (Secure Copy Protocol) is used for secure file transfer.

39. What kind of malware disguises itself as legitimate software? a) Worm b) Trojan c) Virus d) Ransomware Answer: b) Trojan - A Trojan disguises itself as legitimate software to trick users.

40. What is the most secure method of authentication among the following? a) Password b) Token c) Biometric d) Smart Card Answer: c) Biometric - Biometric authentication is generally considered the most secure among these options.

Tips: Boosting your test-taking confidence and skills

The process of preparing for and taking exams can be stressful, especially when it concerns career-defining certifications like CompTIA Security+. Here are several tips to boost your test-taking confidence and skills, ensuring you are well-prepared on the day of the exam:

1. Understand the Exam Format and Objectives:
   - Familiarize yourself with the CompTIA Security+ exam format, including the types of questions you will encounter (multiple-choice, performance-based, etc.), and the exam objectives. Knowing what to expect will help reduce anxiety and allow you to tailor your study plan accordingly.

2. Practice Regularly with Mock Exams:
   - Practice exams are invaluable resources. They simulate the actual exam environment, helping you get comfortable with the format and the types of questions you will encounter. Additionally, they provide immediate feedback, helping you identify areas that need further review.

3. Maintain a Steady Study Schedule:
   - Establish a consistent study schedule well in advance of your exam date. Spreading out your study sessions over time is more effective and less stressful than cramming at the last minute.

4. Join Study Groups:
   - Engaging with others who are also preparing for the exam can provide fresh perspectives and new studying strategies. It also gives you a community to lean on when you come across challenging topics.

5. Utilize Diverse Learning Resources:
   - Use a mix of learning resources such as books, online courses, and interactive labs. Diversifying your study materials will help reinforce concepts and keep the learning process engaging.

6. Relax and Sleep Well Before the Exam:
   - Ensure you get a good night's sleep before the exam day. Avoid last-minute cramming and try to relax. Being well-rested will help you think clearly and perform better on the exam.

7. Read Each Question Carefully:
   - During the exam, read each question and its options carefully before selecting an answer. It's easy to misinterpret a question if you're rushing.

8. Manage Your Time Wisely:
   - Keep track of the time during the exam, ensuring you have enough time to answer all questions. Don't spend too much time on any single question.

9. Stay Positive:
   - Maintain a positive mindset. Confidence can significantly impact your performance. Believe in your preparation and ability to pass the exam.

10. Review and Learn from Mistakes:
    - After the exam, whether you pass or not, review the areas you struggled with and learn from your mistakes for future exams.

Interactive Assessment: Simulated exam environment for practice

The CompTIA Security+ exam is a stepping stone for individuals aspiring to forge a career in cybersecurity. However, passing this exam requires not only a deep understanding of security concepts but also the ability to perform under exam conditions. An interactive assessment through a simulated exam environment is instrumental in preparing candidates for the real exam scenario. This section elucidates the myriad benefits and components of engaging in a simulated exam environment for practice.

1. Accurate Simulation:

- A simulated exam environment closely mirrors the actual exam setting, offering a realistic interface, question formats, and time constraints akin to the CompTIA Security+ exam. This accurate simulation aids in acclimating candidates to the exam ambiance, thus reducing anxiety and improving performance.

2. Immediate Feedback:
   - Engaging in interactive assessments allows candidates to receive immediate feedback on their performance. This instant feedback is pivotal in identifying strengths and weaknesses, enabling targeted study and improved understanding of the subject matter.

3. Time Management:
   - Practicing in a time-bound simulated environment helps hone time management skills, a critical aspect of successfully completing the CompTIA Security+ exam within the stipulated time.

4. Customized Practice Exams:
   - Some simulated exam environments provide the flexibility to create customized practice exams focusing on specific topics or domains. This feature is invaluable for targeted preparation, allowing candidates to concentrate on areas they find challenging.

5. Understanding and Analysis:
   - Detailed explanations accompanying each question in the simulated exams promote a deeper understanding and analysis of the concepts. This feature is instrumental in clarifying doubts and reinforcing learning.

6. Enhanced Confidence:
   - Familiarity with the exam format through simulated practice significantly boosts confidence. Knowing what to expect and having tackled similar questions in a simulated environment alleviates exam-day anxiety.

7. Repetition and Review:
   - The option to retake the simulated exams and review the answers fosters a thorough understanding and retention of the material. It also enables tracking progress over time, encouraging continuous improvement.

8. Up-to-Date Question Bank:
   - It's imperative that the simulated exam environment is updated regularly to reflect the current exam objectives and question formats. An up-to-date question bank is crucial for relevant and effective practice.

9. Accessibility:
   - Online simulated exam environments offer the convenience of practicing anytime, anywhere. This accessibility is beneficial for candidates juggling exam preparation with other commitments.

10. Peer Interaction:
    - Some simulated exam platforms foster a community of learners, enabling peer interaction, discussions, and shared experiences, which can be very enriching.

11. Cost-Effectiveness:
    - Many simulated exam environments are cost-effective or even free, providing a valuable resource for exam preparation without a hefty price tag.

Real-world Scenario: Crafting a Study and Preparation Schedule

Embarking on the journey to attain the CompTIA Security+ certification is a commendable endeavor that demands a structured and disciplined approach. Crafting a robust study and preparation schedule is pivotal in navigating this journey successfully. This section delineates a real-world scenario of a professional aspiring to achieve this certification while balancing a full-time job. The narrative aims to provide insights and a pragmatic blueprint for readers to formulate their own preparation schedules.

1. Profile of the Aspirant:
   - Meet John, a full-time network administrator with a keen interest in advancing his cybersecurity skills. John decides to pursue the CompTIA Security+ certification to bolster his career prospects. Given his demanding job, he aims to develop a meticulous study schedule to prepare for the exam over the next three months.

2. Assessment of Current Knowledge:

- John begins by assessing his current knowledge against the exam objectives. He identifies areas he's well-versed in and those that require more attention. This self-assessment is crucial in allocating time efficiently across different topics.

3. Gathering Resources:
  - He procures reputable study guides, enrolls in an online training course, and gathers a variety of practice exam questions. John also joins a study group to interact with fellow aspirants and share resources.

4. Creating a Study Plan:
  - Based on his self-assessment, John devises a study plan. He allocates more time to topics he's less familiar with. His plan includes reading, watching training videos, hands-on practice, and attempting practice questions.

5. Time Management:
  - Despite his full-time job, John dedicates weekday evenings and weekend mornings to his study plan. He uses a digital calendar to block study time, ensuring he remains committed to his schedule.

6. Practice Exams:
  - John incorporates practice exams into his preparation to gauge his readiness and improve his time management skills. He reviews every question, understanding why an answer is correct or incorrect.

7. Seeking Feedback:
  - Through the study group and online forums, John seeks feedback on his understanding of complex concepts. This interaction enables him to grasp difficult topics better.

8. Adjusting the Plan:
  - As he progresses, John revisits and adjusts his study plan to allocate more time to areas he finds challenging. This flexibility is crucial in ensuring thorough preparation.

9. Healthy Lifestyle:
  - John maintains a balanced diet and regular exercise routine to keep his mind and body in optimal condition. He also ensures to get enough sleep, which is crucial for effective learning and retention.

10. Review and Revision:
  - In the final weeks leading up to the exam, John focuses on reviewing and revising all topics. He also takes several full-length practice exams to simulate the real exam experience.

11. Relaxation and Confidence-Building:
  - The day before the exam, John relaxes and reviews his notes lightly. He focuses on building confidence and maintaining a positive mindset.

12. Exam Day:
  - On exam day, John arrives early at the exam center, stays calm, and systematically tackles each question. His diligent preparation pays off as he successfully passes the CompTIA Security+ exam.

13. Utilizing Various Study Methods:
  - John explores different study methods to find what works best for him. He discovers that a mix of active learning, such as hands-on practice and interactive online courses, along with passive learning like reading, helps him understand and retain the material better.

14. Engagement with the Community:
  - Beyond his study group, John actively engages with the broader cybersecurity community. He attends webinars, local meetups, and online forums where he could discuss complex topics and stay updated on the latest industry trends.

15. Employing Real-World Scenarios:
  - John tries to correlate his study with real-world scenarios. He often discusses with his colleagues how certain security principles and techniques could be applied in their current network environment.

16. Utilization of Flashcards:
  - To aid in memorization and quick recall, John creates flashcards for crucial concepts, acronyms, and key terms. He reviews these flashcards daily, which helps reinforce his memory.

17. Taking Breaks:

- John understands the importance of taking breaks to avoid burnout. He ensures to have short breaks during his study sessions and also sets aside time for hobbies and relaxation.

18. Employing Mnemonics and Memory Techniques:

   - For memorizing complex concepts, John employs mnemonics and other memory-enhancing techniques. These methods make it easier to recall information during the exam.

19. Seeking Professional Guidance:

   - John also consults with a few professionals who have already passed the CompTIA Security+ exam. Their insights and advice provide invaluable guidance on what to expect and how to prepare effectively.

20. Evaluating Progress:

   - Every week, John evaluates his progress by taking a practice exam. This helps him identify areas where he needs to focus more.

21. Maintaining a Positive Mindset:

   - Throughout his preparation journey, John keeps a positive mindset. He celebrates small victories, like mastering a challenging concept or scoring well on a practice exam.

22. Dealing with Anxiety:

   - John practices mindfulness and relaxation techniques to manage exam anxiety. This includes deep breathing, meditation, and visualization exercises that help him stay calm and focused.

23. Final Review:

   - In the last few days before the exam, John reviews all the key concepts, practices more questions, and goes through his flashcards several times to ensure he's well-prepared.

24. Post-Exam Reflection:

   - After the exam, John reflects on his preparation journey. He notes what worked well and what didn't, and considers how he could improve his study strategies for future certifications.

BONUS

Scan the QR code below to access Tutor Security, and practice AI, works with Chat Gpt 4.

Scan the QR code below to access 600 Bonus Exercises

Scan the QR code below and instantly download the Flashcard App to start practicing right away!

Conclusion: A Milestone Achieved, A Journey Ahead

Congratulations! By reaching this point, you have armed yourself with the knowledge, tools, and resources to conquer the CompTIA Security+ exam. However, remember that passing the exam is not the end, but a significant milestone on your ongoing journey in cybersecurity.

The World Awaits Your Expertise

Security threats are continuously evolving, and as someone who is now well-versed in the subject, your skills are invaluable. Your journey post-exam should involve staying abreast of the latest trends, threats, and technologies. The cybersecurity landscape is always changing; thus, your learning should never stop.

A Badge of Credibility

The CompTIA Security+ certification is more than a piece of paper; it's a badge of credibility. It signifies that you have the skills required to manage, detect, and neutralize security risks in real-world scenarios. Employers will look to you as someone who can uphold the organization's security posture, making you an asset to any team.

The Road Ahead

With your CompTIA Security+ certification, new doors will open. Whether you plan on delving into specialized security roles, pursuing higher-level certifications, or even educating others on security best practices, the sky's the limit.

A Community of Professionals

Remember that you're now part of a community of cybersecurity professionals. Networking, sharing knowledge, and participating in continued education are vital for career growth and personal development. Engage with online forums, attend industry conferences, and contribute to open-source projects to keep your skills sharp and relevant.

Acknowledgments and Gratitude

We thank you for choosing this guide as your companion for the CompTIA Security+ exam preparation. We are confident that the real-world approach, interactivity, and depth of content have provided you with the skills and confidence you need to succeed.

Your Success Is Our Success

Your success is a testament to the effectiveness of a focused and structured approach to exam preparation. We hope that this guide has been instrumental in achieving this milestone. We'd love to hear about your exam success and how this guide helped you in your journey.

Final Thoughts

As you close this guide, remember that the real work starts now. Take this certification and apply your knowledge and skills to make the world a safer place, one network at a time.

Here's wishing you all the best in your future endeavors in the realm of cybersecurity.

Warm regards,

The Team Behind "Mastering the CompTIA Security+ Exam"

Made in the USA
Middletown, DE
18 February 2024

50022835R00097